CICS for the
COBOL programmer

Part 1: An introductory course

CICS for the
COBOL programmer

Part 1: An introductory course

Doug Lowe

Mike Murach & Associates, Inc.

4697 West Jacquelyn Avenue
Fresno, California 93722
(209) 275-3335

Development Team

General editor:	Steve Eckols
Copy editor:	Carrie Gwynne
Designer and production director:	Steve Ehlers
Artist:	Ed Gallock
Technical reviewer:	John R. Burns

Related books from Mike Murach & Associates, Inc.

CICS for the COBOL Programmer, Part 2: An Advanced Course by Doug Lowe

CICS for the COBOL Programmer: Instructor's Guide by Doug Lowe

The CICS Programmer's Desk Reference by Doug Lowe

Thanks to Western Electric for permission to reprint the photograph in figure 2-2.

Thanks to International Business Machines for permission to reprint the photographs in figures 2-4 and 2-5.

20 19 18 17 16 15

Library of Congress Catalog Card Number: 83-62724

ISBN: 0-911625-15-1

Contents

Preface

If you're involved in the development of interactive software for an IBM mainframe, the odds are you're using CICS. If you doubt the popularity of CICS, just scan the employment section of *Computerworld* or any large daily newspaper. You'll be surprised by the number of positions that require CICS experience. In today's market, it seems CICS experience is a must.

The only problem is, how do you get CICS experience? One option is to study the IBM manuals. Unfortunately, you'll soon find that they're designed for reference, not for instruction. If you choose this option, you may end up more confused than you were when you started.

A popular option today is to enroll in a CICS training course. Such courses generally provide one intensive week of CICS instruction. Unfortunately, a week isn't nearly enough time to learn CICS programming. And the printed training materials the courses provide are often less than adequate for the weeks—or months—that follow.

Another option is to try one of the books currently on the market. But if you do, I'm afraid you'll find they dwell on advanced topics without taking the trouble to make sure you know how to use the basics. Unfortunately, CICS programming is far too complex a subject for that approach. To understand CICS programming, you need to grasp many complicated ideas, all at the same time.

What this book does

This book, the first in a two-part series for CICS training, teaches you a basic subset of CICS command-level COBOL programming. In it, you'll learn how to program for 3270 terminals using basic mapping support. You'll learn how to process VSAM files using file control commands. And you'll learn many programming techniques, including pseudo-conversational programming. In the second book of this series, you'll learn how to use advanced features of CICS, like terminal paging, message routing, alternate indexing, and more.

Although I designed this book to stand on its own, it also works well when used with other training programs. In particular, if you attend a CICS training course, this book will be a valuable resource, both before and after the course. If you read through the book beforehand, you'll be that much better prepared for the intensity of the week-long course. And after the course, this book will help you reinforce what you've learned.

Why this book is effective

As I've already said, one of the reasons CICS is difficult to learn is that you must grasp several complex concepts at the same time. This book is effective because I've integrated my presentation of these concepts, carefully explaining how each element relates to the whole. In contrast, most books (and courses) present individual CICS elements separately, without integration. No wonder so many people are baffled by CICS.

In addition, this book is effective for three other reasons. First, I spent much time selecting the content of this book. In doing so, I kept my sights set on a usable—and teachable—subset of CICS. As a result, you won't see every feature of CICS in this book. But you will learn the most useful elements. And this book provides a solid foundation for learning the advanced CICS elements the second book of this series presents.

Second, I emphasize the use of coding models in this book. The programming examples not only illustrate CICS language elements, but also serve as models for similar programs you'll write on the job. In addition, I've included models for common COBOL routines and BMS map definitions. I think you'll increase your productivity significantly if you use these models.

Third, I stress careful program design. Although effective program design is critical to the productivity of any programmer, I've yet to see a book or course that adequately deals with how to design a CICS program. In fact, most of them don't say anything about design at all. So, in this book, I show you not only how to code CICS commands, but also how to design CICS programs using the techniques of structured program design.

Who this book is for

This book is for anyone who wants to learn how to write application COBOL programs in a CICS environment. It assumes no prior CICS experience. As a result, the first three chapters present the hardware and software background you need before you can start learning how to write CICS programs. If you've had CICS experience (or other related experience), you may be able to skip some or all of these chapters.

Although you don't need any CICS background to use this book, you *do* need background in elementary COBOL. This book is designed specifically for the basic subset of COBOL presented in chapters 1 through 5 of *Structured ANS COBOL, Part 1*, by Mike Murach and Paul Noll. Although it isn't necessary, a background in VSAM file handling, such as that presented in my book *VSAM for the COBOL Programmer*, is also helpful. Incidentally, you can order these books from Mike Murach & Associates using the order form at the back of this book.

Because CICS is nearly identical under all of IBM's operating systems, you can use this book regardless of the operating system (or systems) installed at your shop. I tested all of the programs in this book using CICS version 1.6 running under MVS on an IBM 3033. In addition, I didn't use any CICS features that weren't available for the previous CICS release (1.5), so the information in this book applies to both versions.

Conclusion

As I see it, this is the first CICS book based on a sound educational approach. It also represents the first attempt to integrate the principles of structured program design with CICS. As a result, I'm confident you'll find this book to be worth many times its purchase price. If I'm wrong, feel free to return it at any time for a full refund, no questions asked.

As always, we welcome your comments, suggestions, criticisms, and questions. If you have any, please use the postage-paid comment form at the back of this book. Your comments will help us improve this product as well as future products.

Doug Lowe
Fresno, California
October, 1983

Part 1

Required background

Before you can start learning the details of CICS command-level COBOL programming, you need to understand some basic concepts. As a result, this part presents the minimum background you'll need before you can learn how to write a command-level program.

Chapter 1 introduces you to interactive systems. Here, you'll learn what types of interactive application programs you need to know how to develop in CICS. Chapter 1 also describes four special problems you need to recognize when you develop CICS programs.

Chapters 2 and 3 describe what makes up the CICS system environment. Chapter 2 introduces you to the hardware components of a data-communications network. Chapter 3 describes what CICS is and how it relates to the operating system and your application programs.

If you've had some experience with interactive programming in general or with CICS in particular, you may already know some of the material in this part. If so, you can use this material as a review.

Chapter 1

Introduction to interactive systems

Traditionally, computer processing has been *batch processing*. This means transactions are accumulated into groups, or batches, before they're processed. For instance, a full day's orders are collected before they're actually processed by the computer system.

Batch processing has improved in the last 20 years. Technological developments have dramatically increased the speed, capacity, and reliability of CPUs and I/O devices. And operating systems have become more and more sophisticated, providing such features as multiprogramming and virtual storage. Even so, these changes have only made traditional batch systems faster; they haven't changed the fundamental nature of those systems.

However, two major hardware advances *have* changed the nature of computing: (1) the development of low-cost CRT terminals and (2) the development of data-communications facilities. Terminals let users interact directly with the computer rather than through some indirect means like punched cards. With a terminal, a user can send data to the computer through a keyboard and immediately receive output from the computer on a display screen. And with data communications, the user doesn't have to be in the same building as the computer—he can be located hundreds of miles away from the computer and still interact directly with it.

7

Today, a new computer system is more likely to be interactive than batch. In an *interactive system* (also called an *on-line system*), the user enters transactions one at a time through a terminal. As each transaction is entered, it's immediately edited, errors are corrected, and master files are updated. Typically, transactions are *not* accumulated to be processed later, as they are in a batch system.

Most interactive systems on IBM mainframe hardware rely on the software product *CICS* (*Customer Information Control System*). This book introduces you to CICS and teaches you how to develop effective interactive programs in COBOL using command-level CICS. But first, you need to understand the different types of interactive programs that make up an interactive system, as well as some special problems they present that batch programs don't.

As a result, the remainder of this chapter has two sections. In the first, I'll describe the four most common types of interactive programs. In the second, I'll discuss four important considerations of interactive systems.

Interactive programs

As I see it, four types of programs are common to all interactive systems. They are: (1) data-entry programs, (2) inquiry programs, (3) file-maintenance programs, and (4) menu programs. In this section, I'll describe each.

Data-entry programs   The most critical programs in most interactive systems are *data-entry programs*. These programs accept input data from the operator and use it to update the system's files. Figure 1-1 illustrates a typical data-entry program. This program requires three steps: (1) the operator enters the data for one transaction at the terminal, (2) the program updates any related master files, and (3) the program writes the transaction to a transaction file.

Figure 1-2 illustrates five screens from the operation of an order-entry program, a typical data-entry application. The first screen (part 1 of figure 1-2) shows the program waiting for input from the operator. This screen is displayed when the program is started. The top line of the screen identifies the program (ORDER ENTRY). Then, *captions* such as CUSTOMER NUMBER: identify *data-entry fields* the operator must enter. The bottom line is a message that tells the operator how to end the program.

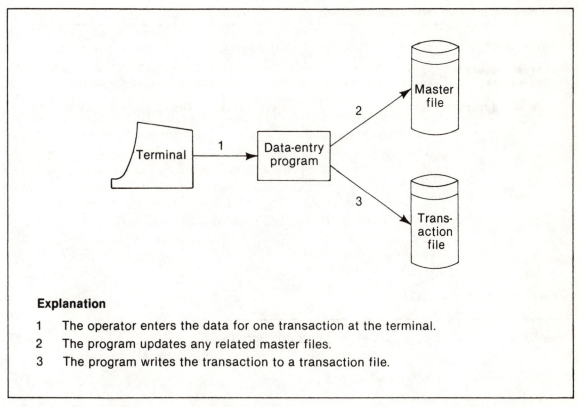

Explanation

1   The operator enters the data for one transaction at the terminal.
2   The program updates any related master files.
3   The program writes the transaction to a transaction file.

Figure 1-1   A data-entry program

Part 2 of figure 1-2 shows the screen after the operator has entered the data for one order. Although you can't tell in this figure, the program displays the screen's headings, captions, and instructions brighter than the data the operator entered. This is called *highlighting*. When the operator presses the enter key, the program edits the order to make sure no detectable errors are present.

Suppose the computer *does* detect an error. In this case, the program displays a screen like the one in part 3 of figure 1-2. Here, the operator entered an item number (293) that doesn't exist. At this point, the operator has three options: (1) correct the error by entering a valid item number, (2) end the terminal session by pressing the clear key, or (3) start the entry over altogether by pressing the erase-input key (this is a function of the terminal that causes all the data on the screen to be erased). Usually, the operator corrects the error.

The order-entry program awaits operator input:

```
ORDER ENTRY

CUSTOMER NUMBER: _
P.O. NUMBER:

ITEM NO   QUANTITY  DESCRIPTION               UNIT PRICE    AMOUNT














PRESS CLEAR TO END SESSION
```

Figure 1-2   Operation of a data-entry program (part 1 of 5)

Even if the computer doesn't detect any errors, that doesn't necessarily mean the entry is correct. As a result, some data-entry programs allow the operator to *sight-verify* the input data to find errors the computer doesn't identify. To allow *sight-verification*, the screen in part 4 of figure 1-2 displays the input data after the operator has corrected the invalid item number. If the operator presses the enter key, the order is processed. On the other hand, if the operator presses PA1, he can modify the order data to correct any remaining errors.

To help the operator sight-verify the data, the program displays additional information on the screen. For example, the customer's name is displayed. If the purchase order did not come from Barry's Hardware Store, the operator could tell immediately that he entered the wrong customer number. Similarly, the description and unit price for each item number are displayed, as well as the line item amount (the quantity times the unit price) and the invoice total.

The operator enters data for an order:

```
ORDER ENTRY

CUSTOMER NUMBER: 1050
P.O. NUMBER:     B3827-2

ITEM NO  QUANTITY  DESCRIPTION             UNIT PRICE    AMOUNT

  101      12
  293      5
  1722     8_




PRESS CLEAR TO END SESSION
```

Figure 1-2 Operation of a data-entry program (part 2 of 5)

The program detects an error and displays an error message:

```
ORDER ENTRY

CUSTOMER NUMBER: 01050        BARRY'S HARDWARE STORE
P.O. NUMBER:     B3827-2

ITEM NO  QUANTITY  DESCRIPTION             UNIT PRICE    AMOUNT

 00101    00012    PVC--3/4" x 20' (50)        9.87      118.44
 00293    00005
 01722    00008    CORNER SPR 1/2" (20)       18.44      147.52




ENTER MODIFICATIONS OR PRESS CLEAR TO END SESSION
ITEM NOT IN INVENTORY FILE
```

Figure 1-2 Operation of a data-entry program (part 3 of 5)

The program asks the operator to verify the order:

```
_ORDER ENTRY

CUSTOMER NUMBER: 01050        BARRY'S HARDWARE STORE
P.O. NUMBER:      B3827-2

ITEM NO   QUANTITY   DESCRIPTION             UNIT PRICE    AMOUNT

00101     00012      PVC--3/4" x 20' (50)         9.87    118.44
00239     00005      ELBOW JNT 3/4" (100)        22.88    114.40
01722     00008      CORNER SPR 1/2" (20)        18.44    147.52




                                INVOICE TOTAL:    380.36



PRESS ENTER TO POST ORDER OR PA1 TO MODIFY ORDER
```

Figure 1-2   Operation of a data-entry program (part 4 of 5)

If the operator verifies the order, the program processes it and awaits entry of another order:

```
ORDER ENTRY

CUSTOMER NUMBER: _
P.O. NUMBER:

ITEM NO   QUANTITY   DESCRIPTION             UNIT PRICE    AMOUNT








ORDER POSTED--ENTER NEXT ORDER OR PRESS CLEAR TO END SESSION
```

Figure 1-2   Operation of a data-entry program (part 5 of 5)

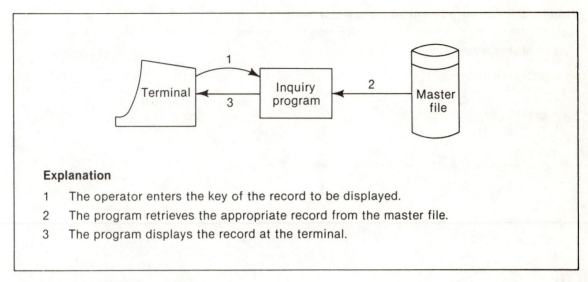

Explanation

1   The operator enters the key of the record to be displayed.
2   The program retrieves the appropriate record from the master file.
3   The program displays the record at the terminal.

Figure 1-3   An inquiry program

In any event, once the program edits the order and the operator verifies it, the program processes the order and displays the fresh screen shown in part 5 of figure 1-2.

I should point out that the sight-verification step is often omitted from data-entry programs. If that's the case, the program automatically processes the data if it doesn't find any errors. Whether or not you should include a verify step in a data-entry program depends mostly on who will be using the program and how often it will be used. If the program will be used by clerks in a large data-entry department, and if the transaction volume is high, you should probably omit the verify step. Unfortunately, most data-entry operators would press the enter key for the verify screen without looking at it anyway. If, however, the program will be run by an end-user (for example, a salesperson), or if the transaction volume is low, the verify step is a must.

Inquiry programs   An *inquiry program* is designed to provide a response to a user's inquiry. Figure 1-3 illustrates a typical inquiry program. As you can see, the inquiry program requires three steps: (1) the operator enters the key of the record to be displayed (such as a customer number or a part number), (2) the program retrieves the appropriate record from the master file, and (3) the program displays the record at the terminal.

The customer-inquiry program awaits operator input:

```
CUSTOMER INQUIRY                                              10/31/83

CUSTOMER NUMBER: _

NAME:                                      CURRENT BALANCE DUE:
ADDRESS:
                                           YEAR-TO-DATE SALES:
                                           MONTH-TO-DATE SALES:

    INVOICE     DATE     DUE DATE     AMOUNT     BALANCE














PRESS CLEAR TO END SESSION
```

Figure 1-4   Operation of an inquiry program (part 1 of 3)

Figure 1-4 shows three screens from a typical inquiry program. This program displays information for a selected customer. In the first screen (part 1), the program is waiting for the operator to enter a customer number. The second screen (part 2) shows the customer number the operator entered. When the operator presses the enter key, the program retrieves and displays the data for customer 1050, as shown in the third screen (part 3).

Inquiry programs can be simple, retrieving one record from a master file and displaying it on a single screen, or quite complex, retrieving several records from several files. The program in figure 1-4 probably retrieves data from two files: a customer master file and an invoice file. The most complicated inquiry program I've written retrieves data from 13 files and displays it with 29 different screen formats. Fortunately, most inquiry programs are considerably less complex.

The operator enters a customer number:

```
CUSTOMER INQUIRY                                              10/31/83

CUSTOMER NUMBER: 1050_

NAME:                                    CURRENT BALANCE DUE:
ADDRESS:
                                         YEAR-TO-DATE SALES:
                                         MONTH-TO-DATE SALES:


    INVOICE     DATE     DUE DATE     AMOUNT     BALANCE







PRESS CLEAR TO END SESSION
```

Figure 1-4   Operation of an inquiry program (part 2 of 3)

The program retrieves the customer's record and displays it:

```
CUSTOMER INQUIRY                                              10/31/83

CUSTOMER NUMBER: 01050

NAME:       BARRY'S HARDWARE STORE          CURRENT BALANCE DUE:    2,049.50
ADDRESS:    2105 N. FIRST STREET
            FRESNO        CA 93726          YEAR-TO-DATE SALES:    10,118.68
                                            MONTH-TO-DATE SALES:    3,328.55

    INVOICE     DATE     DUE DATE     AMOUNT      BALANCE
    078666    08/27/83   09/27/83      149.50      149.50
    079026    09/16/83   10/16/83    1,200.00    1,200.00
    080028    10/01/83   11/01/83      250.00      250.00
    081374    10/27/83   11/27/83    3,078.55      450.00




PRESS CLEAR TO END SESSION
```

Figure 1-4   Operation of an inquiry program (part 3 of 3)

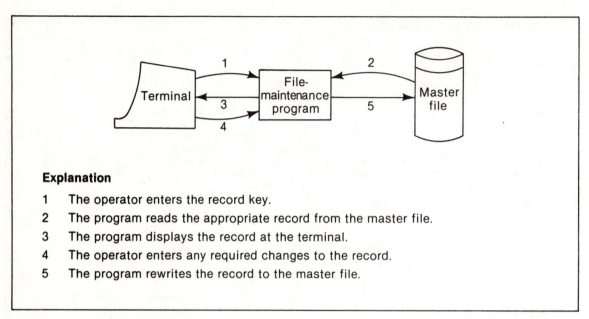

Explanation

1   The operator enters the record key.
2   The program reads the appropriate record from the master file.
3   The program displays the record at the terminal.
4   The operator enters any required changes to the record.
5   The program rewrites the record to the master file.

Figure 1-5   A file-maintenance program

File-maintenance programs   A *file-maintenance program* can update a file by adding, changing, or deleting records. Figure 1-5 shows a typical file-maintenance program. In this case, the program only allows changes. Here, five steps are required: (1) the operator enters the record key, (2) the program reads the appropriate record, (3) the program displays the record at the terminal, (4) the operator enters any required changes to the record, and (5) the program rewrites the record to the master file.

In many ways, a file-maintenance program is a combination of an inquiry program and a data-entry program. Like an inquiry program, a file-maintenance program must accept a record key, read a record, and display it. And like a data-entry program, a file-maintenance program must accept input data (the changes), edit it, verify the changes, and update the system's files.

Menu programs   A *menu program* allows an operator to select the functions he wishes to perform. Figure 1-6 shows a typical menu program. Three steps are required: (1) the program sends a list of processing selections to the terminal, (2) the operator chooses one of the selections, and (3) control is passed to the appropriate program. Systems that use menu programs are often called *menu-driven systems*.

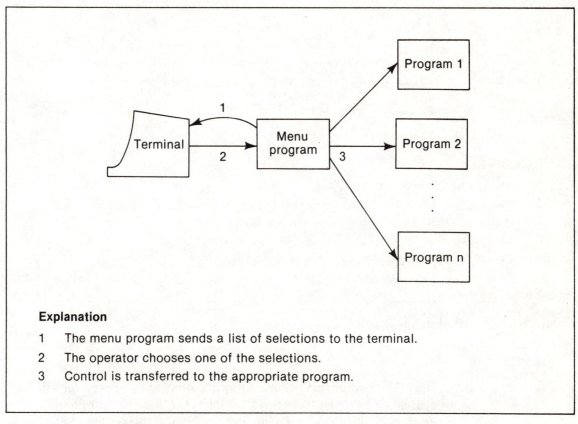

Explanation

1   The menu program sends a list of selections to the terminal.

2   The operator chooses one of the selections.

3   Control is transferred to the appropriate program.

Figure 1-6   A menu program

Figure 1-7 shows a typical menu screen. In many interactive systems, several layers of menus are required. For example, if the operator selects number one in figure 1-7, another menu showing functions related to order entry might be displayed.

Some interactive systems don't use menus. Instead, the operator begins a program by entering a memorized command. For example, the operator might enter:

```
ORD1
```

to begin an order-entry program. In some cases, the command might indicate what type of processing the program should do, like this example from an airline reservation system:

```
A30MARSFOJFK
```

```
        MASTER MENU


        1. ORDER ENTRY

        2. CUSTOMER MAINTENANCE

        3. CUSTOMER INQUIRY

        4. INVOICING


        YOUR SELECTION: _





 PRESS CLEAR TO END SESSION
```

Figure 1-7   A typical menu screen

Here, the operator is using an inquiry program to check for all
available flights (A) on March 30 (30MAR) leaving from San
Francisco (SFO) and arriving at New York (JFK).

Systems that use commands such as these are often called
command-driven systems. Because command-driven systems are
difficult to use and error-prone, most of today's systems are
menu-driven.

Interactive system considerations

Now that you understand the types of programs found in an interactive system, you should be aware of some of the problems these
programs must be able to handle. In this section, I'll cover four
basic problems common to all interactive systems: shared files,
response time, security, and recovery.

Shared files   A batch program typically has complete control of the
files it uses, so there's no chance another program can interfere
with its processing. In an interactive system, however, many terminal operators use the system simultaneously, and all must have
access to the files they require. As a result, an interactive system

must provide for *shared files* by coordinating all file updates so two users aren't allowed to update the same record at the same time.

If two users accessing the same file at the same time creates problems, imagine the problems when hundreds of users are updating the same file! Fortunately, by taking a few simple precautions, you can completely avoid all of these problems. I'll describe these precautions later in this book.

Response time   *Response time* is another special consideration for interactive systems that isn't a concern with batch systems. Quite simply, response time is the amount of time a user must wait while a transaction is being processed. A response time of several seconds is probably good; several minutes is probably not so good.

Many factors affect response time: the number of users on the system, the size of the CPU, the speed of the disk drives, how the system parameters are set, the speed of the communication lines, and how the application programs are written. In this book, I'm only concerned with the last one: how the application programs are written. The other factors are usually out of your control anyway. As for application program efficiency, I'll recommend a few basic techniques that can have a significant effect on program efficiency rather than many obscure techniques that would have only a marginal effect.

Security   In a batch system, computer *security* is relatively easy to maintain because there's only one access to the computer: the computer room. However, in an interactive system, terminals are located in many places, and security is a problem.

The main security technique used in today's interactive system is the *logon procedure*. Unless a terminal user completes the logon procedure, the system prevents him from using the computer. To complete the logon procedure, the user must enter his name and a *password* known only to him. If the name doesn't appear in the list of authorized users, or if he enters the password incorrectly, he can't access the system.

In addition to the logon procedure, most interactive systems have a multi-level security system that allows some users to access certain files, while other users have access to other files. In other words, each user is allowed to access only those files he's authorized to use. For example, an order-entry clerk might have access to order-processing files but not to payroll files.

Recovery   All interactive systems must provide for *recovery* in the event of a system failure. In a batch system, it's easy to recreate the events preceding a system failure. However, in an interactive system with hundreds of users, recovery can be a nightmare if not properly planned. Fortunately, from an application programmer's point of view, recovery is a design consideration that's largely the system programmer's responsibility. I mention it here, though, so you'll be aware that recovery is a consideration in the design of an interactive system.

Discussion

If your programming experience has been limited to batch systems, I think you can now appreciate the complexities interactive systems present. Obviously, to develop programs for an interactive system, you need to know how they differ from the traditional edit, update, and report programs of a batch system. But, just as important, you need to know how the hardware components of an interactive system differ from those of a batch system. So, in the next chapter, I'll give you the hardware background you need to be able to develop command-level CICS programs.

Terminology

batch processing
interactive system
on-line system
CICS
Customer Information Control System
data-entry program
caption
data-entry field
highlight
sight-verify
sight-verification
inquiry program
file-maintenance program
menu program
menu-driven system
command-driven system
shared files

response time
security
logon procedure
password
recovery

Objectives

1. Describe the four major types of interactive programs.

2. Explain the following considerations for interactive systems:

       shared files
       response time
       security
       recovery

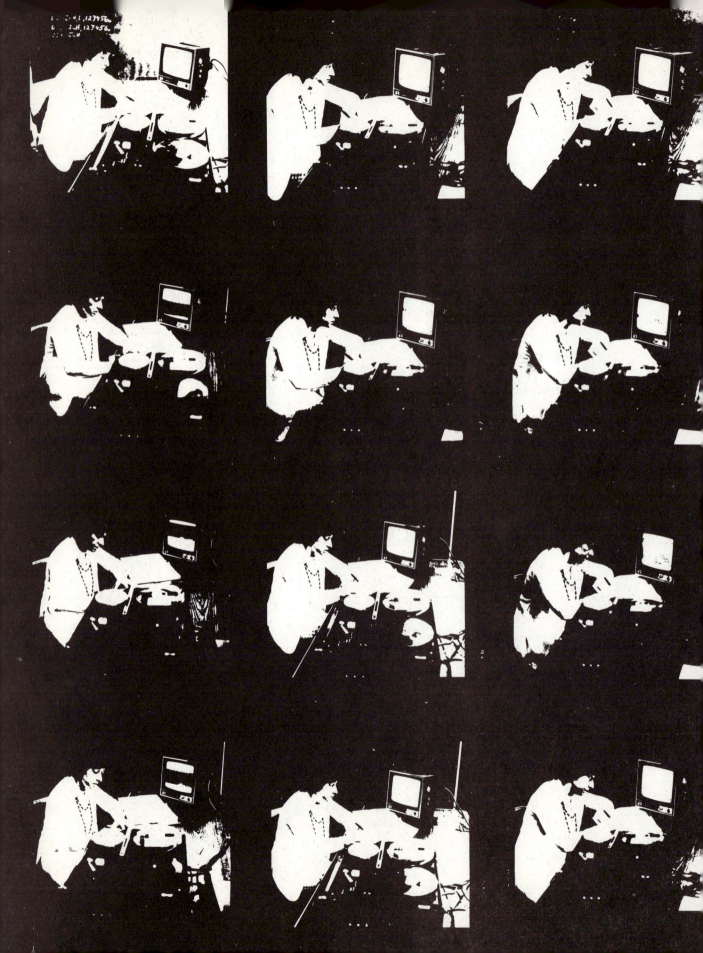

Chapter 2

Introduction to data-communication networks

A *data-communication network* (often called a *telecommunication network*) allows users at *remote terminals* (terminals that aren't located at a computer site) to access a *host computer* (or *host system*). In this chapter, I'll discuss the elements of a data-communication network. Then, I'll briefly present IBM's most popular terminal system, the 3270 Information Display System.

Elements of a data-communication network

Figure 2-1 shows a typical data-communication network. Basically, five elements make up a network: a host system (in the case of CICS, an IBM System/370-family mainframe), a communication controller, modems, communication lines, and terminal systems. A *terminal system* can be a single CRT display station, or several, connected to the network through a terminal controller.

Communication lines   One of the major components of a communication network is a phone connection, often called a *communication line* (or *telecommunication line*, or just *TC line*). The TC line can be set up through the public telephone system or may be privately owned.

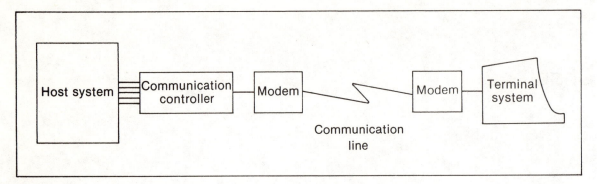

Figure 2-1 Elements of a data-communication network

The most common type of TC line is called a *switched*, or *dial-up*, *line*. Dialing establishes the connection in a switched line. In general, a switched line is the least expensive type of line, unless a high volume of long-distance work is done.

In contrast, a *non-switched line* (or *dedicated line*) does not require dialing; the connection is always established. If a non-switched line is set up through the public telephone system, it's called a *leased line*. If it's privately owned, it's called a *private line*. Leased or private lines are commonly used when a high volume of data is transmitted over long distances.

Non-switched lines have less interference than switched lines and, as a result, can transmit data accurately at higher speeds. Transmission speed is measured in units called *baud*. Typical transmission speeds for switched lines are 1,200 or 2,400 baud. For leased or private lines, 9,600 baud is a common transmission speed.

In addition, some lines permit *full-duplex* (or just *duplex*) transmission. When full-duplex transmission is used, data is transmitted in both directions at the same time. When *half-duplex* transmission is used, data is transmitted only one direction at a time.

Modems   The second critical component in a data-communication network is a pair of *modems*. As you can see in figure 2-1, a modem is required at each end of a TC line. A modem's function is to convert digital signals to audio frequency signals that can be sent over the phone line, and to reconvert audio frequency signals back into digital signals that can be processed by the computer system.

Figure 2-2 A dial-up modem

Figure 2-2 shows a type of modem that's typically connected to a dial-up line. To establish a connection, the user dials the correct number and waits for the host computer to answer. When the computer answers, the user hears a high-pitched squeal on the phone. The user then pushes the DATA button on the phone and hangs up. This connects the modem to the line.

Communication controllers   In figure 2-1, the modem at the left side of the TC line is connected to the host system via a *communication controller*, the third critical component of a data-communication network. The communication controller performs the functions necessary to control the transmission of data over the communication line.

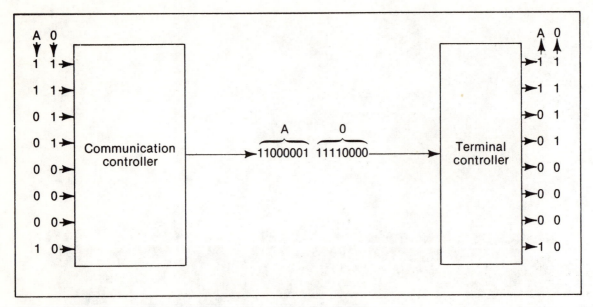

Figure 2-3 Serialization and deserialization of input data

One of the main functions of a communication controller is *data conversion*—that is, converting data into a form that a modem can process. This process is sometimes called *serialization* because it involves converting eight-bit bytes into a continuous stream of bits the modem processes one at a time. Figure 2-3 illustrates serialization. Here, two bytes—A and 0—are converted from their eight-bit byte patterns to a stream of serial bits. Then, the terminal controller at the other end of the line converts that serial stream back to the eight-bit byte patterns for A and 0. This opposite process is called *deserialization*.

Another main function of a communication controller is *data-link control*. Data-link control ensures the successful transmission of data over the communication line. Some of the functions required for data-link control are synchronizing the host with the terminal, identifying the source and destination of a transmission, and detecting and correcting transmission errors.

In addition, data-link control must convert data so it conforms to a standard *line discipline* (sometimes called a *protocol*). A line discipline is a set of rules that governs data transmission. The two most common line disciplines in an IBM communication network are *BSC (Binary Synchronous Control)* and *SDLC (Synchronous Data Link Control)*.

Figure 2-4 IBM 3705 communication controller

The two most common **IBM** communication controllers are the
3705 and the 3704. Both contain their own microprocessor and
memory (up to 512K for the 3705) and execute a special network
control program that performs data-link control functions. The
3705, illustrated in figure 2-4, can control up to 352 communication lines. The 3704, designed for smaller communication networks, can control up to 32 communication lines.

Host system   The fourth critical component of a data-communi-
cation network is the host system. To control communication func-
tions, the host system uses a telecommunications access method.
The three most common are *BTAM* (*Basic Telecommunications
Access Method*), *TCAM*(*Telecommunications Access Method*), and
VTAM (*Virtual Telecommunications Access Method*).

Terminal systems   A terminal system is the fifth critical component of a data-communication network. As I've said, a terminal system consists of a terminal controller plus one or more CRT display stations. Commonly, *terminal* refers to a single CRT display station, and that's how I use the term in this book. Some terminal systems may also include printers.

A variety of terminal systems can be part of an IBM data-communication network. Some are general-purpose, like the 3270 Information Display System and the 3770 Data Communication System. Others are specific to particular applications, like the 3600 Finance Communication System and the 3660 Supermarket System. Although CICS supports all of these terminal systems, by far the most common is the 3270.

The 3270 Information Display System

The 3270 Information Display System is not a single terminal, but rather a system of CRT display stations and printers connected to a controller that communicates with a host system through a communication network. Figure 2-5 illustrates the components of a typical 3270 system.

A single 3270 terminal controller (a 3274) can control up to 32 display stations and printers. The controller is usually attached to the host system through a modem and a communication line. Alternatively, the controller can be equipped for direct attachment to one of the host system's channels.

3270 display station models   3270 display stations are available in a variety of configurations offering anywhere from 12 lines of 40 characters each to 43 lines of 80 characters, with one model that displays 27 lines of 132 characters. One of the most common 3270 display stations is the 3278 Model 2. This terminal displays 24 lines with 80 characters in each, plus a special status line at the bottom of the screen. In this book, I'll sometimes give a screen's dimensions as a pair of numbers separated by an "x," like 24 x 80. This means the screen has 24 lines of 80 characters each, not including the status line.

The 3270 display stations can be configured with many options, including alternate keyboard configurations for special applications. Less common options are a selector light pen that allows an operator to communicate with the host system without using the keyboard, a magnetic slot reader or magnetic hand scan-

Figure 2-5 Components of a 3270 Information Display System

ner, a lock and key to prevent unauthorized use, four- or seven-color display capability, extended highlighting capabilities including underscore, blink, and reverse video (dark characters against a light background), and graphics.

3270 printers   In addition to display stations, printers can be attached to a 3270 system. Many 3270 systems have a local-print feature that allows the data on the screen of a 3270 display station to be transferred to the terminal controller and then printed by one of the 3270 printers. Since this print operation does *not* involve transmission of data between the 3270 system and the host, it's an efficient mode of printing.

You should be aware that there's little distinction between a display station and a printer as far as CICS is concerned. When output is directed to a terminal, it's displayed at the screen if the terminal is a display station; if the terminal is a printer, the output is printed. The major difference is, of course, that printers cannot accept input data, while display stations can.

3270-compatible devices and emulators Because of the enormous popularity of the 3270 system, many manufacturers other than IBM offer compatible terminals, controllers, and printers. And most manufacturers of minicomputers and microcomputers offer *emulator programs* that allow their computers to behave as if they were 3270 devices. As a matter of fact, most of the programs in this book were tested using two emulator programs: one for a large minicomputer system manufactured by Wang Laboratories and the other for IBM's Personal Computer. Because of the cost advantages, it's becoming more and more common to see such products in use in 3270 networks. In the future, I suspect that IBM's Personal Computer will become an integral part of many 3270 systems. In any event, the application programming requirements are the same whether you're using an IBM 3270 device, a 3270-compatible device, or a minicomputer or microcomputer emulating a 3270.

Discussion

Now that you've been introduced to the basic elements of a data-communication network and the 3270 Information Display System, consider figure 2-6, a typical IBM mainframe installation with interactive capability. Here, the System/370 CPU has the usual devices attached via channels: disk drives, tape drives, a high-speed printer, and an operator's console. In addition, a local 3270 system is attached directly to one of its channels, and two remote 3270 systems are attached to it through a 3705 communication controller. You can easily see how complicated the interactive environment can become.

Fortunately, all of this hardware is managed by system software products: the operating system (DOS/VSE or OS/MVS, for example), the telecommunications access method (such as TCAM, VTAM, or BTAM), and, of course, CICS. As an application programmer, all you need to know is how to invoke the CICS functions that control the hardware this topic describes. So, the next chapter explains at a conceptual level what CICS is and how it operates.

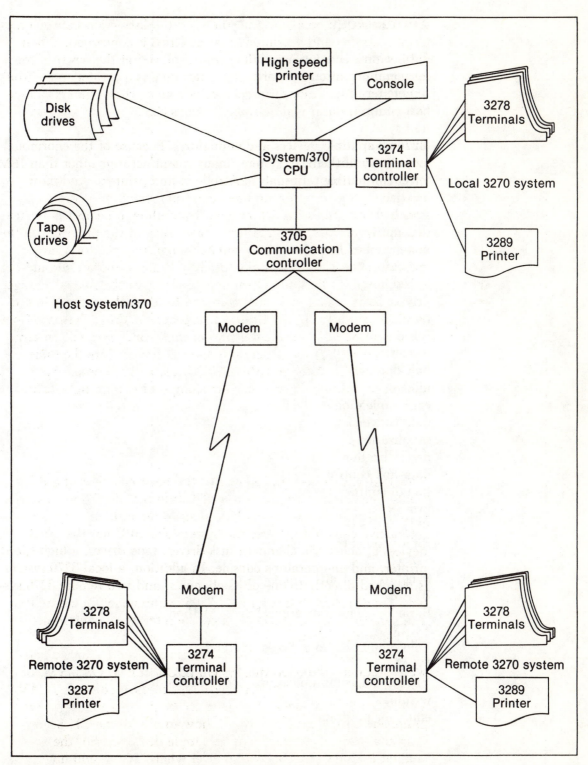

Figure 2-6 A typical System/370 and 3270 configuration

Terminology

data-communication network
telecommunication network
remote terminal
host computer
host system
terminal system
communication line
telecommunication line
TC line
switched line
dial-up line
non-switched line
dedicated line
leased line
private line
baud
full-duplex
duplex
half-duplex
modem
communication controller
data conversion
serialization
deserialization
data-link control
line discipline
protocol
BSC
Binary Synchronous Control
SDLC
Synchronous Data Link Control
BTAM
Basic Telecommunications Access Method
TCAM
Telecommunications Access Method
VTAM
Virtual Telecommunications Access Method
terminal
emulator program

Objectives

1. Describe the components of a data-communication network.
2. Describe the components of a 3270 system.

Chapter 3

Introduction to CICS: Concepts and terminology

To begin with, *CICS* stands for *Customer Information Control System*. And that's just about what CICS is: a system designed to control information in a modern interactive environment. Since CICS controls data-base operations as well as data-communication operations, it's often called a *data-base/data-communication system* (or just *DB/DC system*).

CICS (sometimes called *CICS/VS*) runs on all of IBM's Virtual Storage operating systems: DOS/VS, DOS/VSE, OS/VS1, and OS/MVS. Regardless of the operating system in use, CICS is the same. As a result, the information in this book applies to any CICS system.

Just what does CICS do? Quite simply, CICS is an interface between the application programs in an interactive system and the host operating system, as figure 3-1 illustrates. As you can see, the application program communicates with CICS. In turn, CICS communicates with access methods through the host operating system. Then, the access methods (such as VTAM, BTAM, VSAM, or ISAM) communicate with the system's devices (such as terminals, disk drives, or tape drives).

I must make an important point before I go on: As far as the operating system is concerned, CICS is an application program.

35

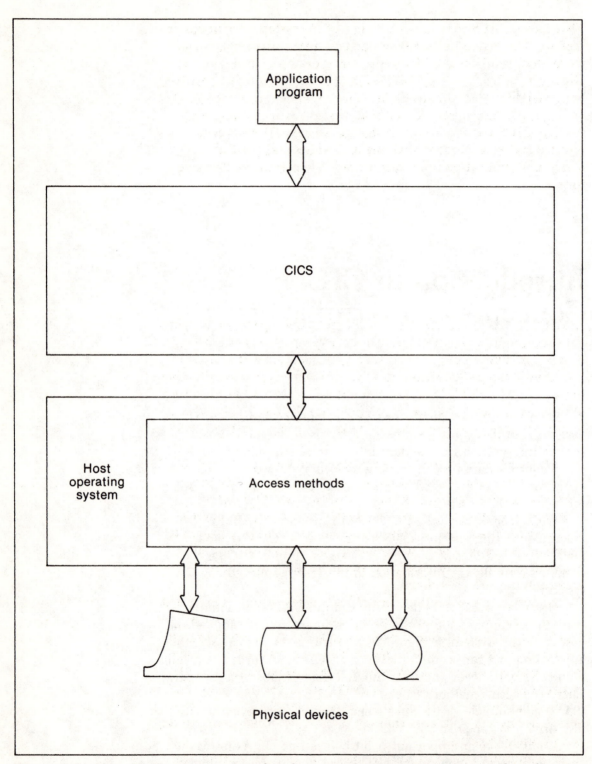

Figure 3-1 How CICS acts as an interface between the operating system and application
programs

That means CICS runs as a job in one of the system's partitions or regions. The region or partition may be a real address space, but more often is a virtual address space. For example, in figure 3-2, CICS is running on a DOS/VSE system in the foreground 1 partition. Usually, CICS requires a large partition or region (2048K isn't an unusually large size). As you read through this chapter, you'll see that CICS requires so much storage because (1) it's a complicated software product with many modules and (2) it allows many user application programs (or tasks) to execute at the same time.

Multitasking

In CICS, a task is the execution of an application program (or perhaps several application programs) for a specific user. For example, if user 1 is running program A, then user 1 has created a task.

One of the basic features of CICS is *multitasking*. Multitasking simply means that CICS allows more than one task to be executing at the same time. For example, consider figure 3-3. It's the same as figure 3-2, except it shows that six tasks are running in the CICS production partition.

Multitasking is similar to multiprogramming. In fact, the difference between multiprogramming and multitasking is subtle. Basically, multiprogramming means that an operating system allows several programs to execute at the same time. In contrast, multitasking means that a program running in a *single* partition or region allows several tasks to execute at the same time. For all practical purposes, multitasking is the same thing as multiprogramming one level down.

Notice in figure 3-3 that three of the users—user 1, user 3, and user 6—are running the same application program: order entry. This would waste valuable storage space if the same program were loaded into storage at three different locations. Under CICS, however, a concept called *multithreading* is used so only one copy of a program is loaded into storage. Multithreading simply means that the area of storage containing a program is not allocated to a specific user—instead, all users running the program have access to the same storage locations.

For multithreading to work, a program must be *reentrant* (or, as you'll see in a moment, must *appear* to be reentrant). A program that's completely reentrant doesn't change itself in any way. In

DOS/VSE	
Supervisor area	
Background	COBOL compiler
Foreground 4	CICS test partition
Foreground 3	Payroll application
Foreground 2	Unused
Foreground 1	CICS production partition

Figure 3-2   CICS in a DOS/VSE partition

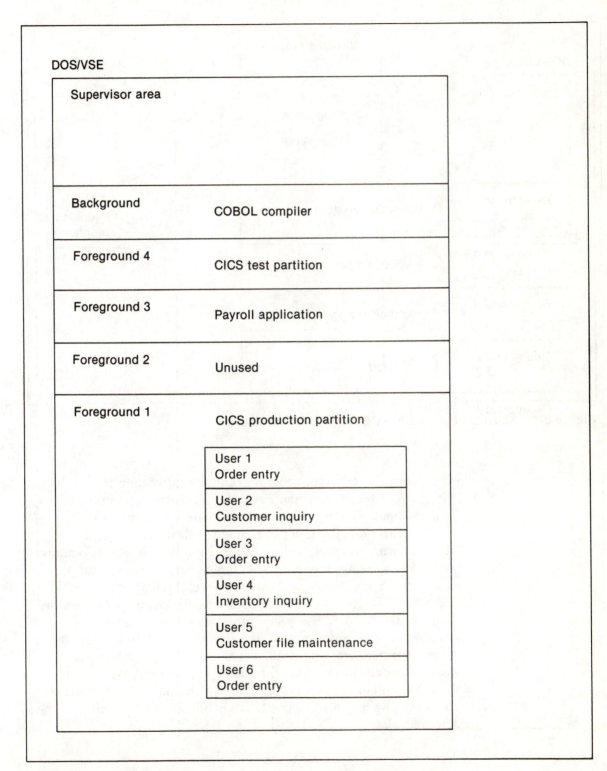

Figure 3-3   Multiprogramming and multitasking in a CICS system

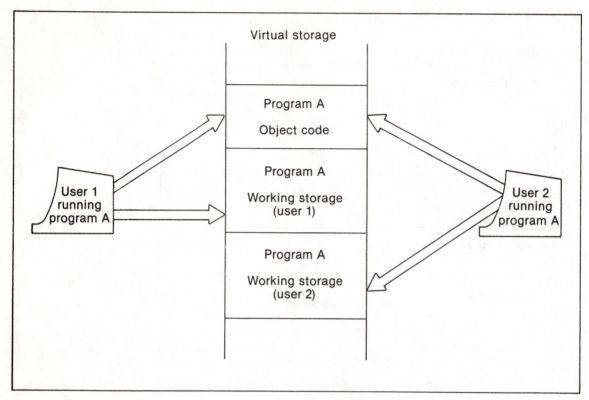

Figure 3-4 Sharing object code: A quasi-reentrant program

other words, a reentrant program cannot modify data in working storage. As a result, any user can enter a reentrant program at any point without affecting other users who are also running it.

You can probably imagine how difficult it is to write a reentrant program. To make things easier, command-level CICS allows you to use working storage by treating all programs as *quasi-reentrant*. Figure 3-4 shows how quasi-reentrant programs work under CICS. Here, two users are running the same application program, PROGRAM A. They share the same storage for the program's object code—that is, the Procedure Division—but each is given a separate working storage area. That way, each can use working storage in the normal fashion. Fortunately, when you write a command-level CICS program, you don't need to worry about making it quasi-reentrant. CICS handles that for you automatically.

Transactions and task initiation

A *transaction* is a predefined unit of work a terminal user can invoke. When a transaction is invoked, a specified application program is loaded into storage (if it isn't already in storage), and a task is started. The difference between a task and a transaction is that while several users may invoke the same transaction, each will be given his own task.

Each transaction is identified by a unique four-character code called a *transaction identifier* (or sometimes just *trans-id*). An operator initiates a transaction by entering the transaction identifier into the terminal. For example, if the operator keys the characters ORD1 and presses the enter key, the transaction named ORD1 is invoked. This is the most common way to invoke a transaction, but there are others I'll explain later.

A special CICS table, called the *Program Control Table* (or *PCT*), defines each transaction. Basically, the PCT contains a list of valid transaction identifiers. Each trans-id is paired with the name of the program CICS will load and execute when the transaction is invoked.

Another CICS table, called the *Processing Program Table* (or *PPT*), contains a list of all valid program names. The PPT indicates each program's location—a storage address if the program has already been loaded or a disk location if the program hasn't been loaded. CICS uses the PPT to determine whether it will load a new copy of the program when the transaction is invoked.

To understand how a task is initiated under CICS, consider figure 3-5. Here, the operator starts a transaction by entering ORD1. Then, CICS searches the Program Control Table to find the program to be executed. As you can see, the program for transaction ORD1 is ORDPGM1. Next, CICS searches the Processing Program Table to determine the location of ORDPGM1. In this case, the program is not currently in storage, so a disk location (location D) is specified. CICS locates the program on the disk and loads it into storage, and a task has been initiated.

On the other hand, suppose the operator enters the trans-id DM01. The entry for DM01 in the PCT indicates that the program DMPGM01 should be executed. In turn, the entry for DMPGM01 in the PPT shows CICS that the program is already in storage. As a result, the object code for DMPGM01 is not retrieved from the disk unit.

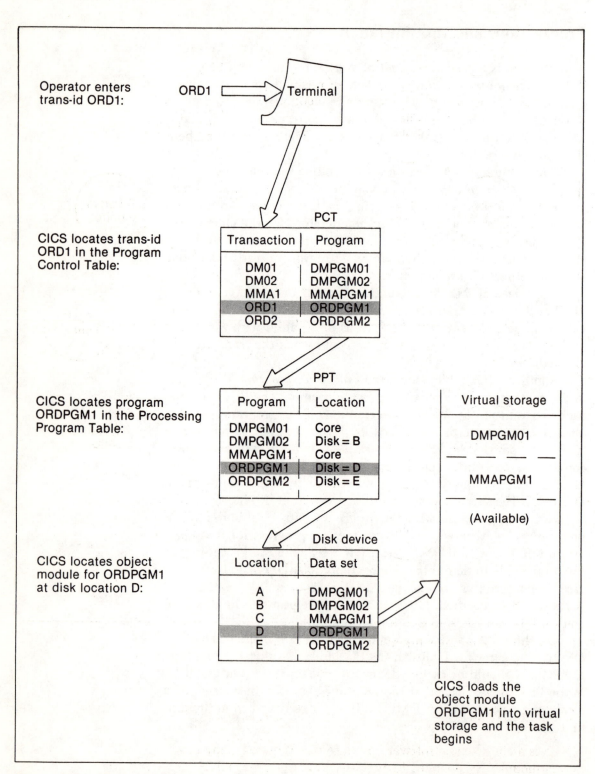

Figure 3-5 CICS task initiation

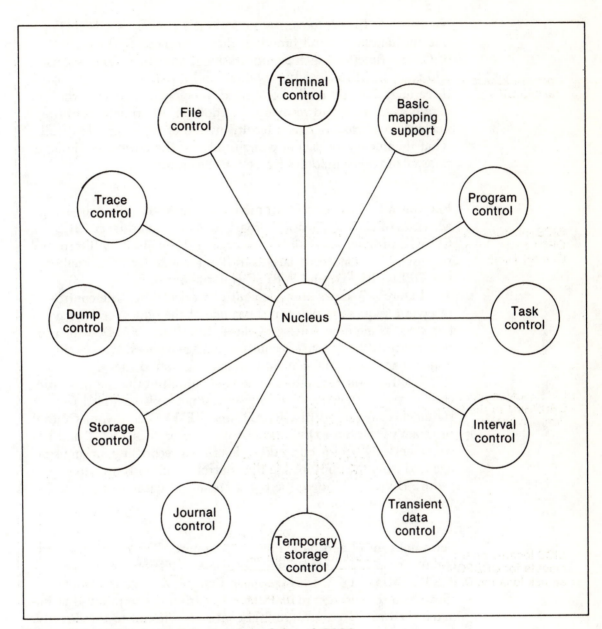

Figure 3-6   The major functional modules of CICS

CICS modules

CICS is a complicated software product that requires many program modules to function. Figure 3-6 shows the major CICS *management modules*.

Nucleus   At the center of figure 3-6 is the *nucleus* of CICS. The nucleus handles general functions that are crucial to the operation of CICS—functions such as multitasking, multithreading, security, and recovery. I've already explained multitasking and multithreading, and you really don't need to be concerned with the details of security and recovery. In addition, the functions of the nucleus are automatic. As a result, instead of explaining in detail what the nucleus does, I'm going to discuss the more specific functions of the other modules figure 3-6 illustrates.

File control   The *file control* module manages the file processing activities of each application program. A command-level CICS COBOL program does all file processing through CICS file control requests. In other words, access to files through COBOL facilities like OPEN, READ, and WRITE is not allowed.

Figure 3-7 shows how file control works. When file control receives a request, it passes it on to one of the host operating system's access methods (such as QSAM, ISAM, or VSAM), which in turn controls the system's secondary storage devices. One of the major functions of file control is managing shared files.

The file control module somewhat simplifies the file processing code in your programs. Not only do you not code standard I-O statements such as OPEN, READ, and REWRITE in your COBOL program's Procedure Division, but you also omit SELECT and FD statements. All you need to do is describe a record in working storage and issue the appropriate file control commands in your Procedure Division. I'll describe the commands to access file control functions in chapter 8.

Terminal control and basic mapping support   The *terminal control* module is CICS's interface with telecommunications access methods like VTAM and BTAM, as shown in figure 3-8. Terminal control allows you to send text to or receive text from the terminal that initiated the task. Even so, terminal control is difficult to use directly. An application program that uses terminal control directly must process complicated strings of control characters and data sent to and received from the terminal.

To relieve you of the task of building and decoding complicated strings of control characters and data, *basic mapping support* (or *BMS*) was developed. As figure 3-9 shows, BMS (a part of CICS) is an interface between the application program and terminal control. To receive data from or send data to a terminal, an application program issues a BMS request. After BMS retrieves the

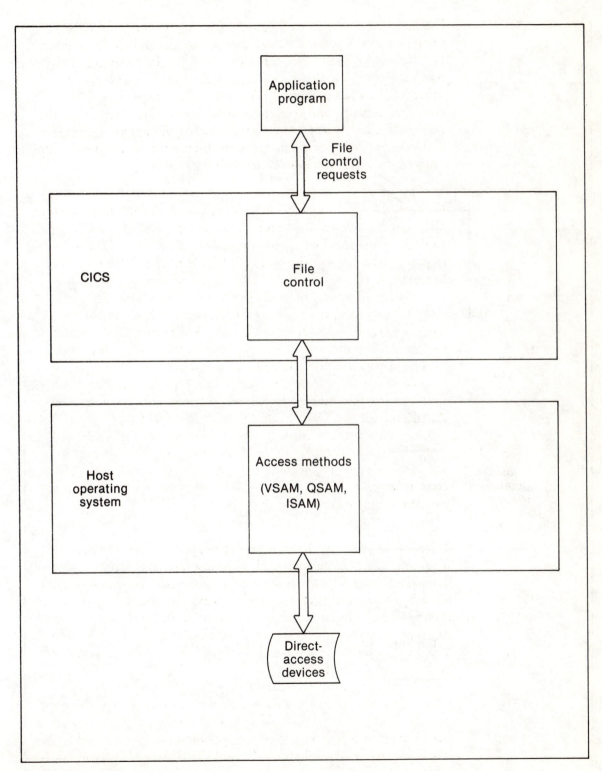

Figure 3-7   File control

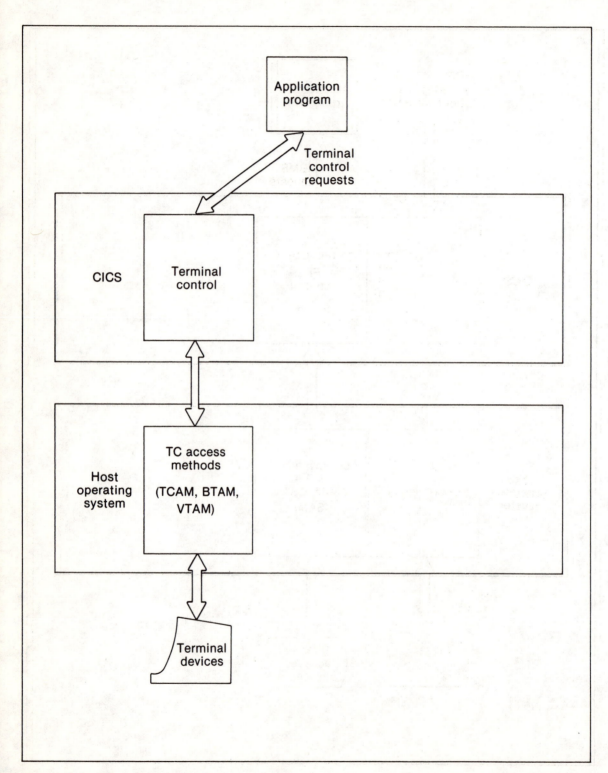

Figure 3-8   Terminal control

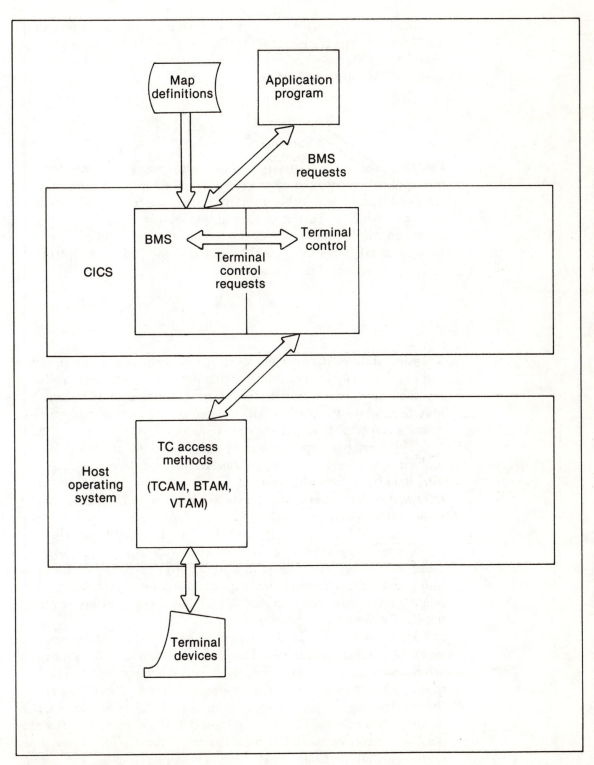

Figure 3-9 Basic mapping support

specified *map definition*, it formats a terminal control request that's valid for the type of terminal that initiated the task and that matches the map definition. In chapter 5, I'll show you how to create a BMS map definition.

Program control   Under CICS, a task may consist of more than one application program. For example, the application program executed when a task is begun may transfer control to a different program, which in turn may invoke yet another program. The *program control* module manages the flow of control from one program to another within a task. I'll describe the program control commands in part 2 of this book.

Transient data control   The *transient data control* module provides a convenient way to use simple sequential files. Each file is called a *transient data queue*, or just *TD queue*. Records in a TD queue may be read or written but not updated or deleted (the only way to delete a record is to delete the entire queue).

There are two types of transient data queues: intrapartition and extrapartition. An *intrapartition transient data queue* can be used only by tasks within a single CICS partition. In contrast, an *extrapartition transient data queue* can be accessed from any partition in the system.

To illustrate, consider figure 3-10. Part 1 of this figure shows an intrapartition TD queue. Here, three CICS users are running an order-entry program that's adding records to the queue. At the same time, another CICS user is running an invoicing program that's reading records from the queue. All four of these users are working within the same CICS partition.

Part 2 of figure 3-10 shows how separate partitions can access an extrapartition TD queue. Here, three users in the CICS partition are running an order-entry program that adds records to a TD queue, while a batch invoicing program running in another partition is reading the data in the TD queue. In this example, a CICS partition is sharing a TD queue with a non-CICS partition. It's also possible for two or more CICS partitions to share a TD queue. For example, if an installation has three partitions running CICS, each can run tasks that access a common TD queue.

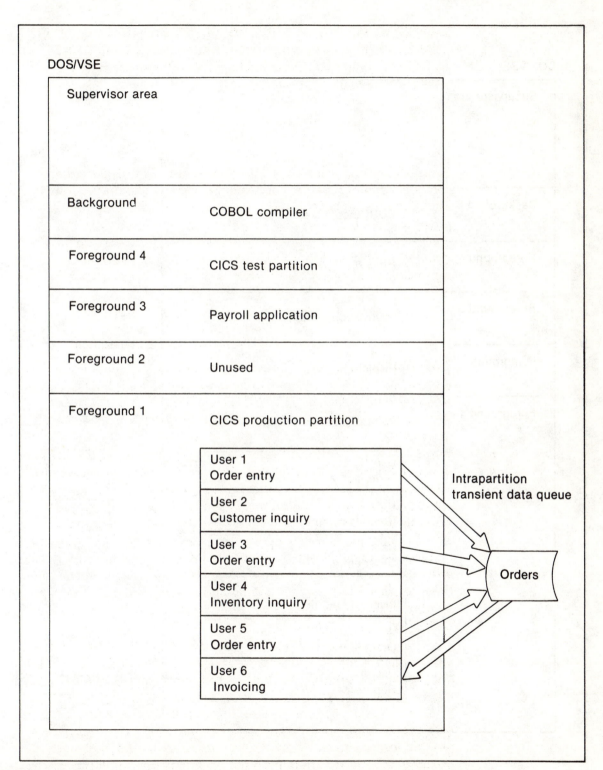

Figure 3-10   Intrapartition and extrapartition transient data queues (part 1 of 2)

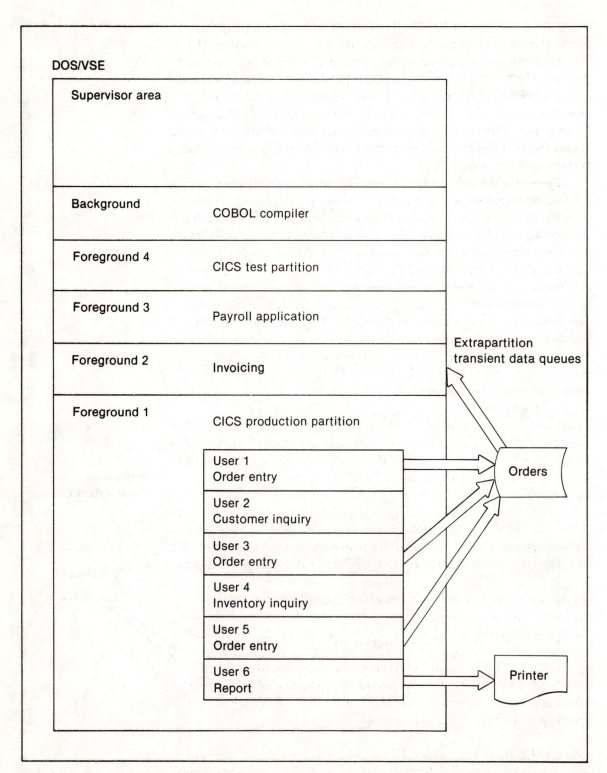

Figure 3-10 Intrapartition and extrapartition transient data queues (part 2 of 2)

Part 2 of figure 3-10 also illustrates that you can assign an extrapartition TD queue to a device other than a disk drive. (In contrast, you can assign an intrapartition TD queue only to a disk device.) Here, the host system's high-speed printer is treated as an extrapartition TD queue. Tape drives, card readers, and card punches can also be treated as extrapartition transient data queues. In fact, any device that's controlled by the host system's sequential access method (SAM on DOS systems, QSAM on OS systems) can be accessed this way.

Transient data control also provides another method of starting a CICS task: *automatic transaction initiation*. When automatic transaction initiation is used, a transient data queue is assigned a transaction identifier and a *trigger level*. As soon as the number of records in the transient data queue reaches the trigger level, the task is automatically started. To illustrate, suppose an order-entry application accumulates orders in a transient data queue. Then, automatic transaction initiation can be used to start an invoicing task that prepares invoices whenever, for instance, 500 or more orders are available in the queue.

Transient data control is an advanced CICS function. I'll describe how to use it in *CICS for the COBOL Programmer, Part 2: An Advanced Course*.

Temporary storage control   The *temporary storage control* module provides a simple method for storing small amounts of data outside an application program's working storage area. Temporary storage is similar to transient data queues in that the data is stored in queues called *temporary storage queues*, or just *TS queues*. However, there are two main differences: (1) temporary storage queues cannot be accessed outside the CICS partition, and (2) temporary storage queues can be stored in main storage as well as on disk. I'll describe temporary storage control in *Part 2: An Advanced Course*.

Dump and trace control   When a CICS application program encounters an unrecoverable error, the *dump control* module produces a storage dump. By using dump control functions, you can force a program dump at specific points in your program.

As an aid to program debugging, the *trace control* module maintains a *trace table* that indicates the sequence of CICS operations performed within a task. In chapter 10, I'll show you how to interpret a storage dump and a trace table.

Other CICS modules   The CICS modules I've just described are the ones you'll be most interested in as you develop command-level

COBOL programs. You will hear references made to others, however. For instance, the *task control* module controls the execution of tasks in the CICS system. For the most part, this is an automatic function.

The *interval control* module allows you to implement time-dependent applications. Interval control provides a method of starting a task that's an alternative to keying in a trans-id. Using interval control functions, you can specify that a task be started at a specific time or after a specific time interval has passed.

The *journal control* module provides a standardized method for creating sequential output files, called *journals*, that are used to restore master files in the event of a system failure.

The *storage control* module allocates storage space to application programs. Since this process is automatic and there are few applications where you need to manage storage control functions yourself, storage control isn't covered in this book.

Quite frankly, you don't have to know what these CICS modules do to be able to write a command-level program. Even so, you'll see the terms I've presented here over and over again in the IBM manuals. In addition, having a general idea about the functions of these modules will give you a better appreciation of how complicated CICS is and how much it's doing for you.

CICS tables

CICS is useful in a variety of installations because it's *table-driven*. In other words, options that vary from one installation to another are defined in tables the user modifies to fit his specific needs. In all, the user must set up 16 CICS tables. You've already seen two of them—the Program Control Table and the Processing Program Table. Two other important tables are the File Control Table and the Sign-On Table.

The File Control Table   Every file a CICS application program can access must be defined in the *File Control Table* (or *FCT*). The FCT lists each file's organization (BDAM, ISAM, or VSAM) and other characteristics such as record format, block length, and record size. In addition, the FCT lists the file-control operations that are valid for each file—whether records can be deleted, new records added, existing records updated, and so on.

The Sign-On Table   The *Sign-On Table* (or *SNT*) contains a list of all authorized CICS users. For each user, a one- to three-character *operator identification*, an *operator name*, and an optional *password* are supplied. To access the system, you have to know your operator name and password. In addition, the SNT provides a security key that's used to determine the resources available to each user.

In most installations, systems programmers create and maintain these, as well as the other, CICS tables. Even so, as an application programmer, you need to be able to describe your needs to the systems programmers. In chapter 9, I'll present the formats of the table entries you need to be familiar with.

CICS service transactions

IBM supplies a set of *service transactions* to perform common CICS functions. The transaction identifier for most of these transactions begins with C. As a result, most user-defined trans-ids begin with something other than C. Now, I'll present a few of the most common service transactions.

The sign-on transaction   In most installations, an operator must sign on to the CICS system before he can use any of its resources. A special transaction, trans-id CSSN, is used for this purpose. The format of the CSSN transaction is:

```
CSSN NAME=name,PS=password
```

For example, if your name is SMITH and your password is BD801X, you can sign on by entering:

```
CSSN NAME=SMITH,PS=BD801X
```

Alternatively, you can enter simply CSSN. In this case, the system displays the sign-on screen in figure 3-11. Then, you key in your name and password. The NEWPASSWORD field is always displayed but normally isn't used.

The sign-off transaction   When an operator has completed a terminal session, he should sign off the system. The CSSF transaction

```
PLEASE SUPPLY PERSONAL DETAILS

NAME= _

PASSWORD=

NEWPASSWORD=
```

Figure 3-11 The CICS sign-on screen

is used for this purpose. If the operator keys:

    CSSF

he's signed off the system, but the terminal remains connected so
that another operator can sign on. If the operator keys:

    CSSF LOGOFF

he's signed off of CICS and the terminal connection is broken. The
connection must be established again before another operator can
sign on.

The master terminal transactions   In a CICS system, certain terminal operators can be designated as *master terminal operators*. A
master terminal operator is entitled to run the master terminal
transaction, CSMT, or the extended master terminal transaction,
CEMT. These transactions allow the operator to perform super-
visory functions that can affect users at other terminals. For example, a master terminal operator can cancel a task running at
another terminal.

One of the most common master terminal operations is updating the Processing Program Table to point to a new version of a program. Whenever you recompile an application program while CICS is up, you must use CSMT to update the PPT so you can access the new version. The command looks like this:

```
CSMT NEW,PGMID=name
```

where *name* is the name of the program. Alternatively, you can use CEMT, like this:

```
CEMT SET PROGRAM=name,NEWCOPY
```

The Execution Diagnostics Facility transaction   A special service transaction, CEDF, invokes a debugging aid called *Execution Diagnostics Facility*, or just *EDF*. When EDF is activated, you can run a CICS program step-by-step, checking the completion of each CICS command and examining working storage as necessary. I'll show you how to use EDF in chapter 10.

Discussion

As I've already said, many of the concepts this chapter presents aren't essential to the COBOL programmer writing CICS application programs. However, I've presented them here because (1) they'll help you understand how CICS works and (2) the IBM manuals are filled with this type of terminology.

If you're having trouble understanding some of these concepts, take heart. I think you'll better understand the concepts and terminology after you've seen them in context. So read on. As you do, you can return to this chapter to review points that are still unclear to you.

Terminology

CICS
Customer Information Control System
data-base/data-communication system
DB/DC system
CICS/VS
task
multitasking
multithreading
reentrant program
quasi-reentrant program
transaction
transaction identifier
trans-id
Program Control Table
PCT
Processing Program Table
PPT
management module
nucleus
file control
terminal control
basic mapping support
BMS
map definition
program control
transient data control
transient data queue
TD queue
intrapartition transient data queue
extrapartition transient data queue
automatic transaction initiation
trigger level
temporary storage control
temporary storage queue
TS queue
dump control
trace control
trace table
task control
interval control
journal control

journal
storage control
table-driven
File Control Table
FCT
Sign-On Table
SNT
operator identification
operator name
password
service transaction
master terminal operator
Execution Diagnostics Facility
EDF

Objectives

1. Explain the most common way a task is started under CICS.

2. Distinguish between multiprogramming, multitasking, and multithreading.

3. Briefly describe the function of each of the following CICS modules:

    a. file control
    b. terminal control
    c. basic mapping support
    d. program control
    e. transient data control
    f. temporary storage control
    g. dump control
    h. trace control

4. Briefly describe the function of each of the following CICS tables:

    a. Program Control Table
    b. Processing Program Table
    c. File Control Table
    d. Sign-On Table

5. Briefly describe the function of each of the following service transactions:

    a. CSSN
    b. CSSF
    c. CSMT
    d. CEMT
    e. CEDF

Part 2

CICS: The core content

This part presents the critical material of your CICS training. If you master it, you'll be able to design and code complete CICS programs in a professional style. What's more, you'll find it relatively easy to build on this base of knowledge by learning how to use additional CICS features. As a result, you should be prepared to put more effort into the mastery of the material in this part than you'll put into subsequent parts of your CICS training.

Chapter 4

The eight steps of
CICS program development

In this chapter, I'm going to show you the sequence of steps you take when you write a CICS command-level program. Figure 4-1 illustrates this sequence. These steps are essentially the same as the steps you take when you develop batch programs. However, there are a few important variations.

Step 1: Get complete specifications

For an interactive program, as for a batch program, you need to have complete specifications before you begin implementation. In general, the specifications for an interactive program and for a batch program have some materials in common: record layouts, file names, processing requirements, and so on. An additional type of specification, the *screen layout*, is required for interactive CICS programs.

Figure 4-2 is the screen layout for a typical 24-line, 80-column 3270 display screen. The screen layout shows where the headings, captions, and data of the screen will be displayed. For instance, the program will display the caption PRINCIPAL AMOUNT: on line 4 beginning at column 2, and the operator will enter the principal amount value on line 4 beginning at column 20.

61

```
1.  Get complete specifications.
2.  Get related source books and subprograms.
3.  Design the program.
4.  Update the CICS tables.
5.  Code the BMS map definitions.
6.  Code the program.
7.  Compile the program.
8.  Test the program.
```

Figure 4-1   The eight steps of CICS program development

Just what you'll receive as program specifications varies from shop to shop. In some installations, the system designer provides complete specifications including detailed processing requirements and layouts for every screen in the program. In other installations, the programmer may end up filling in some or all of the program's processing requirements or designing screen layouts himself. In any event, you must know exactly what a program is to do before you can begin to implement it.

Step 2: Get related source books and subprograms

The next step is to locate any source books (COPY members) or subprograms your program might require. In some shops, the system designer specifies what source books and subprograms your program will use. In others, you'll need to decide for yourself. At the least, all record descriptions (such as for database segments, files, and transient data queues) should be stored as source books in a COPY library, and you should use them. You're also likely to use a couple of IBM-supplied COPY members in your programs. I'll describe these later.

You may also use previously coded processing modules in your programs. In our installation, for example, many of the data-entry programs use a common date-edit routine to determine if a date is in the proper MMDDYY format. Routines like this may be stored either in source or object form.

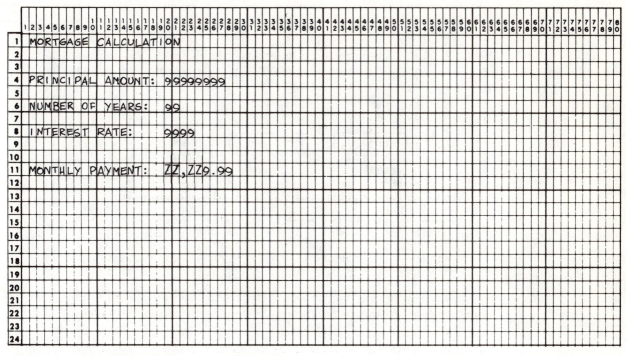

Figure 4-2 A screen layout

Step 3: Design the program

Design is a critical stage in program development. With good design, you can code and test a program efficiently. With poor design, coding is likely to be inefficient, and testing is often a nightmare.

In recent years, a technique called *structured design* (sometimes called *top-down design*) has become increasingly popular. The idea of structured design is to design a program from the top down by first dividing it into major functional modules, then dividing these modules into their major functional modules, and so forth. A structure chart, as in figure 4-3, documents the design.

A related technique, *structured programming*, attempts to improve the readability of a program by limiting the use of control structures, particularly GO TO statements. When combined with the techniques of structured design, structured programming can dramatically improve your productivity.

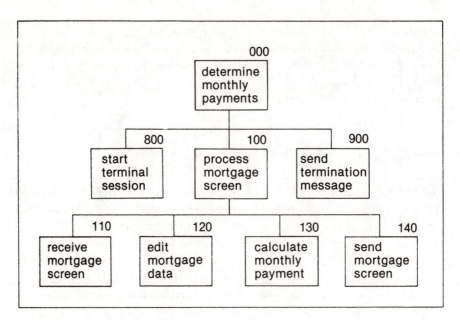

Figure 4-3   A structure chart

Unfortunately, CICS installations have been slow to adopt structured design and programming techniques, even though these techniques can be just as beneficial in a CICS environment as in a batch environment. In chapter 7, then, I'll show you how to apply structured techniques when you design CICS programs.

Step 4: Update the CICS tables

After you've designed your program, you need to make sure the CICS tables are changed so you can run your program to test it. In most installations, a systems programmer will actually change the tables. Even so, you need to be able to tell the systems programmer what changes to make.

Although some may argue with my placement of this step in the overall sequence of program development, I believe it's best to update the CICS tables after the program is designed but before it's coded. Why should the tables be updated *after* the design is completed? Because decisions you make during the design step can affect the required table entries. For example, you might not realize that your program will require a separate subprogram, and thus a separate PPT entry, until you've designed the program. Why should the tables be updated *before* you code the map or program? Because the table entries may affect the code. For example, the systems programmer may assign a name to a transient data queue that your program will require.

Step 5: Code the BMS map definitions

After you've had the CICS tables updated, your next step is to code a basic mapping support (BMS) map definition for each screen your program will display. As you should remember from the last chapter, BMS controls formatted input and output for terminal devices. To use BMS, you first define the screens as they'll appear on the terminal. To do this, you create an assembler language program called a *mapset*. Figure 4-4 is a portion of a typical BMS mapset. For now, don't worry about how to code a BMS mapset. I'll explain that in detail in the next chapter.

Incidentally, many installations use a *map generator* to create mapsets. Quite simply, a map generator automatically generates a BMS mapset based on a screen format entered by the programmer. Since BMS mapsets can be complicated, a good map generator can be a tremendous time-saver.

Step 6: Code the program

Coding a CICS program involves writing a mixture of standard COBOL code and special *CICS commands* to invoke CICS services. The main purpose of this book, of course, is to teach you how to code CICS programs.

Figure 4-5 shows a portion of a CICS command-level program. As you can see, the Environment and Data Divisions are brief. That's because, for example, file-related entries normally included in the Environment Division (SELECT statements) and File Section (FD statements) are not included in CICS programs. Instead, all file processing is done through CICS commands in the Procedure Division. These and other commands are usually thought of as extensions to standard COBOL. In effect, though, the commands transform COBOL into a language with an entirely different flavor. Beginning in chapter 6, and continuing through the rest of this book, I'll explain the forms and functions of many of the CICS commands.

```
          PRINT NOGEN
MORSET1   DFHMSD TYPE=&SYSPARM,                                          X
               LANG=COBOL,                                              X
               MODE=INOUT,                                              X
               TERM=3270-2,                                             X
               CTRL=FREEKB,                                             X
               STORAGE=AUTO,                                            X
               TIOAPFX=YES
***************************************************************************
MORMAP1   DFHMDI SIZE=(24,80),                                          X
               LINE=1,                                                  X
               COLUMN=1
***************************************************************************
          DFHMDF POS=(1,1),                                             X
               LENGTH=20,                                               X
               ATTRB=(BRT,PROT),                                        X
               INITIAL='MORTGAGE CALCULATION'
***************************************************************************
          DFHMDF POS=(4,1),                                             X
               LENGTH=17,                                               X
               ATTRB=(BRT,PROT),                                        X
               INITIAL='PRINCIPAL AMOUNT:'
AMOUNT    DFHMDF POS=(4,19),                                            X
               LENGTH=8,                                                X
               ATTRB=(UNPROT,NUM),                                      X
               PICIN='9(6)V99'
          DFHMDF POS=(4,28),                                            X
               LENGTH=1,                                                X
               ATTRB=ASKIP
***************************************************************************
          DFHMDF POS=(6,1),                                             X
               LENGTH=16,                                               X
               ATTRB=(BRT,PROT),                                        X
               INITIAL='NUMBER OF YEARS:'
YEARS     DFHMDF POS=(6,19),                                            X
               LENGTH=2,                                                X
               ATTRB=(UNPROT,NUM),                                      X
               PICIN='99'
          DFHMDF POS=(6,22),                                            X
               LENGTH=1,                                                X
               ATTRB=ASKIP
***************************************************************************
          DFHMDF POS=(8,1),                                             X
               LENGTH=14,                                               X
               ATTRB=(BRT,PROT),                                        X
               INITIAL='INTEREST RATE:'
RATE      DFHMDF POS=(8,19),                                            X
               LENGTH=4,                                                X
               ATTRB=(UNPROT,NUM),                                      X
               PICIN='V9(4)'
          DFHMDF POS=(8,24),                                            X
               LENGTH=1,                                                X
               ATTRB=ASKIP
***************************************************************************
```

Figure 4-4   Part of a BMS map definition

```
 IDENTIFICATION DIVISION.
*
 PROGRAM-ID.    MORCAL1.
*AUTHOR.        DOUG LOWE.
*DATE.          MAY 10, 1983.
*NOTES.         THIS PROGRAM CALCULATES MONTHLY MORTGAGE PAYMENTS
*               BASED ON PRINCIPAL AMOUNT, NO. OF YEARS, AND
*               INTEREST RATE ENTERED BY THE OPERATOR.
*
 ENVIRONMENT DIVISION.
*
 DATA DIVISION.
*
 WORKING-STORAGE SECTION.
*
 01  SWITCHES.
*
     05  END-SESSION-SW              PIC X              VALUE 'N'.
         88  END-SESSION                               VALUE 'Y'.
     05  VALID-DATA-SW              PIC X              VALUE 'Y'.
         88  VALID-DATA                                VALUE 'Y'.
*
 01  END-OF-SESSION-MESSAGE         PIC X(13)
                                    VALUE 'SESSION ENDED'.
*
 01  COMMUNICATION-AREA            PIC X.
*
 COPY MORSET1.
*
 COPY FACDEFN.
*
 LINKAGE SECTION.
*
 01  DFHCOMMAREA                    PIC X.
*
 PROCEDURE DIVISION.
*
 000-DETERMINE-MONTHLY-PAYMENTS SECTION.
*
     IF EIBCALEN = ZERO
         PERFORM 800-START-TERMINAL-SESSION
     ELSE
         PERFORM 100-PROCESS-MORTGAGE-SCREEN.
     IF END-SESSION
         PERFORM 900-SEND-TERMINATION-MESSAGE
         EXEC CICS
             RETURN
         END-EXEC
     ELSE
         EXEC CICS
             RETURN TRANSID('MOR1')
                    COMMAREA(COMMUNICATION-AREA)
                    LENGTH(1)
         END-EXEC.
*
```

Figure 4-5   Part of a CICS command-level program

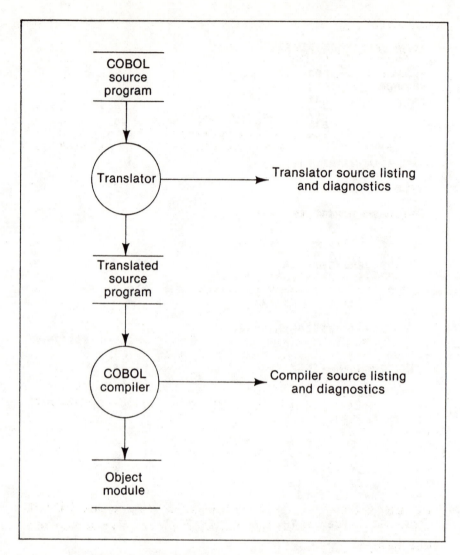

Figure 4-6   The translation and compilation process

Step 7: Compile the program

After you've coded a CICS program, you must compile it. The compilation process, shown in figure 4-6, involves two steps. First, the source program is processed by the *CICS command-level translator*. The translator converts each CICS command into a series of MOVE statements followed by a CALL statement. The MOVE statements assign values to the fields that are the arguments of the following CALL statement. The CALL statement activates the CICS command-level interface to invoke the required CICS ser-

```
Original source code:


    EXEC CICS
        RECEIVE MAP('MORMAP1')
                MAPSET('MORSET1')
                INTO(MORTGAGE-CALCULATION-MAP)
    END-EXEC.


Translated source code:


*EXEC CICS
*     RECEIVE MAP('MORMAP1')
*             MAPSET('MORSET1')
*             INTO(MORTGAGE-CALCULATION-MAP)
*END-EXEC.
      MOVE '                 00079     ' TO DFHEIVO
      MOVE 'MORMAP1' TO DFHC0070
      MOVE 'MORSET1' TO DFHC0071
     CALL 'DFHEI1' USING DFHEIVO  DFHC0070
      MORTGAGE-CALCULATION-MAP DFHDUMMY DFHC0071.
```

Figure 4-7 Sample source and translated code

vices. After the program has been translated, the standard COBOL compiler is used to compile the translated source program into an object module.

Since the translator and compiler execute as separate job steps, you get two sets of source listings and diagnostics. The translator output contains a listing of the source program as you wrote it, plus any diagnostic messages related to CICS commands. The compiler output contains a listing of the translated program, plus any diagnostics related to standard COBOL statements. As a result, you have to look at both listings to determine if your program compiled without errors.

Which source listing should you use when testing and debugging your program? You really need to use both. You need the compiler listing since it contains expansions of all COPY members included in your program. However, it also contains expansions of all CICS commands, code with which you're not concerned.

To illustrate, consider figure 4-7. The top part of this figure shows a typical CICS statement like ones you'll code in your programs. This is how the statement appears in the translator listing. The bottom part of the figure shows how this command appears in the compiler listing. As you can see, the translator placed asterisks in column 7 so the CICS command becomes a comment. Then, it inserted the MOVE and CALL statements necessary to invoke the CICS command-level interface.

Because the translator replaces each command you code with several statements, the structure of your Procedure Division isn't as apparent in the compiler listing as it is in the translator listing. That's why the translator listing is useful when you test a program. By using it, you can refer to the Procedure Division statements just as you coded them.

Besides translating CICS commands, the translator also inserts other code into your program. This code is required for your COBOL program to operate properly under CICS. It consists mainly of field definitions in the Working-Storage and Linkage Sections. Most of it's of little concern to you. However, one segment of code in the Linkage Section, the Execute Interface Block, is important. You'll see how to use the Execute Interface Block later in this book.

Step 8: Test the program

Testing an interactive program is similar to testing a batch program. As a programmer, you must make sure your program performs according to its specifications. To do this, you create test data designed to validate every combination of input data against expected results. When the actual results vary from the expected results, you locate the problem, correct it, and test the program again.

Like a batch program, a CICS program can encounter unrecoverable conditions that can cause it to abend. When this happens, an explanatory message is displayed at the terminal, and a storage dump is spooled for off-line printing. In many cases, the terminal message is sufficient to isolate the problem, so the dump can be suppressed. Otherwise, you need to print and analyze the dump to determine which command was executing when the abend occurred. Alternatively, you can use the Execution Diagnostics Facility (EDF) to locate the error.

In some cases, a program bug may bring the entire CICS system down. When this happens, the problem is more difficult to locate because (1) you usually don't get a message at the terminal and (2) the dump is more difficult to interpret. Because it's surprisingly easy to bring down the CICS system, a separate region or partition is usually set up for testing purposes. That way, you can safely test your programs without taking the risk of bringing down the production system.

Discussion

The sequence of steps you take to develop a CICS program is similar to the sequence you take to develop a standard batch COBOL program. The major differences are: (1) the program specifications must include additional material, particularly screen layouts; (2) you must code and assemble an assembler-language BMS map definition for each screen the program requires; and (3) you use CICS commands in the COBOL program to invoke CICS services. The CICS commands are translated into COBOL by the CICS command-level translator before they're compiled by the standard COBOL compiler.

Terminology

screen layout
structured design
top-down design
structured programming
mapset
map generator
CICS commands
CICS command-level translator

Objectives

1. Describe the eight steps of CICS program development.

2. Explain the translation and compilation process used for a CICS command-level program.

Chapter 5

How to create a BMS mapset

Before you can code an interactive CICS program, you need to
define the screens it will display. In this chapter, I'll show you how
to use basic mapping support (BMS) to do that. This chapter has
two topics. The first describes how the 3270 display station's screen
operates. The second explains how to create a BMS map definition.

Topic 1   Characteristics of the 3270 display screen

Before you can use BMS to define a screen, you need to understand the functional characteristics of the 3270 display station's screen. In this topic, I'll explain those characteristics.

Fields

The 3270 screen is a *field-oriented display*. In other words, the screen consists of a number of user-defined *fields*. As in a record description, a screen field is a specified area that contains a particular category of information. Some screen fields allow the operator to key data into them, while others are protected from data entry.

A special character called an *attribute byte* (or *attribute character*) marks the beginning of a field. The attribute byte takes up one position on the screen—the position immediately to the left of the field it defines—but it's displayed on the screen as a space.

The end of a field is defined by the presence of another attribute byte. So the length of a screen field depends on the position of the next attribute byte. If there's no subsequent attribute byte, the field continues to the end of the screen.

Figure 5-1 shows how attribute bytes precede fields in a 3270 display. Here, the small shaded boxes represent attribute bytes. These boxes don't appear on the actual display. Instead, spaces appear in the attribute-byte positions.

The screen in figure 5-1 has three data-entry fields: principal amount (99999999), number of years (99), and interest rate (9999). (Don't confuse these data-entry fields with the captions that identify the data the operator should key into them.) These data-entry fields each require *two* attribute bytes—one to mark the start of the field, the other to mark the end.

On the other hand, display-only fields—such as captions and data displayed by a program—require only one attribute byte. For example, the monthly payment field in figure 5-1 (ZZ,ZZ9.99) doesn't require an attribute byte to mark where it ends because it's a display-only field. If it were a data-entry field, it would require a terminating attribute byte.

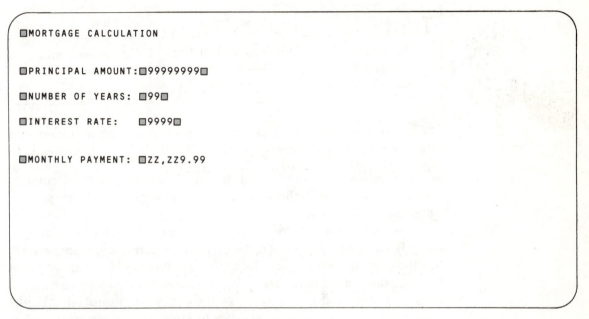

```
□MORTGAGE CALCULATION


□PRINCIPAL AMOUNT:□99999999□

□NUMBER OF YEARS: □99□

□INTEREST RATE:   □9999□


□MONTHLY PAYMENT: □ZZ,ZZ9.99
```

Figure 5-1   Attribute bytes in a 3270 display

Field attributes

As its name implies, the attribute byte does more than just mark
the beginning or end of a field. The attribute byte also determines
a field's characteristics, called its *attributes*. The three attributes
you'll use are: (1) protection, (2) intensity, and (3) shift. Figure 5-2
shows the selections you can make for these attributes. Now, I'll
explain the meaning of each.

The protection attribute   The *protection attribute* indicates
whether or not the operator can key data into a field. If a field is
protected, the operator can't key data into it. On the other hand, if
a field is unprotected, the operator is free to key data into it. As a
result, data-entry fields are often called *unprotected fields*, while
display-only fields are often called *protected fields*.

A third protection attribute option, *auto-skip*, defines a special
kind of protected field called a *skip field*. As with a protected field,
an operator cannot enter data into a skip field. The difference
between a protected field and a skip field is that when the *cursor* (a
marker that indicates where the next character the operator enters
will appear on the screen) is moved to a skip field, it automatically
advances to the first position of the next unprotected field on the
screen. In contrast, when the cursor moves to a protected field

Protection	Intensity	Shift
Protected	Normal	Alphanumeric
Unprotected	Bright	Numeric
Auto-skip (askip)	No-display	

Figure 5-2   Field attributes

without auto-skip, it stops, even though the operator cannot enter data there. Because of this characteristic, protected fields are sometimes called *stop fields*.

You can use skip fields to mark the ends of unprotected data-entry fields. That way, when the operator enters enough characters to fill the unprotected field, the cursor automatically moves on to the next data-entry field, and the operator can continue entering data. If a stop field is used to mark the end of an unprotected field, the operator has to press the tab key to advance to the next data-entry field.

The intensity attribute   The *intensity attribute* indicates how the data in a field is displayed. Normal implies just what it says—the data is displayed with normal intensity. If you specify bright, the data is displayed with brighter than normal intensity. And if you specify no-display, the field isn't displayed at all. If no-display is specified for an unprotected field, spaces are displayed no matter what characters the operator keys into the field. The no-display attribute is often assigned to unprotected fields for security reasons. For example, password fields typically are given the no-display attribute.

The shift attribute   The *shift attribute* indicates whether the keyboard is in *alphanumeric shift* or *numeric shift*. On older 3270 models, the numerals are located on the same keys as some of the letters, so the operator has to shift the keyboard to enter numeric data. However, if a field's attribute byte indicates numeric shift, the keyboard is automatically put into numeric shift so the operator doesn't have to press the numeric shift key.

Newer 3270 display stations have a *numeric lock* feature that allows the operator to enter *only* numeric data (numerals, a sign, and a decimal point) into a field. On these newer terminals, the numeric shift attribute in the attribute byte activates the numeric lock feature. As a result, you'll usually specify the numeric shift

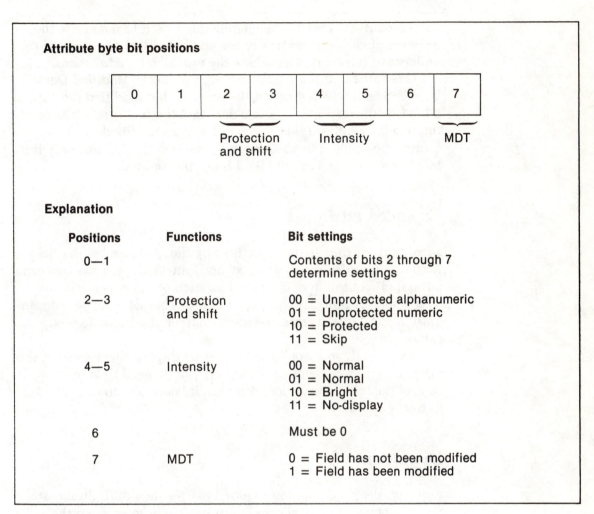

Figure 5-3   Format of the attribute byte

attribute for numeric data-entry fields. Bear in mind, however, that even when the numeric shift attribute is on, the operator can still enter invalid numeric data. For example, the operator can enter data with two decimal points or two minus signs. So, your programs must still edit all numeric data-entry fields to be sure they're valid.

The format of the attribute byte

A field's attributes are determined by the bit settings in the attribute byte, as figure 5-3 shows (the bits within a byte are always numbered from zero). Although you don't need to memorize the meaning of each bit position in the attribute byte, you do need to understand in general terms how the attribute byte functions.

The last bit in the attribute byte, the *MDT* (*Modified Data Tag*) indicates whether or not the operator has modified the data in a field. If the operator keys any data into the field, the MDT is turned on to indicate that the data has been modified. To save transmission time, the 3270 sends a field over the TC line only if its MDT is set. Otherwise, the field is not transmitted.

Extended attributes

In addition to the attributes defined by the attribute byte, a field can have *extended attributes*. Extended attributes provide two capabilities: (1) control over the initial location of the cursor on the screen and (2) control over special display characteristics of certain 3270 models, such as reverse-video, underlining, blinking, and color.

In general, you won't use the special display characteristics the extended attributes control. However, you do need to know how to control the initial cursor location. You'll learn how to do that later in this book.

Discussion

Actually, the programming required to operate a 3270 display station is much more complicated than you might guess from the information I've presented here. Fortunately, basic mapping support handles most of this programming for you. So, on now to topic 2, where you'll learn how to use BMS to define a 3270 screen.

Terminology

field-oriented display
field
attribute byte
attribute character
attribute
protection attribute
unprotected field
protected field

auto-skip
skip field
cursor
stop field
intensity attribute
shift attribute
alphanumeric shift
numeric shift
numeric lock
MDT
Modified Data Tag
extended attribute

Objective

Explain the three primary functions of attribute bytes in a 3270
display.

Topic 2   How to code BMS macro instructions

This topic shows you how to create a BMS mapset. As you know, you must code a *mapset*, a special kind of assembler language program, to define the format of each screen your programs display. After you've completed this topic, you'll be able to create mapsets for most of the screens you'll ever use.

Incidentally, if your shop uses a map generator to create BMS mapsets, you may feel you don't need to learn the material this topic presents. Still, I think it's important to know how to create mapsets of your own. So I suggest you read this topic even if you have access to a map generator.

Once you've created a mapset, you must assemble it. A job to assemble a mapset requires two steps. The first transforms your mapset into a physical map. The second creates a symbolic map from your mapset. Though both the physical and symbolic maps are required for BMS to operate properly, you only need to create one version of your mapset since both types of map are derived from it.

A *physical map* is a load module that contains a table BMS uses to determine the screen locations of data transmitted to and received from the display station. For example, a physical map might indicate that a particular field is displayed on the screen at column 16 of line 4. A physical map also indicates the attributes of each field, such as protection and intensity.

A *symbolic map*, in COBOL, is a COPY library member that defines the format of data sent to or received from the terminal screen. When an application program requests that a map be sent to a terminal, BMS takes data from the symbolic map, formats (or *maps*) it according to the physical map, and sends it to the terminal. Likewise, when an application program requests that data be retrieved from a terminal, BMS uses the physical map to map the data from the screen into the symbolic map.

Incidentally, the term *mapset* actually refers to a collection of one or more map definitions. For efficiency, most mapsets contain only one map definition. As a result, the terms *map* and *mapset* are often used to mean the same thing.

The rest of this topic is divided into three sections. First, I'll show you how to code an assembler language BMS mapset. Second,

I'll give you some models you can follow for most of the BMS field definitions you'll ever need to code. And third, I'll describe the symbolic map BMS creates and show you how you can create a better symbolic map yourself.

HOW TO CODE A MAPSET

Figure 5-4 shows a screen used by a program that calculates monthly mortgage payments based on principal amount, term of the loan in years, and interest rate. This screen has three input fields (principal amount, number of years, and interest rate) and one output field (monthly payment). The input (data-entry) fields are shaded. The next chapter presents the COBOL program for this application. For now, I want to discuss how to define the screen it displays.

The mapset in figure 5-5 defines this screen. In addition, it includes instructions to display a standard operator communication zone at the bottom of the screen. This communication zone, though not shown in screen layouts, will be included in *all* mapsets in this book. You'll see how it's used later in this book.

Remember that a BMS mapset like the one in figure 5-5 is an assembler language program. Don't let that scare you, though. Although some mapsets can be long, they're all simple assembler language programs. Moreover, one mapset is about the same as another. As a result, once you've coded one, you've mastered the skills you need to code almost any other you'll ever be called upon to create.

To create a mapset, you only need to know the two assembler commands and three BMS macro instructions that are shaded in figure 5-5. A *macro instruction*, or just *macro*, is a single instruction that's replaced by two or more other instructions. The first and last lines of the mapset are the assembler commands; the other lines make up the macro instructions.

The first line in figure 5-5, PRINT NOGEN, causes the assembler not to print statements generated by the BMS macro instructions. If you don't include a PRINT NOGEN command, your assembler listing will contain hundreds of lines that aren't important to you. So always start your mapsets with PRINT NOGEN.

The last line in the mapset, END, is required. END, like PRINT, is also an assembler command. Logically, it tells the assembler that there are no more source statements in the mapset program.

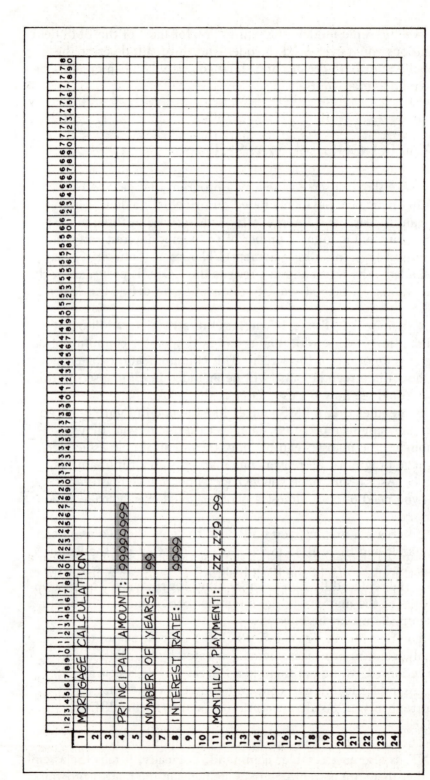

Figure 5-4 Screen layout for a mortgage-calculation program

The three BMS macros you code in a mapset are DFHMSD, DFHMDI, and DFHMDF. First, a DFHMSD macro marks the beginning of the mapset. Then, a DFHMDI macro marks the beginning of each map in the mapset (remember that most mapsets contain only one map). Next, each field on the screen is defined by one or more DFHMDF macros. Finally, you code the DFHMSD macro with TYPE = FINAL to mark the end of the mapset. In a moment, I'll describe each of these assembler language macros in detail. But first, I want to give you the rules for coding them.

How to code an assembler language statement

When you code an assembler language statement (including a BMS macro), you have to follow a few rules. Basically, all assembler language statements follow this general pattern:

    label   op-code   parameters...

Now, I'll explain the meaning of each part of an assembler language statement.

Label   The *label* supplies a symbolic name for the statement and begins in column 1. For a BMS macro, the label must begin with a letter and can be up to seven characters long. (This is in contrast to a standard assembler language label that can be up to eight characters long; that's because CICS adds a one-character suffix to some of the labels you code.) The label field is optional in some instances, so you may omit it if it isn't required.

Op-code   The *op-code* specifies the instruction to be executed (in a mapset, usually one of the BMS macros). It begins in column 10. For a BMS macro instruction, the op-code is DFHMSD, DFHMDI, or DFHMDF. The op-codes for the two assembler commands you use in a mapset are PRINT and END.

Parameters   The *parameters* (sometimes called *operands*) provide information the instruction requires to work properly. They're separated by commas with no intervening spaces. The first parameter should follow the op-code after one space. Although parameters usually begin in column 16, the first parameter following a BMS macro op-code begins in column 17 because the BMS macro op-codes are all six characters long and start in column 10.

```
             PRINT NOGEN
MORSET1   DFHMSD TYPE=&SYSPARM,                                               X
                 LANG=COBOL,                                                  X
                 MODE=INOUT,                                                  X
                 TERM=3270-2,                                                 X
                 CTRL=FREEKB,                                                 X
                 STORAGE=AUTO,                                                X
                 TIOAPFX=YES
*****************************************************************************
MORMAP1   DFHMDI SIZE=(24,80),                                               X
                 LINE=1,                                                      X
                 COLUMN=1
*****************************************************************************
          DFHMDF POS=(1,1),                                                  X
                 LENGTH=20,                                                   X
                 ATTRB=(BRT,PROT),                                           X
                 INITIAL='MORTGAGE CALCULATION'
*****************************************************************************
          DFHMDF POS=(4,1),                                                  X
                 LENGTH=17,                                                   X
                 ATTRB=(BRT,PROT),                                           X
                 INITIAL='PRINCIPAL AMOUNT:'
AMOUNT    DFHMDF POS=(4,19),                                                 X
                 LENGTH=8,                                                    X
                 ATTRB=(UNPROT,NUM),                                         X
                 PICIN='9(6)V99'
          DFHMDF POS=(4,23),                                                 X
                 LENGTH=1,                                                    X
                 ATTRB=ASKIP
*****************************************************************************
          DFHMDF POS=(6,1),                                                  X
                 LENGTH=16,                                                   X
                 ATTRB=(BRT,PROT),                                           X
                 INITIAL='NUMBER OF YEARS:'
YEARS     DFHMDF POS=(6,19),                                                 X
                 LENGTH=2,                                                    X
                 ATTRB=(UNPROT,NUM),                                         X
                 PICIN='99'
          DFHMDF POS=(6,22),                                                 X
                 LENGTH=1,                                                    X
                 ATTRB=ASKIP
*****************************************************************************
          DFHMDF POS=(8,1),                                                  X
                 LENGTH=14,                                                   X
                 ATTRB=(BRT,PROT),                                           X
                 INITIAL='INTEREST RATE:'
RATE      DFHMDF POS=(8,19),                                                 X
                 LENGTH=4,                                                    X
                 ATTRB=(UNPROT,NUM),                                         X
                 PICIN='V9(4)'
          DFHMDF POS=(8,24),                                                 X
                 LENGTH=1,                                                    X
                 ATTRB=ASKIP
```

Figure 5-5   BMS mapset for the mortgage-calculation screen (part 1 of 2)

```
**********************************************************************
          DFHMDF POS=(11,1),                                        X
                 LENGTH=16,                                         X
                 ATTRB=(BRT,PROT),                                  X
                 INITIAL='MONTHLY PAYMENT:'
PAYMENT   DFHMDF POS=(11,19),                                       X
                 LENGTH=9,                                          X
                 ATTRB=PROT,                                        X
                 PICOUT='ZZ,ZZ9.99'
**********************************************************************
MESSAGE   DFHMDF POS=(23,1),                                        X
                 LENGTH=79,                                         X
                 ATTRB=(BRT,PROT)
ERROR     DFHMDF POS=(24,1),                                        X
                 LENGTH=77,                                         X
                 ATTRB=(BRT,PROT)
DUMMY     DFHMDF POS=(24,79),                                       X
                 LENGTH=1,                                          X
                 ATTRB=(DRK,PROT,FSET),                             X
                 INITIAL=' '
**********************************************************************
          DFHMSD TYPE=FINAL
          END
```

Figure 5-5   BMS mapset for the mortgage-calculation screen (part 2 of 2)

To specify a parameter's value, use an equal sign, like this:

`LENGTH=15`

If a parameter requires more than one value, separate the values with commas, and enclose them in parentheses, as follows:

`POS=(1,5)`

If a value contains special characters or spaces, enclose it in single quotes, like this:

`INITIAL='MORTGAGE CALCULATION'`

You can include an apostrophe in a parameter's value by coding two consecutive apostrophes, as in this example:

`INITIAL='CUSTOMER''S NAME'`

Here, the parameter's value is CUSTOMER'S NAME.

When I code BMS macro instructions, I code only one parameter per line. Although this results in a longer listing, it makes the mapset easier to read. To code only one parameter per line, you need to use continuation lines.

Continuation lines   To continue a statement on the next line, code a comma after a parameter, and place any non-blank character in column 72. I use an `'X'`. Then, begin the next parameter in column 16 of the following line. The following line is called a *continuation line*. I think you'll find that if you code BMS macros with only one parameter per line, your mapsets will be far easier to read than if you try to code several parameters on a single line.

Comment lines   You can also improve the readability of a mapset by using comment lines to separate groups of related macros from one another. A *comment line* is any line with an asterisk in column 1. For clarity, I separate groups of related DFHMDF macros from one another with lines of asterisks.

Now, I'll explain the format and function of each of the BMS macro instructions.

Use the DFHMSD macro to define a mapset

The format of the DFHMSD macro is shown in figure 5-6. As you can see, you code the DFHMSD macro in one of two formats. You use format 1 at the beginning of a mapset, and you use format 2 at the end of a mapset. Since format 2 is so simple, I won't discuss it any further.

In format 1 (at the beginning of a mapset), you must specify the name of the mapset in the label field. In figure 5-5, the mapset name is MORSET1. This name will appear in the Processing Program Table (PPT) and in the COPY statement for the symbolic map in your COBOL application program. Since the mapset name must be unique within a CICS system, most installations have naming standards for mapsets. Remember that the maximum length of a mapset name (and of any label you code for a BMS macro) is seven characters.

The TYPE parameter   The TYPE parameter indicates whether a physical map (TYPE = MAP) or a symbolic map (TYPE = DSECT) is being generated. Usually, you'll want to generate both. If you do, code TYPE = &SYSPARM, and the job will have two steps.

The DFHMSD macro

Format 1

```
mapset-name   DFHMSD   TYPE= {&SYSPARM}
                              {DSECT   },
                              {MAP     }

                       LANG= {COBOL}
                             {ASM  },
                             {PLI  }

                       MODE= {IN   }
                             {OUT  },
                             {INOUT}

                       TERM=terminal-type,

                       CTRL=(control-option,control-option...),

                       STORAGE=AUTO,

                       TIOAPFX= {YES}
                                {NO }
```

Format 2

```
         DFHMSD TYPE=FINAL
```

Explanation

TYPE	For format 1, specifies whether a physical map (TYPE = MAP), symbolic map (TYPE = DSECT), or both (TYPE = &SYSPARM) are generated. TYPE = &SYSPARM is usually coded. For format 2, marks the end of a mapset (TYPE = FINAL).
LANG	Specifies the programming language: ASM (assembler), COBOL, or PLI (PL/I). LANG = COBOL is usually coded.
MODE	Specifies whether the mapset is used for input (IN), output (OUT), or both (INOUT). MODE = INOUT is usually coded.

Figure 5-6   The DFHMSD macro (part 1 of 2)

Explanation *(continued)*

TERM	Specifies the type of terminal that can be used with this map. Common values are:

	ALL	The map may be used on any terminal.
	3270	Same as ALL.
	3270-1	The map may be used on a 3270 model 1 terminal (40-character lines).
	3270-2	The map may be used on a 3270 model 2 terminal (80-character lines).

See the IBM manual for other valid devices.

CTRL	Specifies a list of control options in effect for each map in the mapset. Two common options are:

	FREEKB	Free the keyboard after each output operation.
	ALARM	Sound the audio alarm at the terminal during each output operation.

STORAGE	If STORAGE = AUTO is coded, the symbolic maps for each map in the mapset occupy separate storage locations; otherwise, they occupy the same storage locations.
TIOAPFX	Always code TIOAPFX = YES.

Figure 5-6   The DFHMSD macro (part 2 of 2)

First, the procedure substitutes MAP for &SYSPARM, assembles the mapset, and saves the physical map in a load library. Second, it substitutes DSECT for &SYSPARM, generates the symbolic map, and saves it in a source statement library.

The LANG parameter   The LANG parameter specifies the language to be used for the symbolic map. The default is assembler (ASM). If you specify COBOL, the symbolic map will be an 01-level group item that can be copied into a COBOL program. If you specify PLI, the symbolic map will be a structure variable that can be included in a PL/I program. If you specify ASM, the symbolic map will be a dummy section (*DSECT*) that can be included in an assembler language program. (Incidentally, you'll sometimes hear programmers refer to a symbolic map as a DSECT even if it isn't assembler language code.)

The MODE parameter   The MODE parameter specifies whether the map is used for input (IN), output (OUT), or both (INOUT). The default is OUT, so if you need the map for input and output, you must code MODE = INOUT. Since coding IN or OUT isn't any more efficient than coding INOUT, there's no reason you can't code MODE = INOUT for all mapsets.

The TERM parameter   The TERM parameter specifies what type of terminal the map can be used with. If you code ALL or 3270, the map can be used with any type of terminal (even non-3270 devices). Although it's a bit less flexible, it's more efficient to spec- ify the exact terminal type if you know it. Figure 5-6 shows the values you can code for 40-column and 80-column 3270 terminals. Since nearly all 3270s have 24x80 screens, you'll probably always code TERM = 3270-2.

CICS adds a one-character suffix to the end of the mapset name for the physical map. The exact character used depends on the terminal type selected. For example, the mapset definition in figure 5-5 generates a symbolic map named MORSET1 and a phys- ical map named MORSET1M, since M is the suffix for 3270 model 2 terminals.

Because of the suffix, it's possible to have several physical map- sets for a single symbolic map. For example, if you want to use the mapset in figure 5-5 on a 3270 model 1 terminal, all you need to do is change the TERM parameter to 3270-1 and reassemble the map. Then, BMS generates a physical mapset named MORSET1L since L is the suffix for 3270 model 1 terminals.

When you refer to the mapset in an application program, you use the seven-character name without the suffix. CICS automat- ically retrieves the physical map that's appropriate for the terminal the program is running on by appending the correct suffix. For example, if you run the program at a 3270 model 1 terminal, CICS retrieves the mapset named MORSET1L; if you run the program at a 3270 model 2 terminal, CICS retrieves the mapset named MORSET1M.

If CICS can't locate the appropriate mapset, it looks for a mapset with no suffix. An unsuffixed mapset is generated when you code TERM = ALL or TERM = 3270; such a mapset can be used for any type of terminal. To accommodate any terminal type, however, considerable run-time overhead is added to the mapset. That's why it's better to specify the terminal type in the mapset.

The CTRL parameter The CTRL parameter specifies the *control options* used by the maps a mapset defines. Alternatively, you can specify control options individually for each map on the DFHMDI macro. Since the same control options usually apply to all maps in a mapset, I normally code the CTRL parameter on the DFHMSD macro.

The most common control option is FREEKB. If you specify FREEKB, the keyboard is unlocked whenever a map is sent to the terminal. If you don't specify FREEKB, the keyboard is locked, and the operator must press the reset key to enter data. So always specify FREEKB in the CTRL parameter.

The ALARM option causes the audio alarm to sound whenever a map is sent to the terminal. In some installations, the audio alarm is used to warn the operator of an error condition. In most installations, however, the alarm isn't used. If you do need to use the alarm, you probably don't want it to sound on every output operation...you want it to sound only when there's an error. So instead of coding the ALARM option in the mapset, you usually specify it in your COBOL program, if you specify it at all.

You can specify many other control options. Some apply to mapsets used for printer output, while others apply to special features that aren't commonly used. As a result, I'm not going to explain those options here.

The STORAGE parameter Use the STORAGE parameter when you define more than one map in a mapset. It indicates how storage will be allocated to the symbolic map. If you code STORAGE = AUTO, each symbolic map will have its own storage area. If you omit the STORAGE parameter, the symbolic maps will overlay the same storage locations—that is, a REDEFINES clause will be included in the 01-level items for the symbolic maps. I recommend you always code STORAGE = AUTO. (Incidentally, the term AUTO comes from PL/I, where items with their own storage are said to have automatic storage.)

The TIOAPFX parameter If you're going to process a map using a command-level program, you *must* specify TIOAPFX = YES on the DFHMSD macro. The TIOAPFX parameter generates a 12-byte FILLER item at the beginning of the symbolic map. The system uses that item to maintain control information.

The DFHMDI macro

```
map-name   DFHMDI   SIZE=(lines,columns),

                    LINE=line-number,

                    COLUMN=column-number,

                    CTRL=(control-option,control-option...)
```

Explanation

SIZE	Specifies the size of the map in lines and columns. Usually coded SIZE = (24,80) for a 24x80 screen.
LINE	Specifies the starting line number. Usually coded LINE = 1.
COLUMN	Specifies the starting column number. Usually coded COLUMN = 1.
CTRL	Same as CTRL option for DFHMSD macro.

Figure 5-7   The DFHMDI macro

Use the DFHMDI macro to define a map within a mapset

To define a map within a mapset, you use the DFHMDI macro.
The format of the DFHMDI macro is shown in figure 5-7.
Although you can specify many options on the DFHMDI macro
other than those in figure 5-7, they're seldom used.

The label on the DFHMDI macro is the name of the map. In
figure 5-5, the map name is MORMAP1. You'll use this name,
along with the mapset name you specified on the DFHMSD macro,
in your COBOL program. Recall that a mapset name must be
unique within a CICS system. Similarly, a map name must be
unique within a mapset. You'll see in the next chapter that to refer
to a specific map in a CICS command, you specify both the mapset
name and the map name. Of course, if your installation has standards for forming map names, be sure to follow them.

The SIZE parameter specifies the number of lines and columns in the map (*not* the screen). The map can be smaller than the screen, but usually the two are the same size. As a result, you'll usually code SIZE = (24,80) for a standard 24x80 screen.

The LINE and COLUMN parameters specify the starting position of the map on the screen. You'll usually code LINE = 1 and COLUMN = 1. In other words, most maps start at the first column of the first line on the screen.

If you didn't code a CTRL parameter for the entire mapset on the DFHMSD macro, you can still code one on the DFHMDI macro for an individual map. However, since you usually want control options to apply to all maps in a mapset, you should code the CTRL parameter on the DFHMSD macro.

Use the DFHMDF macro to define a field within a map

To define a field on the screen, you use the DFHMDF macro. Actually, the DFHMDF macro defines an attribute byte. To define a protected field, you code one DFHMDF macro. To define an unprotected field, you must code *two* DFHMDF macros, since two attribute bytes are required for each unprotected field. Figure 5-8 gives the format of the DFHMDF macro.

If you code a label on a DFHMDF macro, a data name is generated in the symbolic map. As a result, each screen field your COBOL program processes must have a label on its DFHMDF macro in the mapset. In other words, you should code a label for each data-entry field and for all display-only fields with variable values. You don't need to code a label for a constant field. If you scan the label fields in figure 5-5, you can see the names of the fields that can be processed by the mortgage-calculation program: AMOUNT, YEARS, RATE, PAYMENT, MESSAGE, ERROR, and DUMMY.

The POS and LENGTH parameters   The first parameter in figure 5-8, POS, specifies the line and column position of the attribute byte. Remember that the actual data field follows the attribute byte, so if you want a field to start in column 5 of line 10, you code POS = (10,4).

The next parameter, LENGTH, specifies the length of the data field, *not* including the attribute byte. As a result, if you specify LENGTH = 5, you actually define six screen positions—five positions for the field itself and one position for its attribute byte.

The DFHMDF macro

```
field-name   DFHMDF   POS=(line,column),

                      LENGTH=field-length,

                              (BRT )   (PROT  )
                      ATTRB=( {NORM} , {ASKIP } ,NUM,IC,FSET),
                              (DRK )   (UNPROT)

                      INITIAL='literal',

                      PICIN='picture-string',

                      PICOUT='picture-string'
```

Explanation

POS
Specifies the line and column position of the attribute byte.

LENGTH
Specifies the length of the field, *not* including the attribute byte.

ATTRB
Specifies the setting of the attribute byte for the field:

BRT	The field is displayed with high intensity.
NORM	The field is displayed with regular intensity.
DRK	The field is *not* displayed on the screen.
PROT	The field is protected; data may not be keyed into the field.
ASKIP	The field is protected, and the cursor will automatically skip over it.
UNPROT	The field is unprotected; data may be keyed into the field.
NUM	The field is numeric and is right-justified and zero-filled. If omitted, the field is assumed to be alphanumeric and is left-justified and space-filled.
IC	Specifies that the cursor should be located at the start of the data field.
FSET	Specifies that the MDT bit in the attribute character should be turned on before the map is sent to the terminal.

Figure 5-8   The DFHMDF macro (part 1 of 2)

Explanation *(continued)*

INITIAL   Specifies the initial value of the field.

PICIN   Specifies a COBOL PICTURE string that defines the format of
                 the data on input. Example: PICIN = '999V99'. The length
                 defined by PICIN must agree with the LENGTH parameter. If
                 omitted, PICIN = 'X(n)' will be assumed where 'n' is the value
                 specified for the LENGTH parameter.

PICOUT   Specifies a COBOL PICTURE string defining the format of the
                 data on output. Example: PICOUT ='Z9.99'. The length defined
                 by PICOUT must agree with the LENGTH parameter.

Figure 5-8   The DFHMDF macro (part 2 of 2)

As you create a BMS mapset, you often need to calculate the
location of the first available screen position following a field. To
do this, simply take the column position of the attribute byte (specified in the POS parameter), and add the length plus 1 to it. For
example, suppose you defined a field like this:

```
DFHMDF POS=(5,13),
       LENGTH=14
```

To calculate the next available position, add 14 plus 1 to the starting column, 13. In this example, the next available position is column 28 of line 5.

The ATTRB parameter   The next parameter in figure 5-8,
ATTRB, specifies the characteristics of the attribute byte. The first
set of options for the ATTRB parameter controls the intensity attribute. If you code NORM, the field displays at normal intensity. If
you code BRT, the field displays at bright intensity. If you code
DRK, the field won't be displayed at all. If you don't specify the
display intensity, NORM is assumed.

The second set of options for the ATTRB parameter specifies a
field's protection attribute. If you code PROT, the field is protected—that is, the operator cannot key data into the field. PROT
is the normal attribute for captions and display-only fields. ASKIP
has the same effect as PROT, except that the cursor automatically

jumps over the field to the next unprotected field. You normally use ASKIP at the end of a data-entry field so the cursor automatically skips to the next data-entry field. If you code UNPROT, the field is unprotected—that is, data can be keyed into the field.

For most data-entry applications, protected fields are displayed at a different intensity than unprotected fields. Whether data-entry fields are bright and captions are normal, or the other way around, depends on your installation's standards. In the examples in this book, data-entry fields are displayed with normal intensity, and constants are displayed with bright intensity. In either case, though, most shops require that error messages or other important operator messages be displayed with bright intensity.

The NUM option of the ATTRB parameter specifies a numeric unprotected field. The NUM option causes data to be automatically right-justified and zero-filled. In contrast, if the NUM option is omitted, data is left-justified and padded with blanks. In addition, the NUM option places the keyboard in numeric shift, and, if the appropriate option is installed on the terminal, allows only numeric characters to be keyed into the field.

The IC option indicates that the cursor should be positioned at the beginning of the data field. IC can be coded for the first data-entry field in the map. However, I don't recommend you code the IC option at all. In the next chapter, I'll explain a more flexible way to control the position of the cursor from your COBOL programs.

The last ATTRB option, FSET, causes the MDT bit to be turned on before the map is transmitted to a terminal. Usually, you don't specify the FSET option, since the MDT bit is set automatically when an operator keys data into an unprotected field. However, if you want a *protected* field to be transmitted to your program, you should specify the FSET option.

Notice the last DFHMDF macro in figure 5-5. This field, named DUMMY, is one byte long and specifies these ATTRB options: DRK, PROT, and FSET. As a result, this field can't be seen or modified by the operator but is always transmitted to your program. I'll explain why this field is required later in this book. For now, just remember that you should define a field like this on *all* your maps.

The INITIAL parameter   The INITIAL parameter gives an initial value to a constant field. The value is enclosed in single quotes, like this:

```
INITIAL='ORDER ENTRY'
```

The number of characters you code in the literal should agree with the field length you specify in the LENGTH parameter. If you omit the INITIAL parameter, the field is set to hexadecimal zeros (LOW-VALUE).

In the DUMMY field in figure 5-5, an INITIAL parameter assigns an initial value of one space to the field. If the INITIAL parameter is omitted from this field, the field is *not* transmitted to your program, even though FSET is specified. That's because hexadecimal zeros are *never* transmitted between your program and the terminal.

The PICIN and PICOUT parameters   The next two parameters, PICIN and PICOUT, describe the PICTURE clauses that will be generated in the symbolic map for input and output fields. The picture-string must be a valid COBOL picture string and must agree in length with the LENGTH parameter.

If you omit PICIN or PICOUT, BMS assigns a default alphanumeric picture. For a six-byte field, the default picture is X(6), whether you want the field to be alphanumeric or numeric. In almost all cases, that's what you'd want the picture of a six-byte alphanumeric field to be. As a result, you seldom code PICIN or PICOUT for an alphanumeric field.

However, if the field is numeric, an alphanumeric picture is unacceptable. Even if you code the NUM option, BMS still assigns an alphanumeric picture to the field. As a result, you need a way to control the PICTURE clauses assigned to numeric fields. PICIN and PICOUT give you that control.

You use the PICIN parameter to specify the proper numeric picture for a numeric data-entry field. Of course, the picture can indicate an assumed decimal position. For example:

```
DFHMDF POS=(5,10),
       LENGTH=6,
       ATTRB=(UNPROT,BRT,NUM),
       PICIN='9999V99'
```

means that a decimal point is assumed between the fourth and fifth digits of this six-digit field. For a data-entry field like this, the operator doesn't actually key the decimal point. For example, if the operator enters 123456, the assumed value of the field is 1234.56.

Suppose the operator enters less than six digits. Since the NUM attribute causes the data to be right-justified and zero-filled, an entry of 1234 is converted to 001234, or an assumed value of 12.34.

You use the PICOUT parameter to edit output numeric data, to insert commas and decimal points, to suppress lead zeros, and so on. For example, if you code PICOUT = 'ZZ,ZZ9.99' and move a numeric value of 1234.56 to the field, the data displays as 1,234.56 with a leading space.

Although you need to understand the functions of the parameters I've just described, in actual practice you'll use only a few combinations of them. Fortunately, you can create almost all BMS mapsets by basing your coding on a few simple models of field definitions.

MODEL BMS FIELD DEFINITIONS

In my experience, I've found that the DFHMDF macros used to define screen fields almost always follow a few patterns. As a result, this section presents six models you can use to define your screen fields. These models should cover most BMS requirements you're likely to encounter.

As for the DFHMSD and DFHMDI macros, they're almost always coded just as they are in figure 5-5. So you can refer to that figure for models of those macro instructions.

In general, you need to know how to define five types of fields: (1) constant fields, whose values never change; (2) alphanumeric data-entry fields; (3) numeric data-entry fields; (4) alphanumeric display-only fields; and (5) numeric display-only fields. The five examples that follow are models for each of these five types of fields. The sixth example is a model for a standard operator communication zone in which your program can display operator instructions and error messages.

Example 1: A constant field   Figure 5-9 shows a sample constant field. Constant fields are typically used as headings to identify the screen or individual fields on the screen. In this case, the constant field is a screen heading beginning in column 2 of line 2 and containing the words MORTGAGE CALCULATION.

The map definition for this constant field requires a single DFHMDF macro. The POS parameter locates the attribute byte, immediately to the left of the constant data. The LENGTH parameter specifies the number of characters in the constant field. The ATTRB parameter indicates that the field is protected and is to be displayed with bright intensity. In this book, constant data is displayed with bright intensity, and data-entry or display fields are

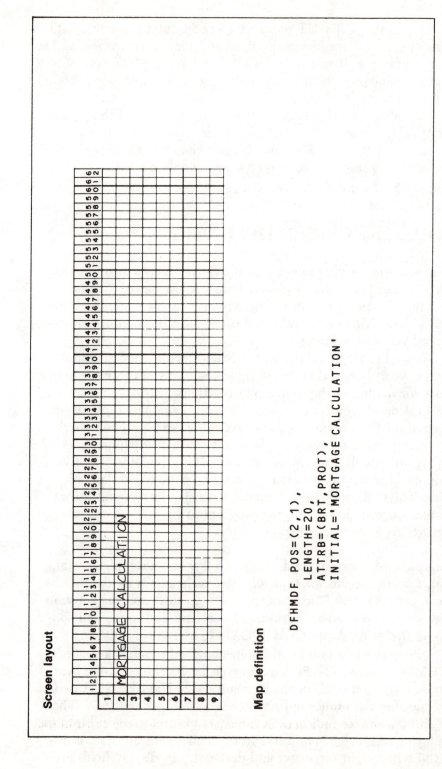

Figure 5-9 Model definition for a constant field

displayed with normal intensity. In some shops, this standard is reversed, so the attribute would be defined like this:

```
ATTRB=PROT,
```

The last parameter in figure 5-9, INITIAL, supplies the value of the constant.

Example 2: An alphanumeric data-entry field   Figure 5-10 is an example of a data-entry field that accepts alphanumeric data. Typically, a data-entry field contains two parts: a caption and the entry field itself. In this case, the caption is CUSTOMER NAME: and the data-entry field is 20 bytes long.

Three DFHMDF macros are required to define this entry field and its caption. The first one is for the caption, so it's similar to the example in figure 5-9.

The next DFHMDF macro in figure 5-10 defines the entry field itself. Since you want this field to appear in the symbolic map, a label is assigned to it (in this case, NAME). The POS parameter indicates that the attribute byte is in column 16 of line 2, and the LENGTH parameter indicates that the entry field is 20 bytes long. The ATTRB parameter says that the field is unprotected, so the operator can enter data into it.

The last DFHMDF macro marks the end of the entry field. As you know, BMS doesn't automatically generate an attribute byte to mark the end of an unprotected field. So you have to do it yourself. If you don't, the rest of the line will be unprotected.

You mark the end of an entry field with an attribute byte that immediately follows it, in this case column 37 of line 2 (POS = (2,37)). The ATTRB parameter should specify ASKIP so if the operator keys to the end of the preceding field, the cursor automatically skips to the next unprotected field.

Example 3: A numeric data-entry field   Figure 5-11 shows a typical numeric data-entry field. Like the example in figure 5-10, this field consists of two parts: a caption and a data-entry field. The main difference is that the entry field contains numeric data. Again, three DFHMDF macros are required. The first one defines the caption, the second defines the entry field, and the third marks the end of the entry field.

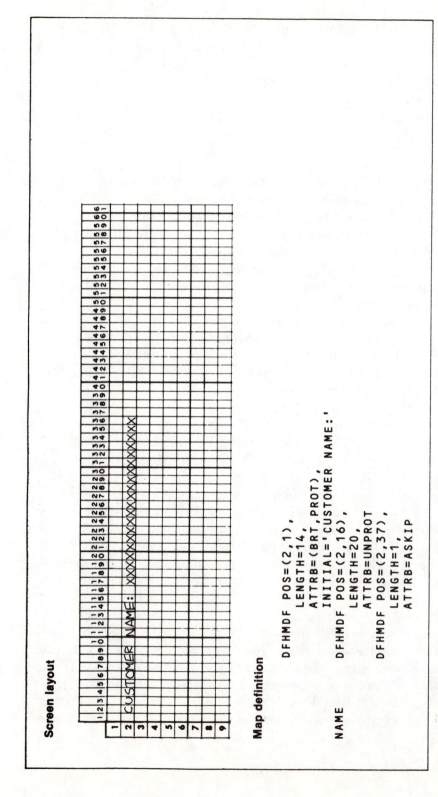

Figure 5-10 Model definition for an alphanumeric data-entry field

Screen layout

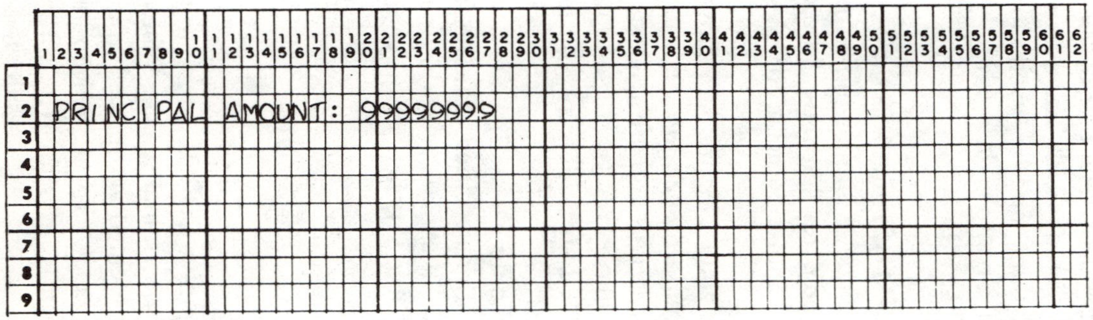

```
   1234567890111111111122222222223333333333444444444455555555556666
             012345678901234567890123456789012345678901234567890012
1
2  PRINCIPAL AMOUNT: 9999999
3
4
5
6
7
8
9
```

Map definition

```
       DFHMDF POS=(2,1),
              LENGTH=17,
              ATTRB=(BRT,PROT),
              INITIAL='PRINCIPAL AMOUNT:'
AMOUNT DFHMDF POS=(2,19),
              LENGTH=8,
              ATTRB=(UNPROT,NUM)
              PICIN='9(6)V99'
       DFHMDF POS=(2,28),
              LENGTH=1,
              ATTRB=ASKIP
```

Figure 5-11 Model definition for a numeric data-entry field

In the second DFHMDF macro, the ATTRB parameter specifies the NUM option so that only numeric data can be entered. In addition, the PICIN parameter supplies a numeric picture with an assumed decimal location for the input field. If you don't code PICIN, BMS generates an alphanumeric PICTURE clause for the field in the symbolic map.

Example 4: An alphanumeric display-only field   Figure 5-12 shows a typical alphanumeric display-only field. The data to be displayed in the field is supplied by a COBOL program.

Two DFHMDF macros define this field. The first defines the field caption. The second defines the display field. The attribute for this display-only field is protected, so data can't be keyed into it. Since the field is protected, you don't have to code a third DFHMDF macro to mark its end.

Example 5: A numeric display-only field   Figure 5-13 shows a typical numeric display-only field. This model is similar to figure 5-12, except that the PICOUT parameter indicates that the field should be zero-suppressed with comma and decimal-point insertion.

Example 6: Operator communication zone   Figure 5-14 shows a set of DFHMDF macros that set up a standard *operator communication zone* for displaying operator instructions and error messages. Here, a field named MESSAGE is displayed on line 23, and a field named ERROR is displayed on line 24. Later, I'll show you how these fields are used.

As I've already mentioned, you should always include a one-byte protected field with the FSET option specified, like the field DUMMY in figure 5-14. In chapter 8, I'll explain why this field is required. For now, just be sure to include this field in all your mapsets.

THE SYMBOLIC MAP

As you know, you use a symbolic map in a COBOL program to access data sent to and received from a terminal screen. When you assemble a mapset, a symbolic map is created and placed in a COBOL COPY library. Then, you use a COPY statement to include the symbolic map in a COBOL program. Unfortunately, the symbolic map generated by BMS isn't easy to use. As a result, I recommend that you discard the symbolic maps BMS creates, and code your own instead.

Screen layout

```
        1111111112222222222333333333344444444445555555555666
123456789012345678901234567890123456789012345678901234567890012
```

1																															
2	ADDRESS:	XXXXXXXXXXXXXXXXXXXX																												
3																															
4																															
5																															
6																															
7																															
8																															
9																															

Map definition

```
          DFHMDF  POS=(2,1),
                  LENGTH=8,
                  ATTRB=(BRT,PROT),
                  INITIAL='ADDRESS:'
ADDRESS   DFHMDF  POS=(2,11),
                  LENGTH=20,
                  ATTRB=PROT
```

Figure 5-12 Model definition for an alphanumeric display-only field

Screen layout

```
     1234567891111111111222222222233333333334444444444555555555566
              0123456789012345678901234567890123456789012345678901
   1
   2  MONTHLY PAYMENT: ZZ,ZZ9.99
   3
   4
   5
   6
   7
   8
   9
```

Map definition

```
         DFHMDF POS=(2,1),
                LENGTH=16,
                ATTRB=(BRT,PROT),
                INITIAL='MONTHLY PAYMENT:'
PAYMENT  DFHMDF POS=(2,19),
                LENGTH=9,
                ATTRB=PROT,
                PICOUT='ZZ,ZZ9.99'
```

Figure 5-13   Model definition for a numeric display-only field

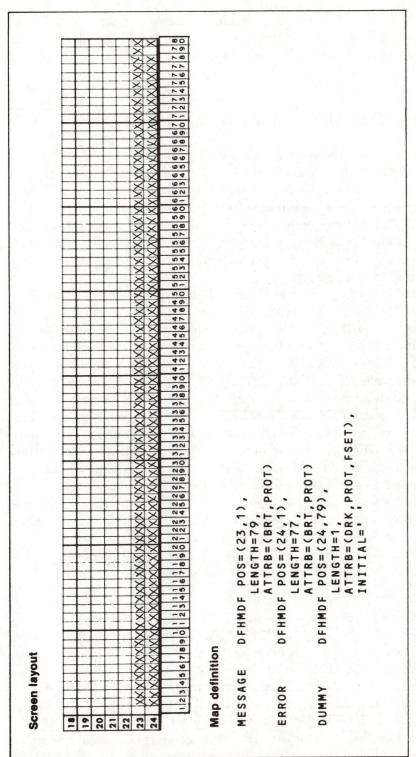

Screen layout

Map definition

```
MESSAGE  DFHMDF POS=(23,1),
                LENGTH=79,
                ATTRB=(BRT,PROT)
ERROR    DFHMDF POS=(24,1),
                LENGTH=77,
                ATTRB=(BRT,PROT)
DUMMY    DFHMDF POS=(24,79),
                LENGTH=1,
                ATTRB=(DRK,PROT,FSET),
                INITIAL=' '
```

Figure 5-14 Model definition for the operator communication zone

The rest of this topic is divided into two sections. First, I'll show you how BMS creates its symbolic maps. Then, I'll show you an easy way to create your own symbolic maps.

How BMS generates the symbolic map

Figure 5-15 is the symbolic map BMS generated from the mapset in figure 5-5. I think you can see why I don't care for this symbolic map. It's difficult to read because it follows no consistent rules of abbreviation or indentation. Data names are created that aren't used. And the names generated by BMS are fine for assembler language but less than adequate for COBOL programming. But before you can create your own symbolic maps, you need to understand how BMS generates its own.

The symbolic map in figure 5-15 has two 01-level items named MORMAP1I and MORMAP1O. Since the second 01-level item contains a REDEFINES clause, these items overlay each other. The fields in the first 01-level group are intended for use in input operations (hence the suffix I), while the fields in the second 01-level group are meant for output (suffix O).

Each of these 01-level groups begins with a 12-byte FILLER item generated because TIOAPFX = YES was specified in the mapset. Then, within these 01-level groups, five data names are created for each DFHMDF macro coded with a label. The data names for these fields are created by adding a one-character suffix to the seven-character label coded on the DFHMDF macro.

The shaded areas of figure 5-15 show the code generated for the data-entry field labelled AMOUNT in figure 5-5. As you can see, five data names have been created for this field: AMOUNTL, AMOUNTF, AMOUNTA, AMOUNTI, and AMOUNTO. Now, I'll explain the function of each data name.

The length field The first field generated in the symbolic map is a two-byte binary field (COMP PIC S9(4)) that contains the length of the data entered by the operator. The value of this field is the actual number of characters entered—not the length of the field specified in the LENGTH parameter on the DFHMDF macro.

To illustrate, suppose the operator enters ABCD into a field defined with LENGTH = 20. The value of the length field will be four since the operator entered four characters. Embedded spaces are included in the count, so if the operator entered JOHN SMITH, the length would be ten.

```
01  MORMAP1I.
    02  FILLER PIC X(12).
    02  AMOUNTL    COMP  PIC  S9(4).
    02  AMOUNTF    PICTURE X.
    02  FILLER REDEFINES AMOUNTF.
        03  AMOUNTA    PICTURE X.
    02  AMOUNTI  PIC 9(6)V99.
    02  YEARSL     COMP  PIC  S9(4).
    02  YEARSF     PICTURE X.
    02  FILLER REDEFINES YEARSF.
        03 YEARSA     PICTURE X.
    02  YEARSI  PIC 99.
    02  RATEL      COMP  PIC  S9(4).
    02  RATEF      PICTURE X.
    02  FILLER REDEFINES RATEF.
        03 RATEA      PICTURE X.
    02  RATEI  PIC V9(4).
    02  PAYMENTL    COMP  PIC  S9(4).
    02  PAYMENTF    PICTURE X.
    02  FILLER REDEFINES PAYMENTF.
        03 PAYMENTA    PICTURE X.
    02  PAYMENTI  PIC X(9).
    02  MESSAGEL    COMP  PIC  S9(4).
    02  MESSAGEF    PICTURE X.
    02  FILLER REDEFINES MESSAGEF.
        03 MESSAGEA    PICTURE X.
    02  MESSAGEI  PIC X(79).
    02  ERRORL     COMP  PIC  S9(4).
    02  ERRORF     PICTURE X.
    02  FILLER REDEFINES ERRORF.
        03 ERRORA     PICTURE X.
    02  ERRORI  PIC X(77).
    02  DUMMYL     COMP  PIC  S9(4).
    02  DUMMYF     PICTURE X.
    02  FILLER REDEFINES DUMMYF.
        03 DUMMYA     PICTURE X.
    02  DUMMYI  PIC X(1).
01  MORMAP1O REDEFINES MORMAP1I.
    02  FILLER PIC X(12).
    02  FILLER PICTURE X(3).
    02  AMOUNTO  PIC X(8).
    02  FILLER PICTURE X(3).
    02  YEARSO  PIC X(2).
    02  FILLER PICTURE X(3).
    02  RATEO  PIC X(4).
    02  FILLER PICTURE X(3).
    02  PAYMENTO PIC ZZ,ZZ9.99.
    02  FILLER PICTURE X(3).
    02  MESSAGEO  PIC X(79).
    02  FILLER PICTURE X(3).
    02  ERRORO  PIC X(77).
    02  FILLER PICTURE X(3).
    02  DUMMYO  PIC X(1).
```

Figure 5-15   Symbolic map generated by BMS for the mortgage-calculation screen

If the operator doesn't enter any data, the field's length value is set to zero. As a result, you can test the length field for a value of zero to see whether or not the operator entered any data.

The data name for the length field is formed by adding the letter L to the end of the label on the DFHMDF macro. So the length field for AMOUNT is AMOUNTL.

The attribute and flag fields   The next two fields generated in the symbolic map are redefinitions of a single byte of storage:

```
02   AMOUNTF      PICTURE X.
02   FILLER REDEFINES AMOUNTF.
 03   AMOUNTA      PICTURE X.
```

After an input operation, AMOUNTF contains a *flag byte* that is normally set to hexadecimal zero (LOW-VALUE). However, if the operator modifies the field but does *not* enter data into it (for example, by using the delete key to erase data in the field), the flag byte is set to hexadecimal 80.

AMOUNTA is used for output operations to override the field attributes defined in the physical map. You'll learn how to use this field in the next chapter.

The data field   Two data names are generated in the symbolic map for the actual data field. In figure 5-15, the names are AMOUNTI and AMOUNTO. (If you count up the bytes in MORMAPI and MORMAPO, you'll see that AMOUNTI and AMOUNTO occupy the same storage location.) AMOUNTI is used for input operations, while AMOUNTO is used for output. Two data names are provided to allow the PICTURE clauses to differ if you specify a PICIN or PICOUT parameter on the DFHMDF macro.

How to create your own symbolic map

As I've already mentioned, I don't like to use the symbolic map BMS generates. Instead, I prefer to create my own, like the one in figure 5-16. I think you'll agree that my map is easier to read and use than the one in figure 5-15.

To create a symbolic map like mine, work from your assembler language mapset. Quite simply, you create a group of 05-level data

```
   01   MORTGAGE-CALCULATION-MAP.
 *
      05   FILLER                      PIC X(12).
 *
      05   MCM-L-PRINCIPAL-AMOUNT      PIC S9(4)    COMP.
      05   MCM-A-PRINCIPAL-AMOUNT      PIC X.
      05   MCM-D-PRINCIPAL-AMOUNT      PIC 9(6)V99.
 *
      05   MCM-L-NO-OF-YEARS           PIC S9(4)    COMP.
      05   MCM-A-NO-OF-YEARS           PIC X.
      05   MCM-D-NO-OF-YEARS           PIC 99.
 *
      05   MCM-L-INTEREST-RATE         PIC S9(4)    COMP.
      05   MCM-A-INTEREST-RATE         PIC X.
      05   MCM-D-INTEREST-RATE         PIC V9(4).
 *
      05   MCM-L-MONTHLY-PAYMENT       PIC S9(4)    COMP.
      05   MCM-A-MONTHLY-PAYMENT       PIC X.
      05   MCM-D-MONTHLY-PAYMENT       PIC ZZ,ZZ9.99.
 *
      05   MCM-L-OPERATOR-MESSAGE      PIC S9(4)    COMP.
      05   MCM-A-OPERATOR-MESSAGE      PIC X.
      05   MCM-D-OPERATOR-MESSAGE      PIC X(79).
 *
      05   MCM-L-ERROR-MESSAGE         PIC S9(4)    COMP.
      05   MCM-A-ERROR-MESSAGE         PIC X.
      05   MCM-D-ERROR-MESSAGE         PIC X(77).
 *
      05   MCM-L-DUMMY                 PIC S9(4)    COMP.
      05   MCM-A-DUMMY                 PIC X.
      05   MCM-D-DUMMY                 PIC X.
 *
```

Figure 5-16   Improved symbolic map for the mortgage-calculation screen

names for each field you labelled in your mapset. Here are some guidelines to follow:

1. Code only one 01-level item, and choose a name for it that describes the function of the map. In figure 5-16, I named the symbolic map MORTGAGE-CALCULATION-MAP.

2. Don't forget to code a 12-byte FILLER item for the TIOAPFX at the beginning of the map.

3. For each map field, code three data names. I use the following rules for forming the names:

    a. Start each data name with a two-or three-character prefix that relates the data name to the group item. In this example, I start each name with MCM.

    b. Include one character to define the field's function: L for the length, A for the attribute, and D for the data.

    c. Use a meaningful name, such as PRINCIPAL-AMOUNT, rather than a short name, like AMOUNT.

    d. Separate each component of the name with a hyphen.

4. Separate each set of data names with a blank comment line.

5. Align the elements of the symbolic map so it's easy to read.

Incidentally, when you create your own symbolic map, you don't need to keep the symbolic map BMS generated. As a result, you can modify the standard map assembly procedure so the symbolic map is routed to a printer (SYSOUT = A) rather than saved in a source library. Then, you can use the printed BMS-generated symbolic map to verify the map you create.

Some programmers object to the practice of creating your own symbolic map because of the chance of error. In fact, creating your own symbolic map may even violate your shop's standards. If that's the case, there's little you can do. Still, I believe that as long as you're careful, the benefits gained by creating your own symbolic maps outweigh the danger of introducing errors.

DISCUSSION

Right now, you're probably thinking that the process of BMS map definition is overly complicated. Quite frankly, you're right. That's why many shops use map generators to ease the burden of creating mapsets. When you use a map generator, you create an image of the screen on a terminal, using special codes for unprotected fields, numeric fields, and so forth. Next, you assign names to the fields that you want in the symbolic map. Then, the map generator analyzes the screen image and creates a BMS mapset you can assemble in the usual way. At the same time, many map generators produce screen documentation that's more useful than a BMS assembler listing. The map generator may also allow you to save your screen image so you can recall it later to make modifications without having to reenter it. Obviously, a map generator can be a tremendous time-saver. If one is available, by all means use it.

Still, it's important to know how to create BMS mapsets. Since map generators cannot handle all situations, you may need to create your own mapsets for complicated screen layouts. Also, you may need to modify output produced by the map generator.

Terminology

mapset
physical map
symbolic map
map
macro instruction
macro
label
op-code
parameter
operand
continuation line
comment line
DSECT
control option
operator communication zone
flag byte

Objectives

1. Given a sample screen layout, code the BMS mapset for it.

2. Given a BMS mapset and a listing of the symbolic map created by BMS, create a symbolic map that's easy to read and use.

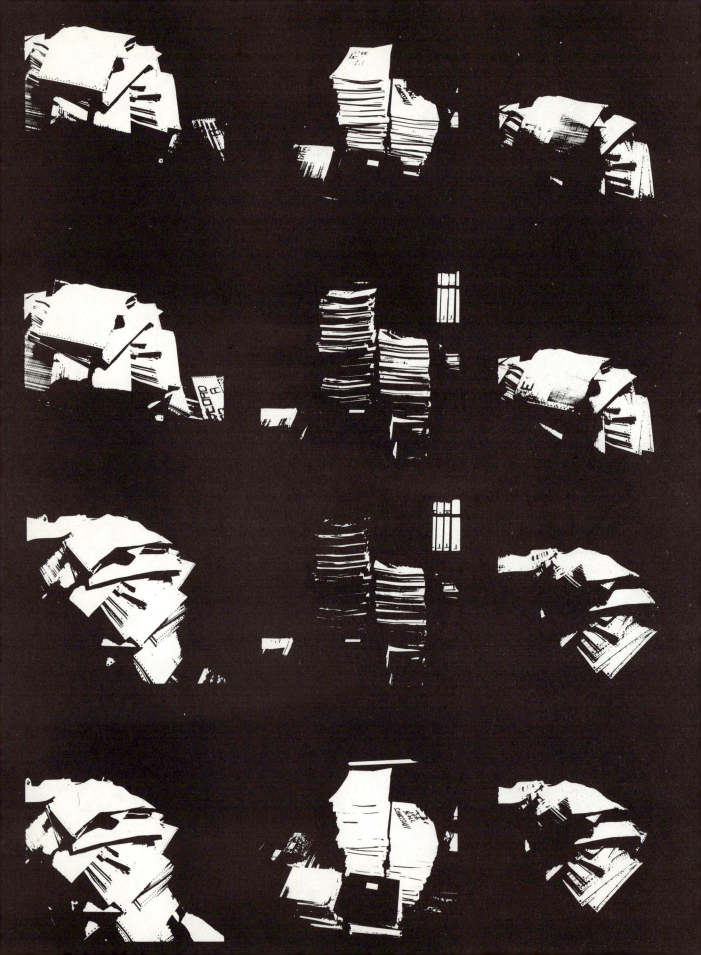

Chapter 6

A basic subset
of command-level CICS

In the last chapter, I showed you how to create a BMS mapset for
the screen a simple mortgage-calculation program displays. In this
chapter, I use the mortgage-calculation program to present a basic
subset of CICS command-level programming in COBOL. The subset includes programming techniques and CICS commands you'll
use in a wide range of CICS applications. Because this chapter presents the most difficult CICS programming concepts, you can
expect to work hard to master this material.

This chapter has four topics. The first presents a programming
technique you'll have to use in almost all of the CICS programs
you'll ever write: pseudo-conversational programming. The second
explains in detail the COBOL and CICS of the mortgage-
calculation program. The third shows the formats of the CICS
commands the mortgage-calculation program uses. And the fourth
describes some additional CICS programming techniques you need
to know. When you finish this chapter, you'll be able to code simple CICS command-level programs.

Topic 1   Pseudo-conversational programming

Before you can write a command-level CICS program that's
acceptable in a typical COBOL shop, you need to understand the
technique of pseudo-conversational programming. Basically, a
pseudo-conversational program is an interactive program that has
actually ended while it appears to be waiting for an operator to
enter data. To illustrate, let me show you how the mortgage-
calculation program works.

A typical terminal session

The five parts of figure 6-1 represent steps during a terminal session
that executes the mortgage-calculation program. You'll recall from
chapter 3 that an operator can begin a terminal session by entering a
transaction identifier. To begin the mortgage-calculation program,
the operator enters the trans-id MOR1, as in part 1 of figure 6-1.
    Once the program is started, it displays the screen shown in
part 2 of figure 6-1. The operator keys in the data to do a
mortgage-calculation, as in part 3, and presses the enter key. The
program calculates the monthly payment for the data the operator
entered and displays it on the screen, as in part 4. Then, the operator can enter data for another calculation or end the terminal session. In this case, the operator decided to end the terminal session
and pressed the clear key. The program displays the termination
message in part 5 of figure 6-1, and the terminal session ends.

Conversational programming

In parts 2, 3, and 4 of figure 6-1, the mortgage-calculation program
appears to be sitting idle, waiting for the operator to enter data. An
interactive program that *does* sit idle and wait for data is called a
conversational program. That's because it carries on a conversation
with the operator.
    You can easily imagine that a conversational program spends
almost all of its time doing nothing but waiting. On a single-user
system, that's not a problem. But on a CICS system with many
users, it *is* a problem.

The operator enters the transaction identifier MOR1 and presses the enter key:

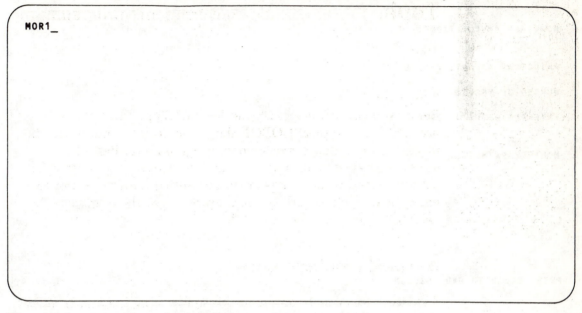

```
MOR1_
```

Figure 6-1   Operation of the mortgage-calculation program (part 1 of 5)

The program displays the data-entry screen:

```
MORTGAGE CALCULATION

PRINCIPAL AMOUNT: _

NUMBER OF YEARS:

INTEREST RATE:

MONTHLY PAYMENT:




PRESS CLEAR TO END SESSION
```

Figure 6-1   Operation of the mortgage-calculation program (part 2 of 5)

The operator enters data and presses the enter key:

```
MORTGAGE CALCULATION


PRINCIPAL AMOUNT: 7500000

NUMBER OF YEARS:   30

INTEREST RATE:     0975


MONTHLY PAYMENT:








PRESS CLEAR TO END SESSION
```

Figure 6-1   Operation of the mortgage-calculation program (part 3 of 5)

The program calculates and displays the monthly payment:

```
MORTGAGE CALCULATION


PRINCIPAL AMOUNT: 07500000

NUMBER OF YEARS:   30

INTEREST RATE:     0975


MONTHLY PAYMENT:      639.49








ENTER NEXT SET OF DATA OR PRESS CLEAR TO END SESSION
```

Figure 6-1   Operation of the mortgage-calculation program (part 4 of 5)

The program sends a message to the terminal and ends the session:

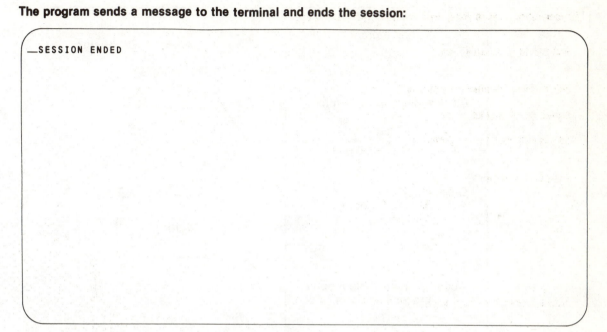

—SESSION ENDED

Figure 6-1   Operation of the mortgage-calculation program (part 5 of 5)

To illustrate, figure 6-2 shows a CICS system with five users, four of them running conversational programs. As you can see, two of the programs are waiting for data, while the other two are actually processing data. Because the four programs occupy nearly all of the available main storage, the fifth user can't work because there isn't enough storage available to load his program.

In figure 6-2, half of the programs are waiting for input data. That's actually pretty good. Consider a more typical system with 30 users. If it takes 30 seconds for an operator to enter a typical transaction and the system takes one second to process it, then only one of the 30 users' programs is actually processing data at any given moment. The other 29 are waiting, taking up space in main storage. And what if the CICS system supports 300 users instead of 30? Clearly, conversational programs can be tremendously inefficient.

Pseudo-conversational programming

The solution to this efficiency problem is to remove a program from storage when it's waiting for data from a terminal. And that's just what happens with a *pseudo-conversational program*. Although the

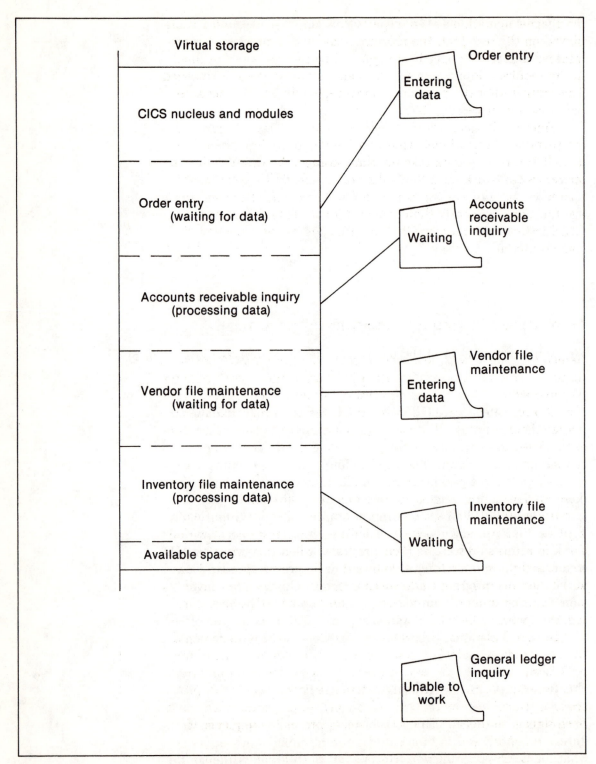

Figure 6-2   Conversational programs in a multitasking environment

mortgage-calculation screen in parts 2, 3, and 4 of figure 6-1 is displayed on the terminal, the mortgage-calculation program has terminated and is no longer in storage. When the operator has filled in the required data, the mortgage-calculation program is restarted. The result is that the program is in storage only when it needs to be: when it's processing data.

Figure 6-3 shows what happens if the programs in figure 6-2 are pseudo-conversational. Here, only the two programs that are actually processing data take up main storage. As a result, all five operators can work, and storage is even available for additional operators. Because pseudo-conversational programs use main storage far more efficiently than conversational programs, almost all CICS installations require CICS programs to be pseudo-conversational.

How a pseudo-conversational program works

Remember that when the screen in parts 2, 3, and 4 of figure 6-1 is displayed, the mortgage-calculation program is no longer executing. As the operator keys in data, it's displayed on the screen. That's a function of the terminal, though, and not of the program. After the operator has filled in all of the required data, the program needs to be reloaded to process it. But just how does CICS know when to restart a pseudo-conversational program?

Basically, an operator signals CICS to restart a pseudo-conversational program by pressing one of the terminal's *AID* (*attention identifier*) *keys*. (AID keys are the enter key, the clear key, the PF keys, and the PA keys.) Of course, most operators don't think in terms of restarting their programs when they press an AID key. Usually, an operator just knows that he presses specific AID keys to get his program to do specific things. On the other hand, as a CICS programmer, you do need to think of an AID key as causing a program to be loaded and executed.

In part 3 of figure 6-1, the operator keys in the data required to do a mortgage calculation and presses the enter key (one of the AID keys). Then, CICS reloads the mortgage-calculation program. The program in turn retrieves the data the operator entered, processes it (calculates the monthly payment), displays the results on a fresh screen, and ends. That's the typical processing sequence in most CICS programs.

A CICS program retrieves the data the operator entered by issuing a CICS command: RECEIVE MAP. For now, don't worry

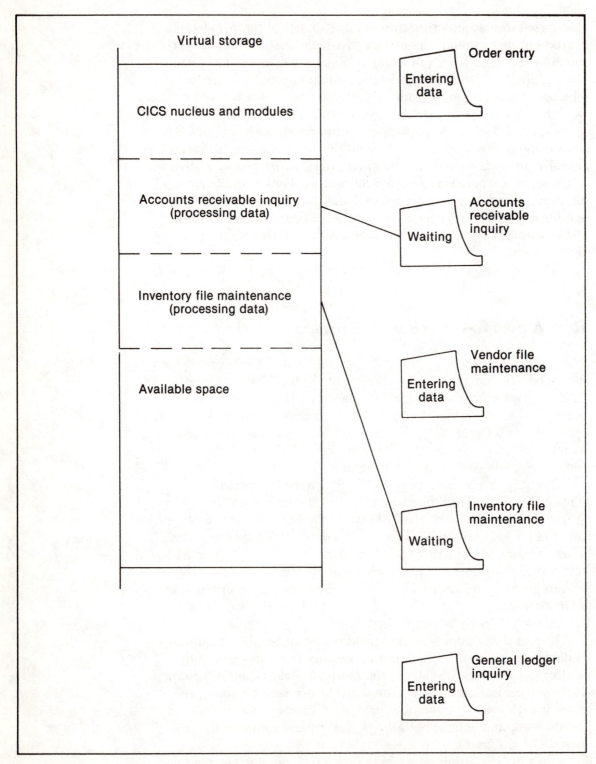

Figure 6-3 Pseudo-conversational programs in a multitasking environment

about the format or complexities of the RECEIVE MAP command. I just want you to realize that the command simply transfers data from the screen to the symbolic map in the program. If you'd like, you can think of RECEIVE MAP as a READ statement that retrieves data from a terminal.

After the program retrieves the data the operator entered, it processes it. In this program, the processing is done by a simple series of standard COBOL statements that edit the input data and calculate the monthly payment. However, in other programs, some CICS commands may be required to do the necessary processing.

Next, the program issues a CICS SEND MAP command to display the results of the calculation on the screen, as shown in part 4 of figure 6-1. If RECEIVE MAP is like a READ statement, then SEND MAP is like a WRITE statement.

After the program issues a SEND MAP command, it issues a RETURN command. The RETURN command ends the program just as a STOP RUN or a GOBACK statement does in a batch COBOL program. In addition, the RETURN command specifies what trans-id CICS should invoke the next time the operator presses an AID key. In this example, the trans-id specified in the RETURN command is MOR1, the same one the operator used to initiate the task in part 1 of figure 6-1. As a result, when the operator presses an AID key, the mortgage-calculation program is loaded and executed again.

Suppose the operator presses the clear key to end the terminal session. Since the clear key is an AID key, CICS restarts the program automatically. When the program sees that the operator pressed the clear key rather than the enter key, it sends the message in part 5 of figure 6-1 to the terminal. Then, it issues a RETURN command *without* a trans-id. That ends the pseudo-conversational cycle, and the operator must enter another trans-id to start a new program.

Discussion

Unfortunately, pseudo-conversational programming complicates the logic of your COBOL programs and, as a result, makes your job harder. However, as I've already mentioned, almost all CICS programs are pseudo-conversational because conversational programs are so inefficient.

Probably the one factor that has the greatest effect on the efficiency of a CICS system is the total number of tasks active at any given moment. If programs are conversational, the number of active tasks is relatively large. In contrast, if programs are pseudo-conversational, relatively few tasks are active at any given moment, even though many operators may be using the system. That's why production CICS programs must be pseudo-conversational in almost all installations.

Now that you've seen a sample terminal session for the mortgage-calculation program, you should understand how this program works and what pseudo-conversational programming is. The next topic presents and describes the COBOL source code for the mortgage-calculation program.

Terminology

conversational program
pseudo-conversational program
AID key
attention identifier key

Objective

Explain the operation of a pseudo-conversational program.

Topic 2   A command-level CICS program: An overview

Now that you've learned about BMS mapsets, 3270 terminals, CICS modules, and the pseudo-conversational programming technique, you have the background you need to understand a CICS command-level COBOL program. Figure 6-4 presents the source listing for a simple command-level program: the mortgage-calculation program I described in topic 1. If you study this figure, you'll see many similarities to a standard batch COBOL program. However, you'll also see many differences. This topic describes those differences in detail, division by division. In addition, it introduces you to several basic CICS commands using the mortgage-calculation program as an example.

As you read this topic, try to understand how this CICS command-level program works in general terms. In topic 3, I explain the format of each of the CICS commands this program uses, and in topic 4, I describe some of the programming techniques the mortgage-calculation program illustrates. You'll better understand the CICS details in topics 3 and 4 if you're already familiar with the COBOL source code for the mortgage-calculation program.

Identification Division

There's no difference between the Identification Division for a CICS program and a normal batch COBOL program. As you can see in figure 6-4, the Identification Division for the mortgage-calculation program specifies the PROGRAM-ID (MORCAL1), as well as some optional information (author, date, and notes). If your shop has standards that dictate how to code the Identification Division, be sure to follow them.

Environment Division

If you look at the Environment Division in figure 6-4, you'll notice it's empty. Environment Division entries, such as SELECT statements, aren't used in CICS programs. Files are defined once in CICS's File Control Table rather than in the Environment Division of each program.

```
 IDENTIFICATION DIVISION.
*
 PROGRAM-ID.   MORCAL1.
*AUTHOR.       DOUG LOWE.
*DATE.         MAY 10, 1983.
*NOTES.        THIS PROGRAM CALCULATES MONTHLY MORTGAGE PAYMENTS
*              BASED ON PRINCIPAL AMOUNT, NO. OF YEARS, AND
*              INTEREST RATE ENTERED BY THE OPERATOR.
*
 ENVIRONMENT DIVISION.
*
 DATA DIVISION.
*
 WORKING-STORAGE SECTION.
*
 01  SWITCHES.
*
     05   END-SESSION-SW            PIC X         VALUE 'N'.
          88  END-SESSION                         VALUE 'Y'.
     05   VALID-DATA-SW             PIC X         VALUE 'Y'.
          88  VALID-DATA                          VALUE 'Y'.
*
 01  END-OF-SESSION-MESSAGE         PIC X(13)
                                    VALUE 'SESSION ENDED'.
*
 01  COMMUNICATION-AREA             PIC X.
*
 COPY MORSET1.
*
 COPY FACDEFN.
*
 LINKAGE SECTION.
*
 01  DFHCOMMAREA                    PIC X.
*
 PROCEDURE DIVISION.
*
 000-DETERMINE-MONTHLY-PAYMENTS SECTION.
*
     IF EIBCALEN = ZERO
         PERFORM 800-START-TERMINAL-SESSION
     ELSE
         PERFORM 100-PROCESS-MORTGAGE-SCREEN.
     IF END-SESSION
         PERFORM 900-SEND-TERMINATION-MESSAGE
         EXEC CICS
             RETURN
         END-EXEC
     ELSE
         EXEC CICS
             RETURN TRANSID('MOR1')
                    COMMAREA(COMMUNICATION-AREA)
                    LENGTH(1)
         END-EXEC.
*
```

Figure 6-4   Source listing for the mortgage-calculation program (part 1 of 4)

```
    100-PROCESS-MORTGAGE-SCREEN SECTION.
*
    PERFORM 110-RECEIVE-MORTGAGE-SCREEN.
    IF NOT END-SESSION
        PERFORM 120-EDIT-MORTGAGE-DATA
        IF VALID-DATA
            PERFORM 130-CALCULATE-MONTHLY-PAYMENT
            MOVE 'ENTER NEXT SET OF DATA OR PRESS CLEAR TO END SE
-               'SSION' TO MCM-D-OPERATOR-MESSAGE
            MOVE SPACE TO MCM-D-ERROR-MESSAGE
            MOVE -1 TO MCM-L-PRINCIPAL-AMOUNT
            PERFORM 140-SEND-MORTGAGE-SCREEN
        ELSE
            MOVE 'ERRORS DETECTED--MAKE CORRECTIONS OR PRESS CLEA
-               'R TO END SESSION' TO MCM-D-OPERATOR-MESSAGE
            PERFORM 140-SEND-MORTGAGE-SCREEN.
*
    110-RECEIVE-MORTGAGE-SCREEN SECTION.
*
    EXEC CICS
        HANDLE AID CLEAR(110-CLEAR-KEY)
                   ANYKEY(110-ANYKEY)
    END-EXEC.
    EXEC CICS
        RECEIVE MAP('MORMAP1')
                MAPSET('MORSET1')
                INTO(MORTGAGE-CALCULATION-MAP)
    END-EXEC.
    GO TO 110-EXIT.
*
    110-CLEAR-KEY.
*
    MOVE 'Y' TO END-SESSION-SW.
    GO TO 110-EXIT.
*
    110-ANYKEY.
*
    MOVE 'N' TO VALID-DATA-SW.
    MOVE -1 TO MCM-L-PRINCIPAL-AMOUNT.
    MOVE 'INVALID KEY PRESSED' TO MCM-D-ERROR-MESSAGE.
*
    110-EXIT.
*
    EXIT.
*
    120-EDIT-MORTGAGE-DATA SECTION.
*
    MOVE FAC-UNPROT-NUM-MDT TO MCM-A-PRINCIPAL-AMOUNT
                               MCM-A-NO-OF-YEARS
                               MCM-A-INTEREST-RATE.
*
    IF MCM-L-INTEREST-RATE = ZERO
        MOVE FAC-UNPROT-NUM-BRT TO MCM-A-INTEREST-RATE
        MOVE -1 TO MCM-L-INTEREST-RATE
        MOVE 'YOU MUST ENTER AN INTEREST RATE'
            TO MCM-D-ERROR-MESSAGE
```

Figure 6-4   Source listing for the mortgage-calculation program (part 2 of 4)

```
          ELSE IF MCM-D-INTEREST-RATE NOT NUMERIC
              MOVE FAC-UNPROT-NUM-BRT TO MCM-A-INTEREST-RATE
              MOVE -1 TO MCM-L-INTEREST-RATE
              MOVE 'INTEREST RATE MUST BE NUMERIC'
                  TO MCM-D-ERROR-MESSAGE
          ELSE IF MCM-D-INTEREST-RATE NOT > ZERO
              MOVE FAC-UNPROT-NUM-BRT TO MCM-A-INTEREST-RATE
              MOVE -1 TO MCM-L-INTEREST-RATE
              MOVE 'INTEREST RATE MUST BE GREATER THAN ZERO'
                  TO MCM-D-ERROR-MESSAGE.
*
          IF MCM-L-NO-OF-YEARS = ZERO
              MOVE FAC-UNPROT-NUM-BRT TO MCM-A-NO-OF-YEARS
              MOVE -1 TO MCM-L-NO-OF-YEARS
              MOVE 'YOU MUST ENTER NO OF YEARS'
                  TO MCM-D-ERROR-MESSAGE
          ELSE IF MCM-D-NO-OF-YEARS NOT NUMERIC
              MOVE FAC-UNPROT-NUM-BRT TO MCM-A-NO-OF-YEARS
              MOVE -1 TO MCM-L-NO-OF-YEARS
              MOVE 'NO OF YEARS MUST BE NUMERIC'
                  TO MCM-D-ERROR-MESSAGE
          ELSE IF MCM-D-NO-OF-YEARS NOT > ZERO
              MOVE FAC-UNPROT-NUM-BRT TO MCM-A-NO-OF-YEARS
              MOVE -1 TO MCM-L-NO-OF-YEARS
              MOVE 'NO OF YEARS MUST BE GREATER THAN ZERO'
                  TO MCM-D-ERROR-MESSAGE.
*
          IF MCM-L-PRINCIPAL-AMOUNT = ZERO
              MOVE FAC-UNPROT-NUM-BRT TO MCM-A-PRINCIPAL-AMOUNT
              MOVE -1 TO MCM-L-PRINCIPAL-AMOUNT
              MOVE 'YOU MUST ENTER PRINCIPAL AMOUNT'
                  TO MCM-D-ERROR-MESSAGE
          ELSE IF MCM-D-PRINCIPAL-AMOUNT NOT NUMERIC
              MOVE FAC-UNPROT-NUM-BRT TO MCM-A-PRINCIPAL-AMOUNT
              MOVE -1 TO MCM-L-PRINCIPAL-AMOUNT
              MOVE 'PRINCIPAL AMOUNT MUST BE NUMERIC'
                  TO MCM-D-ERROR-MESSAGE
          ELSE IF MCM-D-PRINCIPAL-AMOUNT NOT > ZERO
              MOVE FAC-UNPROT-NUM-BRT TO MCM-A-PRINCIPAL-AMOUNT
              MOVE -1 TO MCM-L-PRINCIPAL-AMOUNT
              MOVE 'PRINCIPAL AMOUNT MUST BE GREATER THAN ZERO'
                  TO MCM-D-ERROR-MESSAGE.
*
          IF MCM-D-ERROR-MESSAGE NOT = LOW-VALUE
              MOVE 'N' TO VALID-DATA-SW.
*
      130-CALCULATE-MONTHLY-PAYMENT SECTION.
*
          COMPUTE MCM-D-MONTHLY-PAYMENT =
              MCM-D-PRINCIPAL-AMOUNT /
                  ((1 - (1 / (1 + MCM-D-INTEREST-RATE / 12)
                      ** (MCM-D-NO-OF-YEARS * 12)))
                          / (MCM-D-INTEREST-RATE / 12))
              ON SIZE ERROR
                  MOVE ZERO TO MCM-D-MONTHLY-PAYMENT.
*
```

Figure 6-4   Source listing for the mortgage-calculation program (part 3 of 4)

```
    140-SEND-MORTGAGE-SCREEN SECTION.
*
        EXEC CICS
            SEND MAP('MORMAP1')
                 MAPSET('MORSET1')
                 FROM(MORTGAGE-CALCULATION-MAP)
                 DATAONLY
                 CURSOR
        END-EXEC.
*
    800-START-TERMINAL-SESSION SECTION.
*
        MOVE LOW-VALUE TO MORTGAGE-CALCULATION-MAP.
        MOVE 'PRESS CLEAR TO END SESSION' TO MCM-D-OPERATOR-MESSAGE.
        MOVE -1 TO MCM-L-PRINCIPAL-AMOUNT.
        EXEC CICS
            SEND MAP('MORMAP1')
                 MAPSET('MORSET1')
                 FROM(MORTGAGE-CALCULATION-MAP)
                 ERASE
                 CURSOR
        END-EXEC.
*
    900-SEND-TERMINATION-MESSAGE SECTION.
*
        EXEC CICS
            SEND TEXT FROM(END-OF-SESSION-MESSAGE)
                      LENGTH(13)
                      ERASE
                      FREEKB
        END-EXEC.
```

Figure 6-4   Source listing for the mortgage-calculation program (part 4 of 4)

Data Division

The first thing you may notice about the Data Division in figure
6-4 is that it doesn't have a File Section. It's omitted for the same
reason the Environment Division is left empty: all files are defined
in the File Control Table. The mortgage-calculation program is a
somewhat misleading example because it doesn't use any files. But
even if it did, the program wouldn't include a File Section. What's
left in the Data Division, then, is the Working-Storage Section and
the Linkage Section.

Working-Storage Section   You use the Working-Storage Section to
define program variables, just as you do in a batch program. In
addition, all file record layouts, if a program requires them, are
coded in working storage, since there isn't a File Section. Let me
briefly explain each of the Working-Storage Section entries in figure
6-4.

The first Working-Storage Section entry in figure 6-4 is an 01-level group item named SWITCHES. It contains the definition of the data fields I use to control program logic in the Procedure Division. Although you can set up a program switch in many ways, I code a one-byte alphanumeric data field (PIC X) whose value will be Y if the switch is on and N if the switch is off. I use a condition-name (88-level item) to make the Procedure Division statements that test the switch easier to understand. The name of the switch field is the condition-name followed by -SW. Thus, if the condition name is VALID-DATA, the switch name is VALID-DATA-SW.

In figure 6-4, I defined two switches. The first, END-SESSION-SW, is used to tell whether the operator has indicated the end of the terminal session. The second, VALID-DATA-SW, is used to indicate whether the operator entered valid data. You'll see how I use these switches when I describe the mortgage-calculation program's Procedure Division.

After the switches, I included an entry named END-OF-SESSION-MESSAGE. This field contains the message that's sent to the operator when the session ends.

The next working storage entry is an 01-level item named COMMUNICATION-AREA. The *communication area* is a special field used to pass data from one program execution to the next. In a more complicated program, the communication area can contain many fields.

Following the communication area is a COPY statement for the mortgage-calculation screen's symbolic map (MORSET1). This COPY statement expands to the code in figure 6-5. (The symbolic map in figure 6-5 is the same as the programmer-created map in figure 5-16.) Following the COPY statement for the map description, you include other COPY statements for file record layouts if they're required.

The next Working-Storage Section entry in figure 6-4 is a COPY statement for a library member named FACDEFN. This COPY member, illustrated in figure 6-6, contains standardized definitions for attribute characters I use in the program's Procedure Division.

Before I go on, I should point out that each time a program is executed, a fresh copy of working storage is obtained. As a result, any changes you make to the contents of working storage fields are *not* saved between executions of a pseudo-conversational program. If you need to preserve data from one program execution to the next, you can pass the data between executions using the communication area. That's why the communication area in a more

```
    01   MORTGAGE-CALCULATION-MAP.
*
         05   FILLER                    PIC X(12).
*
         05   MCM-L-PRINCIPAL-AMOUNT    PIC S9(4)    COMP.
         05   MCM-A-PRINCIPAL-AMOUNT    PIC X.
         05   MCM-D-PRINCIPAL-AMOUNT    PIC 9(6)V99.
*
         05   MCM-L-NO-OF-YEARS         PIC S9(4)    COMP.
         05   MCM-A-NO-OF-YEARS         PIC X.
         05   MCM-D-NO-OF-YEARS         PIC 99.
*
         05   MCM-L-INTEREST-RATE       PIC S9(4)    COMP.
         05   MCM-A-INTEREST-RATE       PIC X.
         05   MCM-D-INTEREST-RATE       PIC V9(4).
*
         05   MCM-L-MONTHLY-PAYMENT     PIC S9(4)    COMP.
         05   MCM-A-MONTHLY-PAYMENT     PIC X.
         05   MCM-D-MONTHLY-PAYMENT     PIC ZZ,ZZ9.99.
*
         05   MCM-L-OPERATOR-MESSAGE    PIC S9(4)    COMP.
         05   MCM-A-OPERATOR-MESSAGE    PIC X.
         05   MCM-D-OPERATOR-MESSAGE    PIC X(79).
*
         05   MCM-L-ERROR-MESSAGE       PIC S9(4)    COMP.
         05   MCM-A-ERROR-MESSAGE       PIC X.
         05   MCM-D-ERROR-MESSAGE       PIC X(77).
*
         05   MCM-L-DUMMY               PIC S9(4)    COMP.
         05   MCM-A-DUMMY               PIC X.
         05   MCM-D-DUMMY               PIC X.
*
```

Figure 6-5   Symbolic map for the mortgage-calculation screen (MORSET1)

complicated program can contain many fields. I'll explain how to
pass data from one program execution to the next in chapter 8.

Linkage Section   All CICS programs have a Linkage Section. At
the minimum, you need to code a Linkage Section definition for
the communication area with the special name DFHCOMMAREA.
In figure 6-4, the communication area is one byte long. In other
programs, the communication area may contain many fields. In
any event, DFHCOMMAREA must have the same length as the
communication area entry in the Working-Storage Section.

```
01   FIELD-ATTRIBUTE-DEFINITIONS.
*
     05  FAC-UNPROT                    PIC X     VALUE ' '.
     05  FAC-UNPROT-MDT                PIC X     VALUE 'A'.
     05  FAC-UNPROT-BRT                PIC X     VALUE 'H'.
     05  FAC-UNPROT-BRT-MDT            PIC X     VALUE 'I'.
     05  FAC-UNPROT-DARK               PIC X     VALUE '<'.
     05  FAC-UNPROT-DARK-MDT           PIC X     VALUE '('.
     05  FAC-UNPROT-NUM                PIC X     VALUE '&'.
     05  FAC-UNPROT-NUM-MDT            PIC X     VALUE 'J'.
     05  FAC-UNPROT-NUM-BRT            PIC X     VALUE 'Q'.
     05  FAC-UNPROT-NUM-BRT-MDT        PIC X     VALUE 'R'.
     05  FAC-UNPROT-NUM-DARK           PIC X     VALUE '*'.
     05  FAC-UNPROT-NUM-DARK-MDT       PIC X     VALUE ')'.
     05  FAC-PROT                      PIC X     VALUE '-'.
     05  FAC-PROT-MDT                  PIC X     VALUE '/'.
     05  FAC-PROT-BRT                  PIC X     VALUE 'Y'.
     05  FAC-PROT-BRT-MDT              PIC X     VALUE 'Z'.
     05  FAC-PROT-DARK                 PIC X     VALUE '%'.
     05  FAC-PROT-DARK-MDT             PIC X     VALUE '_'.
     05  FAC-PROT-SKIP                 PIC X     VALUE '0'.
     05  FAC-PROT-SKIP-MDT             PIC X     VALUE '1'.
     05  FAC-PROT-SKIP-BRT             PIC X     VALUE '8'.
     05  FAC-PROT-SKIP-BRT-MDT         PIC X     VALUE '9'.
     05  FAC-PROT-SKIP-DARK            PIC X     VALUE '@'.
     05  FAC-PROT-SKIP-DARK-MDT        PIC X     VALUE QUOTE.
```

Figure 6-6   Attribute byte definitions (FACDEFN)

Why define the communication area in both the Working-Storage Section and the Linkage Section? Because, as figure 6-7 illustrates, the Working-Storage Section definition of the communication area is the source of the data passed on to the next execution of the program, while the Linkage Section definition is the destination of the data passed from the previous execution. In other words, two versions of the communication area exist during an execution of the program: one to pass data to the next execution, the other to receive data from the previous execution.

Incidentally, if you don't include an entry for DFHCOMMAREA, the command translator inserts a definition for a one-byte communication area automatically. Even so, I recommend you always code your own definition for DFHCOMMAREA.

Although you can't see it in the source listing in figure 6-4, the command translator also inserts another special field called the *Execute Interface Block* (or *EIB*) in all CICS programs after the DFHCOMMAREA entry. Unlike DFHCOMMAREA, you don't

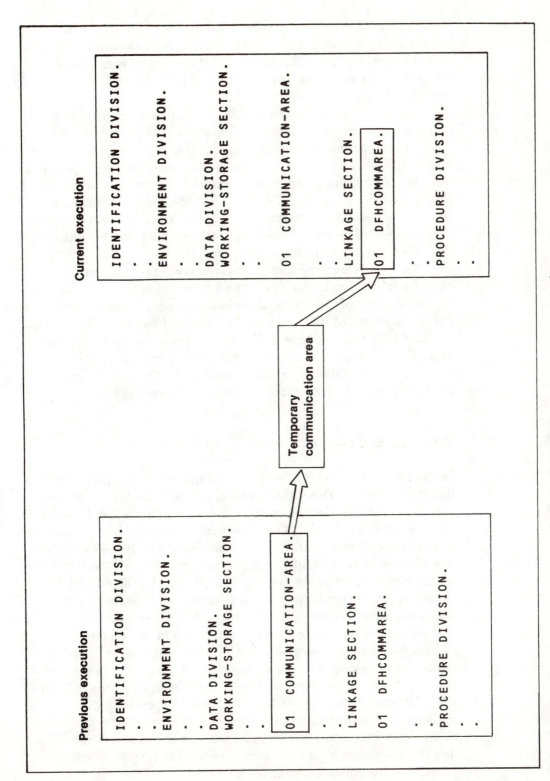

Figure 6-7 How the communication area is passed from one program to the next

code your own definition for the EIB because its fields are the same in all CICS programs. The Execute Interface Block contains several useful items of system information I'll show you how to use in chapter 8. For now, you need to know about one field in particular: EIBCALEN.

When your program starts, EIBCALEN contains a value that represents the length of the communication area passed to your program. If no communication area is passed to your program, EIBCALEN is set to zero. Since no communication area is passed if you start a program by entering a transaction identifier at a terminal, you can evaluate EIBCALEN to detect the first-time condition in a pseudo-conversational program. You'll see in a moment why a program needs to be able to distinguish its first execution in a terminal session from subsequent executions.

The only reason the mortgage-calculation program passes a communication area is to allow its next execution to determine that it's not the first of the terminal session. The next execution will check the length of the communication area (by evaluating EIBCALEN) and find that it did indeed receive a communication area. But it doesn't do anything with the one byte of data it received. In contrast, more complicated programs usually process the data passed to them through the communication area.

Procedure Division

In the Procedure Division, you code a mixture of standard COBOL statements (like MOVE, ADD, and so on) and special *CICS commands* that invoke CICS functions. Before I go on, I should point out that many of the COBOL statements you use in batch programs aren't allowed in CICS programs. Specifically, you can't use any of the standard COBOL features in figure 6-8. CICS commands handle most of the functions performed by these COBOL elements. Other functions, such as Report Writer or the SORT statement, simply aren't available in a CICS environment.

Figure 6-9 shows the structure chart I used to develop the mortgage-calculation program. Each of the boxes (or *modules*) in figure 6-9 represents a major function of the program. In the next chapter, I'll show you how to develop a chart like the one in figure 6-9. For now, I just want you to recognize that each module is implemented as a section in the program in figure 6-4, and PERFORM statements invoke those sections as needed. Now, I'll describe the function of each section of the mortgage-calculation program's Procedure Division.

Operator communication statements	ACCEPT
	DISPLAY
File I/O statements	OPEN
	CLOSE
	READ
	WRITE
	REWRITE
	DELETE
	START
Program termination statements	STOP RUN
	GOBACK
Sort statements	SORT
	RELEASE
	RETURN
Debugging statements	EXHIBIT
	TRACE
String manipulation statements	INSPECT
	UNSTRING
Segmentation feature	
Report Writer feature	

Figure 6-8 Standard COBOL statements and features not supported under CICS

Module 000: Determine monthly payments The key to understanding how the mortgage-calculation program works is understanding module 000. It contains most of the code required to implement pseudo-conversational programming.

The first statement in module 000 checks for the first-time condition by testing EIBCALEN for a value of zero. Module 800 is performed to start the terminal session if the first-time condition is true. If the first-time condition is *not* true, module 100 is performed to process an operator entry (that is, do a mortgage calculation). So, each time the program is executed, module 000 invokes *either* module 800 or module 100.

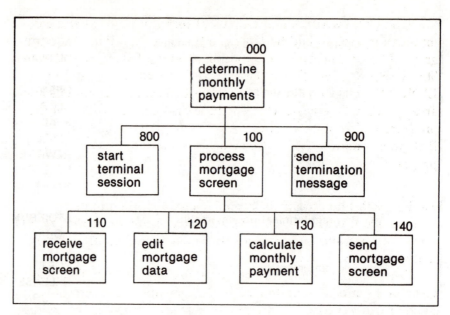

Figure 6-9 Structure chart for the mortgage-calculation program

After module 800 or 100 ends, the program itself must end. As you should remember from topic 1, the RETURN command causes a program to end and control to return to CICS. It's equivalent to the STOP RUN or GOBACK statement in a standard batch COBOL program. (Notice that the RETURN commands begin with the words EXEC CICS and end with the word END-EXEC; all CICS commands are coded this way.)

The IF END-SESSION statement in module 000 causes one of two RETURN commands to be executed, depending on whether the operator pressed the clear key to end the terminal session. If the operator did press the clear key, module 900 is performed to send a termination message to the terminal. Then, the first RETURN statement (without the TRANSID, COMMAREA, and LENGTH options) is executed. Otherwise, the second RETURN statement is executed.

The second RETURN statement includes the TRANSID, COMMAREA, and LENGTH options. As you should remember from the last topic, the RETURN command allows you to specify what trans-id will be invoked the next time the operator presses an AID key. Because I coded TRANSID('MOR1'), transaction MOR1 will be started, and the mortgage-calculation program will be executed again.

The COMMAREA and LENGTH options specify that a communication area should be passed to the next execution of the program. The COMMAREA option identifies the field in the Working-Storage Section (*not* the Linkage Section) to be passed, and the LENGTH option gives the field's length. Because a communication area is passed, the EIBCALEN field for the next execution of the program will contain a value greater than zero. As a result, the first-time condition will *not* be true on subsequent executions of the program.

Module 800: Start terminal session   Since the second line in module 000 invokes module 800, I want you to look at module 800 now. This module formats the first screen of the terminal session and sends it to the terminal.

The module begins with three MOVE statements. The first clears the symbolic map for the mortgage-calculation screen by moving LOW-VALUE to it. The second sets the operator instruction to be displayed. The third causes the cursor to be displayed at the principal amount field. Don't worry if you don't understand why I coded these MOVE statements; you will when you've finished this chapter.

Then, the module issues a SEND MAP command to send a BMS map to the terminal. Notice that I coded the ERASE option on the SEND MAP command in module 800. ERASE clears the screen before the new map is displayed. Later in this chapter, I'll describe the other SEND MAP options I coded.

Module 900: Send termination message   While you're near the end of the listing, look at module 900. It's invoked from module 000 when the operator signals the end of the session by pressing the clear key. Module 900 issues a SEND TEXT command that displays a simple text message at the terminal. The message is the one I defined in the Working-Storage Section: END-OF-SESSION-MESSAGE.

Module 100: Process mortgage screen   Now, look at module 100. It controls all of the functions necessary to do a mortgage calculation. First, it performs module 110 to retrieve input data from the terminal. Then, if the operator doesn't signal the end of the session by pressing the clear key, module 100 performs module 120 to edit the input data.

If the data is valid, modules 130 and 140 are performed to calculate the monthly payment and send the data back to the terminal. Before the program performs module 140 to send the data back to the terminal, it executes three MOVE statements. The first two format the operator communication zone by providing the proper operator instruction and clearing any previous error message. The third MOVE statement causes the cursor to appear at the principal amount field. I'll explain cursor positioning later in this chapter.

If the data is invalid, an error message is formatted, and module 140 is performed to send the data (along with the error message) to the terminal, but module 130 is not performed, so the payment isn't calculated.

Module 110: Receive mortgage screen   Module 110 retrieves input data from the terminal and detects the use of the clear key. To do these functions, the program uses two CICS commands: HANDLE AID and RECEIVE MAP. In almost all cases, you'll code HANDLE AID and RECEIVE MAP together. HANDLE AID doesn't do any processing; it just tells your program what to do when it detects that the operator pressed an AID key. The use of the AID key is actually detected when a RECEIVE MAP command is executed. Basically, the RECEIVE MAP command reads data from the terminal and maps it into the symbolic map. If the operator presses a key specified in a HANDLE AID command, control transfers to the paragraph specified for that key. Usually, however, the program continues with the statement after the RECEIVE MAP command.

Quite simply, the HANDLE AID command in figure 6-4 specifies that if the operator presses the clear key, control will be transferred to the paragraph labelled 110-CLEAR-KEY. The ANYKEY option specifies that control will be transferred to 110-ANYKEY if the operator presses any AID key other than the clear key or the enter key. The ANYKEY option works for any AID key *except* the enter key and other keys explicitly mentioned in the HANDLE AID command (in this case, the clear key).

Figure 6-10 shows the general structure I use when I code a section that contains a HANDLE AID command (or a similar command, HANDLE CONDITION, which I'll explain in chapter 8). As you can see, I place the HANDLE AID and RECEIVE MAP commands at the beginning of the section. Then, I use a GO TO statement to branch to a paragraph at the end of the section that contains an EXIT command. Between that GO TO statement and the EXIT paragraph, I code the paragraphs that process the AID keys I specified in the HANDLE AID command. Each of these

```
xxx-module-name SECTION.

    HANDLE AID and HANDLE CONDITION commands
    RECEIVE MAP command
    other COBOL and CICS commands
    GO TO xxx-EXIT.

xxx-exception-routine-1.

    COBOL and CICS commands for exceptional condition.
    GO TO xxx-EXIT.

xxx-exception-routine-2.

    COBOL and CICS commands for exceptional condition.
    GO TO xxx-EXIT.


        .
        .
        .


xxx-EXIT.

    EXIT.
```

Figure 6-10   General structure of a section containing a HANDLE AID or
HANDLE CONDITION command

paragraphs also ends with a GO TO statement that branches to the
EXIT paragraph. For the last paragraph before the EXIT
paragraph (110-ANYKEY in figure 6-4), the GO TO statement is
optional since control falls through to the EXIT paragraph anyway.

I want to be sure you understand this coding, so recall how the
PERFORM statement works with sections and paragraphs. If a
PERFORM statement specifies a paragraph name, then all
statements in the paragraph are executed. If a PERFORM statement specifies a section name, then execution begins with the first
statement after the section header and continues through the last
statement of the last paragraph in the section (a section may contain many paragraphs). GO TO statements are allowed if they
don't branch to paragraphs outside the section. That way, the
PERFORM statement that invoked the section remains active.

Error condition	IF statement to test condition
Field was not entered	IF MCM-L-PRINCIPAL-AMOUNT = 0
Field is not numeric	IF MCM-D-PRINCIPAL-AMOUNT NOT NUMERIC
Field is not positive	IF MCM-D-PRINCIPAL-AMOUNT NOT > ZERO
Field is zero	IF MCM-D-PRINCIPAL-AMOUNT = ZERO
Field is spaces	IF MCM-D-CUSTOMER-NAME = SPACE

Figure 6-11   Common field edits

When you name paragraphs within a section, I recommend you follow three guidelines. First, use the same module sequence number for all paragraph names within the section. Second, name the paragraphs that process the AID keys with the module sequence number followed by the name of the AID key. (For example, 110-CLEAR-KEY is the name of the paragraph that processes the clear key in module 110.) And third, form the name for the last paragraph in the section with the module sequence number followed by the word EXIT. If you follow these guidelines, there shouldn't be any confusion about the functions of the paragraphs within a section.

Module 120: Edit mortgage data   Module 120 edits the input data to insure that the program processes only valid data. The first statement in this module, a MOVE statement, modifies the attribute character fields in the symbolic map. I'll show you how this statement works and why it's required later in this chapter. The statements that follow detect invalid data in the symbolic map.

Figure 6-11 summarizes the more common error conditions that should be tested and gives a sample IF statement for each test. Besides the conditions in figure 6-11, certain fields have specific editing requirements. For example, you should test a state code field to be sure it contains a valid code (for instance, CA is a valid state code, but CB isn't). Similarly, you should test a social-security-number field to make sure the operator entered nine digits.

Beyond these tests, an edit module must also test whether data-entry fields agree with each other. For example, if one of the input

```
IF error-condition-1 for field-1
    MOVE attribute-character TO attribute-field for field-1
    MOVE -1                  TO length-field for field-1
    MOVE error-message       TO error-message-field
ELSE IF error-condition-2 for field-1
    .
    .
    .


IF error-condition-1 for field-2
    .
    .
    .


IF error-message-field NOT = LOW-VALUE
    MOVE 'N' TO VALID-DATA-SW.
```

Note: Fields should be tested in the reverse order of how they appear on the screen.

Figure 6-12   General structure of an edit module

fields is supposed to be the total of other input fields, you must test
to be sure the numbers agree. (Of course, in this case, it would be
better to let the program calculate the total rather than require the
operator to enter it.)

Figure 6-12 illustrates the basic structure of an edit module.
Basically, the module edits each field with a series of nested IF
statements, like this:

```
IF error-condition-1
    error processing
ELSE IF error-condition-2
    error processing
ELSE ...
```

To avoid a long string of nested IF statements, each field should
have its own series of them.

Notice in figure 6-4 that the program edits the data-entry fields
from the bottom of the screen to the top. As a result, all of the
invalid fields are highlighted, but the error message the program

displays relates to the first invalid field on the screen. If the program edited the fields from top to bottom, the error message would relate to the *last* invalid field on the screen. Of course, you can code an edit module so it edits fields in the same order they appear on the screen, but editing from the bottom to the top results in the simplest code.

When you detect an error, you need to do three things: (1) modify the attribute field so the error is highlighted (I'll explain this later in the chapter), (2) move -1 to the length field so the cursor will be placed under the field in error (you'll see how this cursor-positioning technique works later also), and (3) move an appropriate error message to the error-message field.

If you code the editing module as shown in figure 6-4, you must do these three steps for each IF statement for each data-entry field on the screen. Counting the IF statement, then, you must code four statements for each edit condition. For a screen with twenty input fields, each requiring an average of three field edits, the edit module will contain 240 lines of code. You might be tempted to break this module into several smaller modules, but it's unnecessary. Even though the module is long, it's repetitive and its structure is clear. Breaking it into several smaller modules won't improve the program's readability, so code simple field edits in one straightforward module.

You should, however, consider creating a separate module for complicated edits. For example, you should code edits that require table lookups in separate modules. And if an edit requires a file lookup, by all means feel free to code a separate module. The point is to keep the program clear. As long as the edits are simple, keep them in one module. When they become complex, isolate them in separate modules.

The last IF statement in figure 6-12 (and in module 120 of the mortgage-calculation program) tests the error-message field for a value other than LOW-VALUE. When the RECEIVE MAP command in module 110 is executed, hexadecimal zeros (LOW-VALUE) are moved to any fields in the symbolic map that aren't entered by the operator, including protected fields such as the error-message field. If the edit module detects an error, data is moved to the error-message field. So a value other than LOW-VALUE in the error-message field means the edit module detected an error. In that case, the program moves N to VALID-DATA-SW so module 100 will know an error was detected.

Module 130: Calculate monthly payment Module 130 calculates the monthly payment based on the principal amount, number of years, and interest rate. Although the formula for this calculation is complicated, it doesn't affect the logic of the program. So don't spend too much time trying to figure out how the COMPUTE statement in module 130 works.

Module 140: Send mortgage screen   Module 140 contains a SEND MAP command that sends the symbolic map (including the calculated monthly payment if the data was valid) back to the terminal. After the SEND MAP command, the terminal is ready to accept another set of input data from the operator. The DATAONLY option means that only data in the symbolic map is actually sent to the terminal. Since the screen headings defined in the physical map are already displayed on the screen, there's no reason to send them again.

Discussion

At this point, you should understand how the mortgage-calculation program in figure 6-4 works. Still, you lack a complete understanding of each of the CICS commands I used in this program and of some of the programming techniques it illustrates. So, the next two topics describe these commands and techniques in detail.

Terminology

communication area
Execute Interface Block
EIB
CICS command
module

Objectives

1. Explain the COBOL code that detects the first execution of a program in a terminal session.
2. Explain the COBOL code that processes AID keys.
3. Explain the COBOL code that edits data-entry fields.

Topic 3   CICS commands of the basic subset

Now that you've seen several CICS commands within the context of the mortgage-calculation program, you're ready to learn about them in more detail. First, this topic describes how to code a CICS command. Then, it presents the specific options you can code for the CICS commands in the mortgage-calculation program.

How to code a CICS command   When you code a CICS command, you must follow a few rules. To begin with, all CICS commands must follow this general pattern:

```
EXEC CICS
    command option(value)...
END-EXEC.
```

The words EXEC CICS and END-EXEC are required. The command specifies the operation to be performed, and the *options* (or *parameters*) provide information CICS needs to perform the specified operation.

If an option requires a value, enclose the value in parentheses. An option value may be coded in one of several forms, depending on the requirements of each command. The illustrations for each command indicate whether an option value should be coded as a *data-name* (an elementary or group item defined in the Working-Storage Section), a *numeric-data-value* (a data-name or a numeric literal), an *alphanumeric-data-value* (a data-name or an alphanumeric literal in quotes), or a *procedure-name* (a paragraph or section name).

When a CICS command requires more than one option, use blank spaces to separate them, *not* commas. To make your program listings easier to read, I recommend you code each option on a separate line. Special coding isn't necessary to continue a CICS command from one line to the next.

In the mortgage-calculation program in topic 2 (figure 6-4), I used five CICS commands: RETURN, SEND MAP, SEND TEXT, HANDLE AID, and RECEIVE MAP. I've already explained the basic operation of each of these commands. Now, I'll present the details of how you use them.

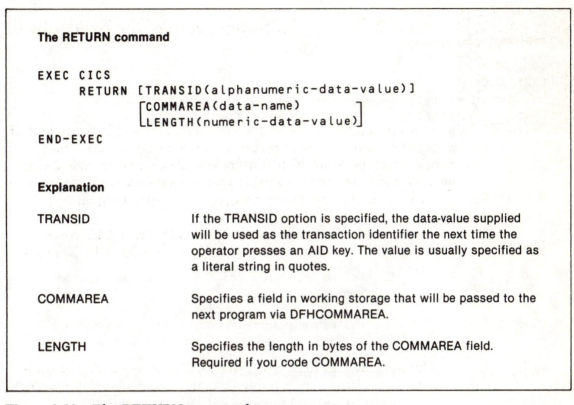

The RETURN command

```
EXEC CICS
     RETURN [TRANSID(alphanumeric-data-value)]
            [COMMAREA(data-name)
            [LENGTH(numeric-data-value)]
END-EXEC
```

Explanation

TRANSID   If the TRANSID option is specified, the data-value supplied
                 will be used as the transaction identifier the next time the
                 operator presses an AID key. The value is usually specified as
                 a literal string in quotes.

COMMAREA   Specifies a field in working storage that will be passed to the
                 next program via DFHCOMMAREA.

LENGTH   Specifies the length in bytes of the COMMAREA field.
                 Required if you code COMMAREA.

Figure 6-13   The RETURN command

The RETURN command   The RETURN command, shown in
figure 6-13, returns control to CICS. If you code the RETURN
command with no options, control simply returns to CICS, and the
terminal session ends. On the other hand, if you code the
TRANSID option, CICS invokes the trans-id you specify the next
time the operator presses an AID key.

The COMMAREA and LENGTH options are used to pass a
communication area to the next program. COMMAREA specifies
the name of the field in working storage containing the data to be
passed, and LENGTH specifies the number of bytes to be passed.
When the next program execution begins, the data passed via the
communication area is available in the DFHCOMMAREA field in
its Linkage Section.

The SEND MAP command   The SEND MAP command, shown in
figure 6-14, sends data from your program to the terminal screen.
The MAP and MAPSET options indicate, respectively, the map and

The SEND MAP command

```
EXEC CICS
    SEND MAP(alphanumeric-data-value)
         MAPSET(alphanumeric-data-value)
         FROM(data-name)
        [MAPONLY/DATAONLY]
        [ERASE/ERASEAUP]
        [CURSOR[(numeric-data-value)]]
END-EXEC
```

Explanation

MAP	Specifies the name of the map. The value is usually supplied as a literal string in quotes.
MAPSET	Specifies the name of the mapset that contains the map. The value is usually supplied as a literal string in quotes.
FROM	Specifies the symbolic map.
MAPONLY	Specifies that only data from the physical map (that is, headings, constants, and attribute characters) is sent to the terminal.
DATAONLY	Specifies that only data from the symbolic map is sent to the terminal. The physical map is used to map the data to its correct location on the screen, but data from the physical map is not actually sent to the terminal.
	If both MAPONLY and DATAONLY are omitted, both the physical and the symbolic map data are sent to the terminal.
ERASE	Indicates that the screen should be erased before the data is displayed.
ERASEAUP	Indicates that all unprotected fields should be erased before the data is displayed.
	If both ERASE and ERASEAUP are omitted, no data is erased from the screen before the map is sent to the terminal.
CURSOR	Indicates cursor positioning.

Figure 6-14   The SEND MAP command

mapset names for the physical map. The FROM option names the symbolic map definition in the program's Working-Storage Section.

If you specify the MAPONLY option on a SEND MAP command, only the data in the physical map is sent to the screen. As a result, only the screen's headings will be displayed. In contrast, if you specify the DATAONLY option, only the data from the symbolic map is sent to the screen. So, only the actual data values are sent to the screen—the headings are *not*. If you omit the MAPONLY and DATAONLY options, the data in the symbolic map is combined with the data in the physical map, and both are sent to the screen.

The first SEND MAP command executed in a terminal session usually sends both headings and initial data to the screen. As a result, you'll code the first SEND MAP with neither the MAPONLY nor the DATAONLY option. Subsequent SEND MAP commands generally use the DATAONLY option so the headings aren't transmitted again. Using the DATAONLY option improves transmission time. I'll have more to say about this efficiency technique in the next topic.

The ERASE option causes CICS to erase the contents of the screen before any data is displayed. If ERASE is not specified, the screen isn't erased, so any characters that aren't overlaid by new data remain on the screen. ERASE is usually specified for the first SEND MAP issued by a program. That way, whatever was on the screen before the SEND MAP command is executed is erased. On subsequent SEND MAP commands, however, you generally do not code the ERASE option, particularly if you code the DATAONLY option.

The ERASEAUP option is similar to the ERASE option. The difference is that the ERASEAUP option specifies that only unprotected fields are erased, while ERASE completely clears the screen. In other words, ERASEAUP causes only data-entry fields to be erased. Whether you use the ERASEAUP option depends on whether you want to erase all data-entry fields between transactions. In most applications, you do, so you code a SEND MAP with the DATAONLY and ERASEAUP options. In some applications, such as the mortgage-calculation program, you want to leave the previous transaction's data on the screen so the operator can enter only the fields that are changed. In this case, you do not code the ERASEAUP option.

Bear in mind that the ERASEAUP option erases only unprotected fields. So if you want to erase protected fields in your symbolic map—such as the error-message field—you must move

---

The SEND TEXT command

```
EXEC CICS
    SEND TEXT FROM(data-name)
              LENGTH(numeric-data-value)
            [ERASE]
            [FREEKB]
END-EXEC
```

Explanation

FROM   Specifies the name of the field containing the data to be
                    transmitted to the terminal.

LENGTH   Specifies the number of characters to be sent. Usually coded
                    as a numeric literal, but may be a data-name.

ERASE   Specifies that the screen should be erased before any data is
                    displayed on the screen.

FREEKB   Specifies that the keyboard should be unlocked after the data
                    is sent. If FREEKB is not specified, the operator must press
                    the RESET key to unlock the keyboard.

Figure 6-15   The SEND TEXT command

SPACE to them. Moving LOW-VALUE to protected fields does not
cause them to be erased because CICS doesn't transmit LOW-
VALUE to the terminal.

The last SEND MAP option in figure 6-14, the CURSOR
option, is used for cursor positioning. I'll explain cursor-positioning
techniques in the next topic.

The SEND TEXT command   In many cases, you want to send a
short message to the terminal without having to create a BMS mapset. The SEND TEXT command, shown in figure 6-15, allows you
to do just that. The FROM option specifies the field in the
Working-Storage Section that contains the message, and the
LENGTH option specifies that field's length. The message is

The HANDLE AID command

```
EXEC CICS
    HANDLE AID
        option(procedure-name)...
END-EXEC
```

Explanation

option
      The name of the AID key to be handled. Up to 12 options may be specified in a single command. More than 12 options may be handled by multiple HANDLE AID commands. Common options are:

PA1—PA3	Program attention keys
PF1—PF24	Program function keys
ENTER	Enter key
CLEAR	Clear key
ANYKEY	Any AID key not previously specified in the HANDLE AID command, except the enter key

Control is passed to the procedure-name when the use of the specified AID key is detected. If procedure-name is omitted, no action is taken when the specified key is detected, even if ANYKEY is also specified.

Figure 6-16 The HANDLE AID command

displayed starting in the top left corner of the screen. If you specify the ERASE option, the screen is erased before the message is displayed; otherwise, the message simply overlays whatever was on the screen before. If you specify the FREEKB option, the keyboard is released after the message has been sent; otherwise, the operator has to press the reset key.

The HANDLE AID command   The HANDLE AID command, illustrated in figure 6-16, tells your program what to do when the operator uses one of the AID keys. To code a HANDLE AID command, you list one or more AID keys, along with the paragraph name that will process the key. Valid AID-key options are:

PA1 - PA3	The program attention keys
PF1 - PF24	The program function keys
ENTER	The enter key
CLEAR	The clear key
ANYKEY	Any AID key (other than the enter key) not previously specified in the HANDLE AID command

When the use of an AID key is detected (remember that the use of the key is detected by the RECEIVE MAP command, not the HANDLE AID command), CICS simply transfers control to the corresponding label specified in a previous HANDLE AID command.

For example, consider this HANDLE AID command:

```
EXEC CICS
    HANDLE AID PF1(110-PF1-KEY)
                CLEAR(110-CLEAR-KEY)
END-EXEC.
```

Here, control is passed to the paragraph or section named 110-PF1-KEY if the operator presses PF1. If the operator presses the clear key, control is passed to 110-CLEAR-KEY. If any other key is pressed, no special action is taken.

The ANYKEY option is provided to process AID keys not specifically mentioned in the HANDLE AID command. For example, consider the HANDLE AID command in the mortgage-calculation program in figure 6-4:

```
EXEC CICS
    HANDLE AID CLEAR(110-CLEAR-KEY)
                ANYKEY(110-ANYKEY)
END-EXEC.
```

Here, control is passed to 110-CLEAR-KEY if the clear key is pressed. If any other key is pressed, control is passed to 110-ANYKEY. Note, however, that the enter key is not handled by the ANYKEY option. The only way to handle the enter key with a HANDLE AID command is to specify ENTER as an option. Usually, though, you don't want to do any special processing for the enter key, so you don't code ENTER as an option on a HANDLE AID command.

If you specify an AID key without a label, that key isn't included as part of the ANYKEY option, and any previous HANDLE AID for that key is ignored. For example, consider these two HANDLE AID commands:

```
EXEC CICS
    HANDLE AID PF1(110-PF1-KEY)
               CLEAR(110-CLEAR-KEY)
END-EXEC.
EXEC CICS
    HANDLE AID PF2(110-PF2-KEY)
               ANYKEY(110-WRONG-KEY)
               PF1
END-EXEC.
```

After the execution of the second of these HANDLE AID commands, the clear key is processed by 110-CLEAR-KEY, PF2 is processed by 110-PF2-KEY, and any other AID keys besides the enter key and PF1 are processed by 110-WRONG-KEY. Since I coded PF1 without a label, no action is taken for it, even though I specified it explicitly in the first command and implicitly in the ANYKEY option in the second.

You can see from this example that a HANDLE AID command doesn't necessarily cancel all of the effects of another executed earlier during a program execution. To avoid potentially confusing program bugs caused by multiple HANDLE AID commands, I recommend you code your programs so only one HANDLE AID is invoked per program execution. That's easy to do because a single execution of a pseudo-conversational program usually invokes only one RECEIVE MAP command and, as a result, only one HANDLE AID command. (Remember that I recommend you pair RECEIVE MAP and HANDLE AID commands.)

The RECEIVE MAP command

```
EXEC CICS
    RECEIVE MAP(alphanumeric-data-value)
            MAPSET(alphanumeric-data-value)
            INTO(data-name)
END-EXEC
```

Explanation

MAP	Specifies the name of the map. The value is usually supplied as a literal string in quotes.
MAPSET	Specifies the name of the mapset containing the map. The value is usually supplied as a literal string in quotes.
INTO	Specifies the symbolic map.

Figure 6-17   The RECEIVE MAP command

The RECEIVE MAP command   The RECEIVE MAP command, shown in figure 6-17, receives input data from the terminal. The MAP and MAPSET options indicate the map and the mapset that contains it. The INTO option names the symbolic map in the Working-Storage Section of your program.

When the operator enters data at the terminal and presses an AID key, the data is transferred to a CICS buffer. Then, when your program executes a RECEIVE MAP command, the data in the buffer is mapped into your symbolic map. As a result, your program must not do a RECEIVE MAP before the operator has sent data from the terminal. This sounds like a problem, but it isn't. As long as your program is pseudo-conversational, data will always be available in the buffer because your program won't be executed until the operator presses an AID key.

Discussion

The CICS commands in this topic are among the most important you'll use. In fact, almost all CICS programs require all of them (except SEND TEXT). As a result, you should be sure you understand the material this topic presents. You'll need to learn other commands as your CICS training progresses, but they'll seem easy after you've mastered the ones presented in this topic.

Terminology

option
parameter
data-name
numeric-data-value
alphanumeric-data-value
procedure-name

Objectives

1. Describe the basic format and coding rules for any CICS command.

2. Describe the function of each of the CICS commands in this topic: RETURN, SEND MAP, SEND TEXT, HANDLE AID, and RECEIVE MAP.

3. Explain when it is and isn't appropriate to code the DATAONLY, MAPONLY, ERASE, and ERASEAUP options on the SEND MAP command.

Topic 4   Programming techniques every CICS programmer should know

This last topic of the basic subset of command-level CICS doesn't introduce any new CICS language elements. Instead, it covers programming techniques. Here, I'll describe two programming techniques that make your programs easier for operators to use: positioning the cursor and modifying attribute characters.

Then, I'll turn to efficiency techniques. As I've stated before, the most important CICS efficiency technique is pseudo-conversational programming. Because I've already covered pseudo-conversational programming in detail, I won't say more about it in this topic. What I do cover here are ways to optimize your programs' transmission times and main storage usage.

How to position the cursor

One way to make your CICS programs easier to use is to position the cursor properly. The cursor should appear automatically at the first field on a screen into which the operator should enter data. Then, the operator doesn't have to move it there himself.

As I mentioned in topic 3, you use the CURSOR option of the SEND MAP command to control cursor positioning on the screen. If you omit the CURSOR option altogether, the cursor is positioned in a map field that has the IC option specified. (IC, as you'll remember from topic 2 of chapter 5, is an option you can code on the DFHMDF macro when you define a BMS mapset. IC indicates the cursor should be positioned at the beginning of the data field for which it's specified.) If none of the map fields have IC options specified, the cursor is placed in the home position (row 1, column 1). Most of the time, however, you'll specify the CURSOR option when you code the SEND MAP command. In general, you can use two kinds of CURSOR positioning through the SEND MAP command: direct and symbolic.

To use *direct cursor positioning*, specify a cursor position in the CURSOR option of the SEND MAP command. This cursor position is a displacement from the start of the screen, not a row/column address. As a result, it must be a number from 0 to 1919 (for 24 x 80 screens), where 0 is row 1/column 1, and 1919 is row 24/column 80. To calculate the displacement from the row/column address, subtract 1 from the row address and multiply the result by 80. Then, subtract 1 from the column address. Add the results of the first two steps. The sum is the displacement you code in the CURSOR option of the SEND MAP command.

To illustrate, suppose you want to place the cursor in column 17 of row 12. The correct displacement is 896:

$$(12 - 1) \times 80 + (17 - 1) = 896$$

Then, you code the CURSOR option like this:

```
CURSOR(896)
```

As a result, the cursor is placed in column 17 of row 12.

Direct cursor positioning has two major drawbacks. First, cursor displacements are awkward to use. Second, and perhaps more important, direct cursor positioning ties your program to specific screen locations. So, if you change your mapset by moving a field from one screen location to another, you have to change your program as well. It's because of these drawbacks that you'll use symbolic cursor positioning more often than direct cursor positioning.

To use *symbolic cursor positioning*, you specify the position of the cursor by field rather than by displacement. To tell CICS which field to place the cursor in, you move −1 to the corresponding length field in the symbolic map. Then, you issue a SEND MAP command with the CURSOR option specified *without* a displacement. (Incidentally, if you move −1 to more than one length field in the symbolic map, the cursor is positioned at the first field containing −1.)

Edit routines often use symbolic cursor positioning. Whenever an edit routine that uses this technique detects invalid data in a field, it moves −1 to the corresponding length field in the symbolic map. That way, when the program issues a SEND MAP command, the cursor is automatically positioned at the start of the field that's in error. If you look back to module 120 of the mortgage-calculation program in figure 6-4 you'll see symbolic cursor positioning in use.

How to modify attribute characters

As I've already mentioned, you can change a field's attribute byte by moving a value to the corresponding attribute field in the symbolic map. Typically, you use this feature to highlight errors detected by an edit module.

In general, CICS looks in one of three places to find the attribute byte for a field: the symbolic map, the physical map, or the screen itself. If you move a value to an attribute field in the symbolic map and issue a SEND MAP command without the MAPONLY option, that value is used as the attribute character for the field. If an attribute field contains hexadecimal zero (LOW-VALUE), the field's attribute byte depends on the options coded for the SEND MAP command: if you code DATAONLY, the attribute byte on the screen remains unchanged; otherwise, the attribute byte in the physical map is used.

The simplest way to move an attribute character to a symbolic map attribute field is to move a literal value, like this:

```
MOVE 'Q' TO MCM-A-PRINCIPAL-AMOUNT.
```

Here, I set the attribute for the principal amount field to unprotected, numeric, and highlighted. (The letter Q is the EBCDIC character for the bit combination that specifies those attributes.) The only problem with this method is that you have to know the EBCDIC character for each attribute-byte bit combination you need to use. And since not all attribute-byte bit combinations have an EBCDIC equivalent, you can't code all attribute bytes this way.

To make it easier for you to modify attribute characters, IBM supplies a standard COPY member named DFHBMSCA. This member, shown in figure 6-18, defines many attribute characters. It has some severe limitations, however. First, the names assigned to the various attributes are cryptic. For example, DFHBMASB is the name for auto-skip and highlighted. Second, IBM's COPY member doesn't include some of the most commonly used attribute characters, and most of the definitions it does include are rarely used. For example, the attribute character for unprotected, numeric, and highlighted isn't supplied, yet attributes for special features like reverse-video and colors are.

Rather than use IBM's COPY member, I recommend you code your own, if your shop hasn't already done so. I showed you the COPY member I use in figure 6-6 when I introduced the mortgage-

```
01          DFHBMSCA.
   02       DFHBMPEM    PICTURE X    VALUE IS    ' '.
   02       DFHBMPNL    PICTURE X    VALUE IS    ' '.
   02       DFHBMASK    PICTURE X    VALUE IS    '0'.
   02       DFHBMUNP    PICTURE X    VALUE IS    ' '.
   02       DFHBMUNN    PICTURE X    VALUE IS    '&'.
   02       DFHBMPRO    PICTURE X    VALUE IS    '-'.
   02       DFHBMBRY    PICTURE X    VALUE IS    'H'.
   02       DFHBMDAR    PICTURE X    VALUE IS    '<'.
   02       DFHBMFSE    PICTURE X    VALUE IS    'A'.
   02       DFHBMPRF    PICTURE X    VALUE IS    '/'.
   02       DFHBMASF    PICTURE X    VALUE IS    '1'.
   02       DFHBMASB    PICTURE X    VALUE IS    '8'.
   02       DFHBMEOF    PICTURE X    VALUE IS    ' '.
   02       DFHBMDET    PICTURE X    VALUE IS    ' '.
   02       DFHSA       PICTURE X    VALUE IS    ' '.
   02       DFHCOLOR    PICTURE X    VALUE IS    ' '.
   02       DFHPS       PICTURE X    VALUE IS    ' '.
   02       DFHHLT      PICTURE X    VALUE IS    ' '.
   02       DFH3270     PICTURE X    VALUE IS    ' '.
   02       DFHVAL      PICTURE X    VALUE IS    'A'.
   02       DFHALL      PICTURE X    VALUE IS    ' '.
   02       DFHERROR    PICTURE X    VALUE IS    ' '.
   02       DFHDFT      PICTURE X    VALUE IS    ' '.
   02       DFHDFCOL    PICTURE X    VALUE IS    ' '.
   02       DFHBLUE     PICTURE X    VALUE IS    '1'.
   02       DFHRED      PICTURE X    VALUE IS    '2'.
   02       DFHPINK     PICTURE X    VALUE IS    '3'.
   02       DFHGREEN    PICTURE X    VALUE IS    '4'.
   02       DFHTURQ     PICTURE X    VALUE IS    '5'.
   02       DFHYELLO    PICTURE X    VALUE IS    '6'.
   02       DFHNEUTR    PICTURE X    VALUE IS    '7'.
   02       DFHBASE     PICTURE X    VALUE IS    ' '.
   02       DFHDFHI     PICTURE X    VALUE IS    ' '.
   02       DFHBLINK    PICTURE X    VALUE IS    '1'.
   02       DFHREVRS    PICTURE X    VALUE IS    '2'.
   02       DFHUNDLN    PICTURE X    VALUE IS    '4'.
   02       DFHMFIL     PICTURE X    VALUE IS    ' '.
   02       DFHMENT     PICTURE X    VALUE IS    ' '.
   02       DFHMFE      PICTURE X    VALUE IS    ' '.
   02       DFHMT       PICTURE X    VALUE IS    ' '.
   02       DFHMFT      PICTURE X    VALUE IS    ' '.
   02       DFHMET      PICTURE X    VALUE IS    ' '.
   02       DFHMFET     PICTURE X    VALUE IS    ' '.
```

Figure 6-18   The IBM-supplied COPY member DFHBMSCA

calculation program. For convenience, I've duplicated it in figure 6-19. In it, each attribute combination has a meaningful name. For example, the name for unprotected, numeric, and highlighted is FAC-UNPROT-NUM-BRT.

```
01   FIELD-ATTRIBUTE-DEFINITIONS.
*
     05   FAC-UNPROT                   PIC X      VALUE ' '.
     05   FAC-UNPROT-MDT               PIC X      VALUE 'A'.
     05   FAC-UNPROT-BRT               PIC X      VALUE 'H'.
     05   FAC-UNPROT-BRT-MDT           PIC X      VALUE 'I'.
     05   FAC-UNPROT-DARK              PIC X      VALUE '<'.
     05   FAC-UNPROT-DARK-MDT          PIC X      VALUE '('.
     05   FAC-UNPROT-NUM               PIC X      VALUE '&'.
     05   FAC-UNPROT-NUM-MDT           PIC X      VALUE 'J'.
     05   FAC-UNPROT-NUM-BRT           PIC X      VALUE 'Q'.
     05   FAC-UNPROT-NUM-BRT-MDT       PIC X      VALUE 'R'.
     05   FAC-UNPROT-NUM-DARK          PIC X      VALUE '*'.
     05   FAC-UNPROT-NUM-DARK-MDT      PIC X      VALUE ')'.
     05   FAC-PROT                     PIC X      VALUE '-'.
     05   FAC-PROT-MDT                 PIC X      VALUE '/'.
     05   FAC-PROT-BRT                 PIC X      VALUE 'Y'.
     05   FAC-PROT-BRT-MDT             PIC X      VALUE 'Z'.
     05   FAC-PROT-DARK                PIC X      VALUE '%'.
     05   FAC-PROT-DARK-MDT            PIC X      VALUE ']'.
     05   FAC-PROT-SKIP                PIC X      VALUE '0'.
     05   FAC-PROT-SKIP-MDT            PIC X      VALUE '1'.
     05   FAC-PROT-SKIP-BRT            PIC X      VALUE '8'.
     05   FAC-PROT-SKIP-BRT-MDT        PIC X      VALUE '9'.
     05   FAC-PROT-SKIP-DARK           PIC X      VALUE '@'.
     05   FAC-PROT-SKIP-DARK-MDT       PIC X      VALUE QUOTE.
```

Figure 6-19 An improved COPY member containing attribute byte definitions

So then, to change an attribute, you simply move the correct value to the attribute field. For example:

```
MOVE FAC-UNPROT-NUM-BRT TO MCM-A-PRINCIPAL-AMOUNT
```

changes the attribute byte in the symbolic map for the principal amount field to unprotected, numeric, and highlighted.

Once you've changed an attribute value, you must be able to restore it to its original value. You can do this several ways. First, you can issue a SEND MAP command with the MAPONLY option. That way, the attribute characters from the physical map are sent to the terminal. Second, you can move LOW-VALUE to the attribute fields in the symbolic map and issue a SEND MAP command without the MAPONLY or DATAONLY options. Again, the attribute bytes from the physical map are used. Third, you can move the original values of the attribute bytes to the attribute fields in the symbolic map and issue a SEND MAP command with the DATAONLY option. That way, the attribute bytes in the symbolic map are sent to the terminal.

I use the third technique in the mortgage-calculation program. That's why the first statement in module 120 of figure 6-4 is:

```
MOVE FAC-UNPROT-NUM-MDT TO MCM-A-PRINCIPAL-AMOUNT
                           MCM-A-NO-OF-YEARS
                           MCM-A-INTEREST-RATE.
```

After the edit module restores all of the attribute bytes to their original values, subsequent statements set the attribute fields of *invalid* fields to FAC-UNPROT-NUM-BRT. As a result, when the edit module has completed, all the attribute bytes are set correctly: fields that aren't in error are normal intensity, and fields that contain invalid data are high intensity.

You may wonder why I specified FAC-UNPROT-NUM-MDT rather than FAC-UNPROT-NUM in the first line of module 120 of the mortgage-calculation program. In other words, why did I specify that the modified data tag (MDT) should be turned on? Quite simply, so that any field containing valid data will be automatically sent to the program when the operator presses an AID key. If I didn't specify MDT here, the field would *not* be transmitted to the program (even though it appeared on the screen) unless the operator modified it.

Again, I recommend you restore *all* of a screen's data-entry field attribute bytes to their original values before you issue a SEND MAP command. That's because you can't assume that all of the attribute bytes in your symbolic map are set to hexadecimal zeros after you issue a RECEIVE MAP command. Usually, they are. However, if an operator modifies a field but does *not* enter data into it (for example, by erasing the field), the attribute field contains a hexadecimal 80 after a RECEIVE MAP command. If you then issue a SEND MAP command, hex 80 is sent as the field's attribute byte. And since hex 80 isn't a valid attribute character, the results are unpredictable. So remember, move an attribute character or LOW-VALUE to each attribute field (or to the entire symbolic map) before you issue a SEND MAP command during normal processing.

(By the way, a fix is available from IBM that eliminates this problem. It's not installed in all CICS shops, however, so I still recommend you restore the attribute byte by moving a valid attribute character or LOW-VALUE to the attribute field before issuing a SEND MAP command.)

How to optimize transmission time

For the sake of efficiency, you should try to optimize the transmission time a SEND MAP command requires. In general, that means you should send as few characters as possible. In particular, it means that once you've sent the physical map to the terminal, subsequent SEND MAP commands should specify the DATAONLY option. That way, the headings, captions, and other constant data in the physical map aren't transmitted unnecessarily.

You should also realize that CICS *never* sends LOW-VALUE to a terminal. As a result, you can save transmission time by moving LOW-VALUE to any fields in the symbolic map that are already on the screen. Then, those fields aren't transmitted.

You shouldn't be overly concerned with transmission time, however. If a program is heavily used, and large amounts of data are transmitted to and from the terminal, you should make sure its SEND MAP commands are as efficient as possible. But use common sense.

How to optimize storage usage

You can optimize storage usage in several ways. Among the most useful are: reducing the size of your Working-Storage Section, using straight-line coding when practical, and placing infrequently used sections of code near the end of the program.

As you read CICS literature, you're likely to encounter the terms *working set* and *locality of reference*. A program's working set is the number of virtual-storage pages normally required in main storage as the program executes. In general, the smaller the working set, the more efficient the program. Locality of reference means that a program shouldn't refer unnecessarily to data that isn't in the working set. If it does, the page containing the required data must be moved into main storage. And that degrades the entire system. The efficiency techniques that follow are designed to optimize a program's working set and locality of reference.

Because each task in a CICS system receives its own copy of working storage, reducing the size of your program's Working-Storage Section can sometimes have a dramatic effect on the overall response time of a CICS system. Of course, you can't eliminate data that's required by your program. However, you can reduce the size of your Working-Storage Section by coding constant data as literals in the Procedure Division rather than as fields in the Working-Storage Section.

Here, I'm thinking especially of error messages. If your program edits 15 data fields, each field has three edit checks, and the error messages average 20 characters each, your program may have as many as 900 bytes of error messages. If you place this data in working storage, each user is given his own copy of it. As a result, if 30 users run the program at the same time, error messages occupy 27K of main storage! However, if you code error messages as literals in the Procedure Division, only one copy is in main storage, no matter how many users run the program. So, placing constant data in the Procedure Division can result in significant savings in main storage. And in a virtual storage environment, that means better response time for the users.

A second efficiency technique you should consider using is straight-line coding. Basically, this means you should avoid using the PERFORM statement excessively. Whenever you invoke a module using a PERFORM statement, a page fault may occur. And paging is one of the major factors affecting the overall response time of a CICS system.

Unfortunately, the use of straight-line coding often compromises the principles of structured design and structured programming. That's because these disciplines depend on the use of well-defined functional modules. If you use straight-line coding exclusively, your entire program becomes a single module, making it difficult to design, code, and test.

In the programs in this book, I've strived for balance in the way I use straight-line coding. For example, I coded the edit module of the mortgage-calculation program (module 120) as a single module in straight-line fashion. Even though it's long, its structure is manageable.

A third efficiency technique, related to the second, is to place seldom-used sections of code at the end of your source program. For each terminal session, modules 800 and 900 of the mortgage-calculation program are executed only once. Putting them at the end of the program results in fewer page faults while the major sections of the program are executing. Again, the result is improved response time throughout an installation.

Discussion

At this point, you should be able to begin writing original CICS programs that receive data from the terminal using BMS, edit the data, manipulate it, and send it back to the terminal. However, a basic element is missing from such programs: they don't manipulate data files. And there aren't many practical business programs that don't require file handling. Even so, don't be discouraged. CICS file-handling is relatively easy to learn compared with BMS and pseudo-conversational programming. Now that you're familiar with the material in this chapter, you'll have no trouble learning additional CICS features.

Up to now, I've given but a superficial treatment to the concepts of structured program design. Yet program design is one of the most important and most often neglected aspects of CICS programming. So, the next chapter shows you how to design a CICS program.

Terminology

direct cursor positioning
symbolic cursor positioning
working set
locality of reference

Objective

Given the specifications for a CICS program that requires the CICS facilities this chapter presents, code a solution.

Chapter 7

How to design
a structured CICS program

You're now familiar with BMS and the complexities of coding a simple command-level CICS program in COBOL. Although you've learned what you need to know to code a simple program, you're still not ready to take on a realistic CICS programming assignment. Before you can do that, you need to know how to design a command-level CICS program. In this chapter, I'll show you how to do that.

In recent years, many shops have adopted the techniques of structured program development. In most cases, they've experienced substantial improvements in both programmer productivity and program quality. Unfortunately, it's difficult to adapt all of the principles of *structured program design* to pseudo-conversational CICS programs.

In this chapter, I'll show you how I use structured techniques to design a CICS program. If you're familiar with other structured programming methodologies, you'll see that mine is adapted specifically to meet CICS and COBOL requirements. As a result, I think you'll find my CICS programs far easier to read and understand than unstructured programs or programs developed with other structured methodologies.

163

The main design document of structured program design is the *program structure chart* (or just *structure chart*). (You saw an example of a structure chart for a CICS program in chapter 6.) Drawing a structure chart helps you design a better program because it forces you to consider functions. When you draw a structure chart, you work from the top down, focusing first on broad functions rather than the kinds of trivial details that can confuse and distract you.

Once the chart is complete, you use it as a guide to code your program. If you look back to chapter 6, you'll see a one-to-one correspondence between boxes on the program structure chart and sections in the COBOL source code. You use the chart to plan the sequence in which you'll code and test your program. Finally, when the program itself is complete, the structure chart becomes an important piece of documentation.

HOW TO CREATE A STRUCTURE CHART

To illustrate how to create a structure chart, I'll present the design for a typical application: an order-entry program. Figure 7-1 presents the specifications for it. This program accepts order transactions from the operator, edits them, and writes valid transactions to an order file (Invoice). If the program detects no errors in the data, it allows the operator to sight-verify the data before it writes a record to the order file. Although the narrative in figure 7-1 is brief, this problem should show you how to create structure charts.

Design by levels

When you begin a structure chart, you draw the top-level, or level-0, module. This module represents the entire program, so you should give it an appropriate functional name. In this case, "accept customer orders" is appropriate.

To name a module, use one verb, one or at most two adjectives, and one noun. Although this may seem limiting, it's all you need. I use this naming technique in all of the structure charts in this book.

How to design level-1 of the structure chart   After you've drawn the top-level module, you determine what functions (modules) it

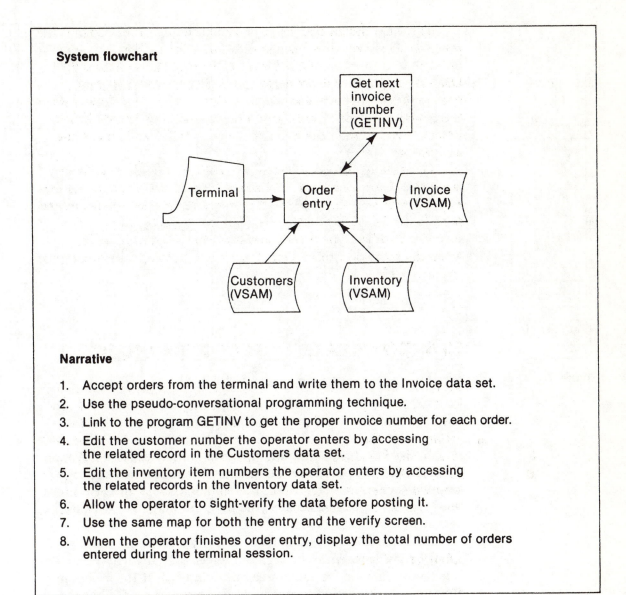

System flowchart

Narrative

1. Accept orders from the terminal and write them to the Invoice data set.
2. Use the pseudo-conversational programming technique.
3. Link to the program GETINV to get the proper invoice number for each order.
4. Edit the customer number the operator enters by accessing the related record in the Customers data set.
5. Edit the inventory item numbers the operator enters by accessing the related records in the Inventory data set.
6. Allow the operator to sight-verify the data before posting it.
7. Use the same map for both the entry and the verify screen.
8. When the operator finishes order entry, display the total number of orders entered during the terminal session.

Figure 7-1 Specifications for an order-entry program (part 1 of 2)

consists of. Figure 7-2 shows the four level-1 modules for the order-entry program: (1) a module that starts the terminal session, (2) a module that processes an entry screen, (3) a module that processes a verify screen, and (4) a module that sends a termination message to the terminal.

```
    ORDER ENTRY

    CUSTOMER NUMBER:  XXXXX    XXXXXXXXXXXXXXXXXXXXXXXXXXXXXX
    P.O. NUMBER:  XXXXXXXXX

    ITEM NO   QUANTITY   DESCRIPTION              UNIT PRICE    AMOUNT

    99999     99999      XXXXXXXXXXXXXXXXXXXXX    ZZ,ZZ9.99    ZZ,ZZ9.99
    99999     99999      XXXXXXXXXXXXXXXXXXXXX    ZZ,ZZ9.99    ZZ,ZZ9.99
    99999     99999      XXXXXXXXXXXXXXXXXXXXX    ZZ,ZZ9.99    ZZ,ZZ9.99
    99999     99999      XXXXXXXXXXXXXXXXXXXXX    ZZ,ZZ9.99    ZZ,ZZ9.99
    99999     99999      XXXXXXXXXXXXXXXXXXXXX    ZZ,ZZ9.99    ZZ,ZZ9.99
    99999     99999      XXXXXXXXXXXXXXXXXXXXX    ZZ,ZZ9.99    ZZ,ZZ9.99
    99999     99999      XXXXXXXXXXXXXXXXXXXXX    ZZ,ZZ9.99    ZZ,ZZ9.99
    99999     99999      XXXXXXXXXXXXXXXXXXXXX    ZZ,ZZ9.99    ZZ,ZZ9.99
    99999     99999      XXXXXXXXXXXXXXXXXXXXX    ZZ,ZZ9.99    ZZ,ZZ9.99
    99999     99999      XXXXXXXXXXXXXXXXXXXXX    ZZ,ZZ9.99    ZZ,ZZ9.99

                                      INVOICE TOTAL:    ZZ,ZZ9.99
```

Figure 7-1   Specifications for an order-entry program (part 2 of 2)

In most cases, determining the level-1 modules for a CICS program is easy. All pseudo-conversational programs have a start-terminal-session module. Then, there's one module for each screen the program processes. Finally, the program may have a send-termination-message module.

Even though the data-entry and verify screens use the same map, I consider them to be separate screens. That's why I created one level-1 module for each screen in figure 7-2. If the order-entry program didn't need to process a verify screen, it would have only three level-1 modules: (1) start terminal session, (2) process entry screen, and (3) send termination message. If, on the other hand, the program processed four screens, it would have six level-1 modules.

In general, the left-to-right placement of modules in the structure chart indicates the probable sequence in which the modules execute. This is certainly true for the level-1 modules in figure 7-2. However, this isn't always the case. In many instances, subordinate modules execute in a sequence that isn't apparent from the structure chart.

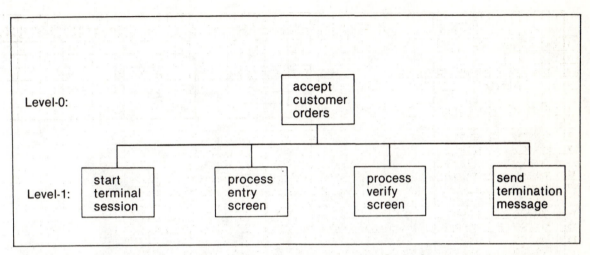

Figure 7-2   The first two levels of the structure chart for the order-entry program

How to design level-2 of the structure chart   After you've created the level-1 modules, you decide whether they consist of subordinate functions. Here, you should think in terms of clearly defined functions.

For the order-entry program, I decided upon the level-2 modules in figure 7-3. Thus, the process-entry-screen module consists of three subordinate modules: (1) receive entry screen, (2) edit order data, and (3) send order screen. The process-verify-screen module consists of three similar modules.

When you decide upon the level-2 modules, bear in mind that for each screen your program processes, you must provide for at least three functions: (1) receive the screen, (2) process the data in some way, and (3) send the next screen. As a result, most of your program designs will have level-2 modules like those in figure 7-3.

As you might guess, the receive and send modules are much the same from one program to the next. The major variation, then, is in the modules that perform the processing functions. In the order-entry program, the processing modules are edit order data and post order data. The processing modules for another program may be entirely different.

There's no rule that says you can have only one processing module at level-2 for each screen. For example, suppose the order-entry program didn't require a verify screen. In that case, the structure chart might look like the one in figure 7-4. This chart has

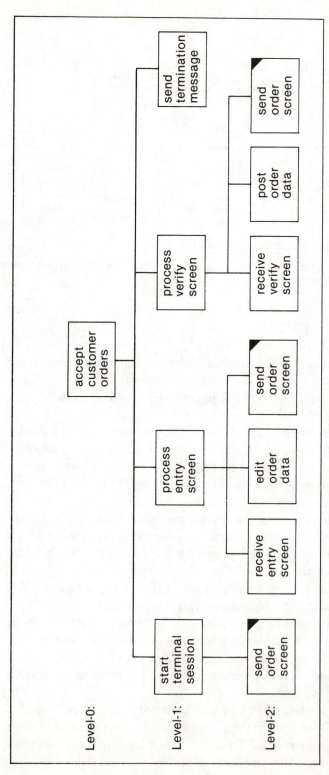

Figure 7-3   The first three levels of the structure chart for the order-entry program

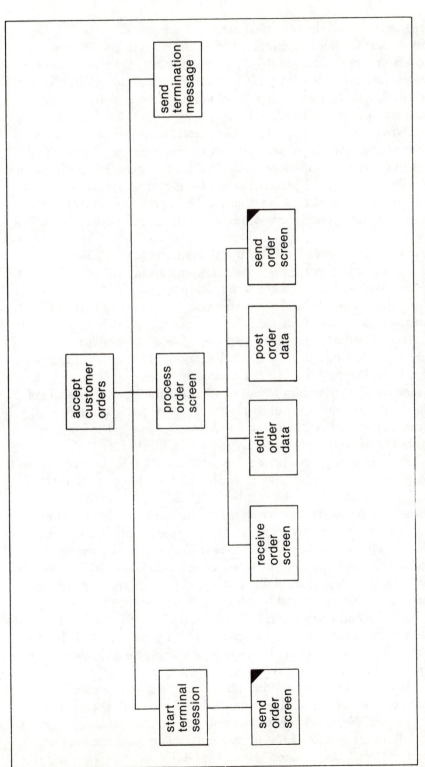

Figure 7-4   Structure chart for the order-entry program without a verify screen

three level-1 modules: (1) start terminal session, (2) process order screen, and (3) send termination message. Subordinate to the process-order-screen module are four modules: (1) receive order screen, (2) edit order data, (3) post order data, and (4) send order screen. As you can see, two level-2 modules (edit and post) are required to process the order data.

When I created the send-order-screen module subordinate to the process-entry-screen and process-verify-screen modules, I realized that the send function is required by the start-terminal-session module as well. So, I placed the send-order-screen module beneath the start-terminal-session module too. As a result, the send-order-screen module appears three times in the structure chart in figure 7-3.

How to design lower levels on the structure chart   The modules below level-2 depend entirely on the application. Figure 7-5 shows the next two levels of the structure chart for the order-entry program. Here, I considered what functions must be done to edit and post the order data. I realized that to edit the data, I needed modules to (1) read a customer record and (2) edit an individual line item. To edit a line item, I needed a module to read an inventory record. And to post an order, I needed modules to (1) format an invoice record (including formatting individual line items and getting the correct invoice number) and (2) write an invoice record. Notice the special symbol I used to show that the get-invoice-number module is a separate program (GETINV).

Because this program uses the same map for both the entry and verify screen, I realized that I needed modules to manipulate the map's attribute bytes. The attributes for all fields on the verify screen should specify protected, while data-entry fields should be unprotected on the entry screen. Thus, I added modules to set and reset the attribute bytes subordinate to the send-order-screen module. Each of these, in turn, requires a module to set or reset the attribute bytes for an individual line item. Be aware that these modules are only required because the program uses the same map for both the entry screen and the verify screen. If the program used different maps for the entry screen and verify screen, or if the program didn't require a verify screen at all, these modules wouldn't be necessary.

At this point, the structure chart in figure 7-5 is logically complete—all modules have been broken down into their functional components. Note, however, that you do not need to be concerned with all of the details of the program to create a structure chart like this. For instance, I created the edit modules without knowing the

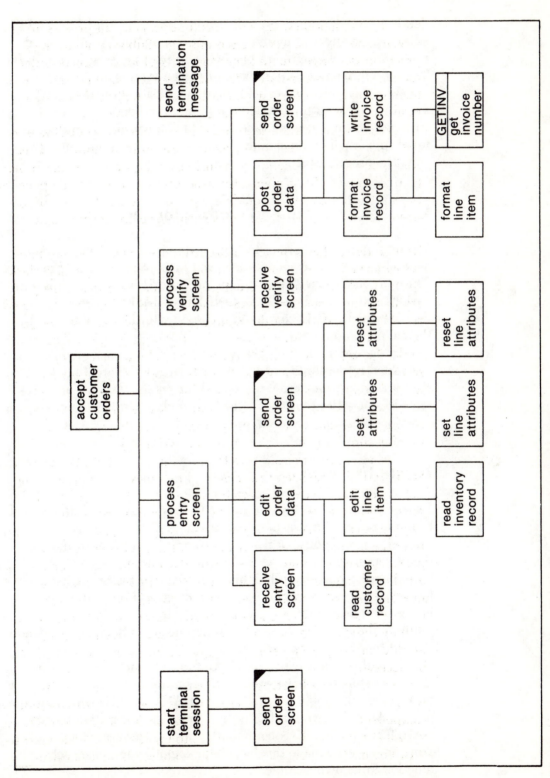

Figure 7-5   Structure chart for the order-entry program

details of the editing rules. I did know, however, that I needed to edit each line item individually. I also knew that I needed to edit the customer and item number fields by reading records from a file. The structure chart reflects both of these requirements.

Whether you're given complete specifications or not, you shouldn't focus on the details of a program when you create a structure chart. Once you're convinced you can program a module, forget the details. You shouldn't have to confront them until you code the program.

Use a generalized send module for each map

To simplify your program design, I recommend you create a single, general-purpose send module for each map your program processes. This send module will contain one or more SEND commands with various options (such as DATAONLY or ERASE). The send module decides which SEND command to issue by testing a switch set by the calling module.

In the order-entry program, the generalized send module has the added responsibility of setting or resetting the attribute bytes so the data-entry fields are unprotected for an entry screen and protected for a verify screen. The calling module also controls this function by setting a switch.

Isolate I/O modules

I also recommend that you isolate I/O functions, including file and terminal operations, in their own modules. That's why figure 7-5 has a separate module to read the customer record, even though this function could be done in the edit module.

I suggest you isolate I/O functions for two reasons. First, they have a significant effect on the design of your program. So, isolating them on the structure chart will help you design your program by showing you which I/O functions must be done and where they fit in your program structure.

Second, in most cases, you have to use branching logic within an I/O module to process exceptional conditions. For example, in a receive module, you'll normally use a HANDLE AID command to process AID keys. Similarly, file I/O modules generally require a HANDLE CONDITION command, as you'll learn in chapter 8. You can better manage this branching logic if you place each I/O function in its own module.

Since it's true that a performed module is less efficient than in-line code, you may object to isolating I/O functions in their own modules. However, you need to keep a clear perspective on efficiency. Although in-line coding does increase program efficiency, it does so only marginally. As I see it, the benefits of isolating I/O functions in performed modules outweigh efficiency considerations for most applications.

Shade common modules

Because the send module in figure 7-5 appears more than once on the structure chart, it's called a *common module*. To indicate a common module, I shade the upper right-hand corner of the box. As you can see in figure 7-5, that makes common modules easy to identify on the structure chart. Also, notice that modules subordinate to common modules appear only once in the structure chart.

HOW TO EVALUATE A STRUCTURE CHART

Once you've completed the first version of a structure chart, you should evaluate it. Are all modules functional? Are they independent? Does the structure chart provide for all required functions?

After you're convinced that your structure chart is complete and proper, you should consider reviewing it with someone else involved with the program—a manager, a systems analyst, another programmer, or even a user. Your primary purpose here is to make sure your structure chart has accounted for everything.

Some companies have specific requirements for reviewing structure charts. For instance, a programmer may be required to review each structure chart with the systems analyst who created the specifications for the program. In other words, the programmer can't code the program until the systems analyst okays the structure chart. Requirements like this can increase the productivity of a programming department.

Based on your review, you're likely to change your structure chart. Usually, this means changing or moving only a block or two. Less often, it means redrawing the entire chart.

When you evaluate your structure chart, you should watch for a number of things. Most important, ask yourself whether all the modules are functional and whether the chart is complete. After that, you should consider verb consistency, module independence, subordination, span of control, and module size.

Are the modules functional?   Perhaps you noticed my emphasis on function as I described how I create a structure chart. This emphasis, as you might guess, is one of the key principles of effective *top-down design*. In brief, *all* modules should represent one, and only one, program function.

You can feel confident that program modules are functional if you can describe them in a single imperative sentence such as "send the entry screen," "update the records in the master file," or "search the customer table." This, of course, is what you do when you name the module by using one verb, one or two adjectives, and a noun. If you can't describe a module this way, it's probably not functional, and your program design may be faulty.

If a module name contains the word *and* or *or*, the module probably contains more than one function. Thus, a "read and sort table records" module should be divided into two functional modules, just as a "print valid or invalid message" module should be two modules.

Strive for functional modules. If your modules are functional, they'll be relatively easy to code and test. If they aren't functional, you'll run into problems as you develop the program.

Is the structure chart complete?   When you're sure that each module represents one and only one function, your next question should be: does the structure chart provide for all functions the program must do? When the structure chart consists of dozens of modules, this is a difficult question to answer.

The way to approach this question is one level at a time, from the top down. In the case of figure 7-5, for example, you should first ask whether the four level-1 modules do everything implied by their boss, the level-0 module. In other words, does processing the first- and last-time conditions and either an entry screen or a verify screen account for all of the functions required by the accept-customer-orders module? In my opinion, level-1 is complete as shown.

After you've analyzed one level for completeness, you continue with the next level down. For example, are all of the functions required by "process entry screen" accounted for? I believe so.

Are the verbs consistent?   Use verbs as consistently as possible in your module descriptions. In other words, one verb should mean the same thing within a structure chart, and, if possible, throughout the programming department.

Many of the verbs I use mean more than their names seem to imply. For instance, I use *receive* to mean not only getting data from a terminal using the RECEIVE command, but also processing AID keys. Similarly, I use *send* to mean both sending data to the screen with a SEND command and formatting attribute characters, if necessary.

Quite frankly, you can debate the way I use these words. However, I use verbs consistently throughout this book. So once you understand what I mean by the verbs I use, you'll be able to understand the module names in any of the structure charts in this book.

Are the modules independent?   Structured programming depends on the use of independent modules. An independent module can do its job without depending on other modules besides those subordinate to it.

Much has been written about module independence, and, quite frankly, much of it is a waste of words. In general, if your modules are functional, they'll be sufficiently independent. Even so, when you review your structure chart, you should watch out for modules that seem to depend unnecessarily on one another.

Is proper subordination shown?   When I refer to proper *subordination*, I mean that called modules are related to the correct calling modules. Since you have many options when you create a structure chart, achieving proper subordination isn't always easy.

To illustrate, look at figure 7-6, an alternative structure chart for the order-entry program. Here, the programmer decided on five level-1 modules. The program could be coded like this, so why do I consider this figure an illustration of improper subordination? The reason is that receiving the entry screen is a logical sub-function of processing the entry screen, along with editing the data and sending the next screen. Therefore, placing the receive module at the same level as the process module reflects improper subordination.

Of course, the question of proper subordination is largely a matter of experience and partly a matter of opinion. Even so, the structure chart should show the subordination of functions logically.

Are the control spans reasonable?   If a module has three modules subordinate to it, its *span of control* is three. In other words, it controls the operation of three modules. Span of control is useful because it can indicate potential program design problems.

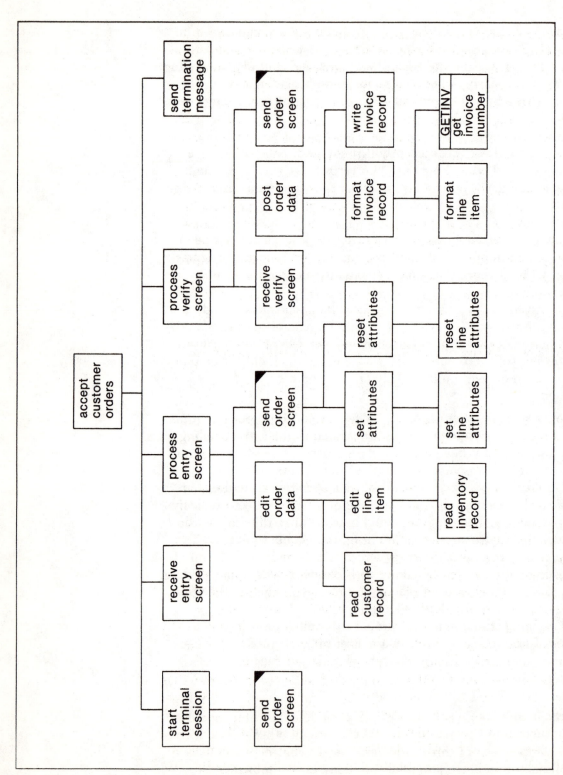

Figure 7-6   An alternative structure chart for the order-entry program showing improper subordination

As a rule of thumb, the span of control for a module should range from two to nine. So figure 7-7 shows two control span problems. In example one, the level-0 module has a control span of ten. That's a sign the module may be overly complex. In example two, several modules have a control span of one. Here, the modules would probably be trivial. Although you can't say absolutely that these structure charts are incorrect, these control spans do indicate that you should reevaluate and consider design alternatives.

Are the modules too large?   Part of the theory of structured design says that each module should be small enough to be manageable. For COBOL programs, this usually means that a module should contain 50 or fewer statements. However, this is not a hard and fast rule. If a module requires 75 simple MOVE statements, there's no need for concern. However, if the module seems too complicated to code in under 50 lines (or maybe even under 20 lines), you should consider making it two or more modules.

HOW TO COMPLETE A STRUCTURE CHART

After you've evaluated your structure chart and feel confident that it's correct, you need to draw a final version of it. To complete the chart, you need to number the modules. Also, for all but the simplest of programs, you'll need an efficient way to draw the chart on more than one page.

Numbering the modules   Once you've decided your structure chart is correct, you should number the modules. When you code the program, you combine these numbers with the module names to form the COBOL section names. Then, you code the sections in numeric sequence in your program.

Although you can use complicated numbering schemes, I recommend you number the modules like I did in figure 7-8. Here, I gave the top-level module the number 0000. Next, I gave the start-terminal-session module the number 8000 and the send-termination-message module the number 9000. You'll recall from the last chapter that I code start-terminal-session and send-termination-message modules at the end of my programs because they're each executed only once during a terminal session. The high numbers, 8000 and 9000, indicate that the source code is at the end of the program. The modules in between are numbered by thousands, beginning with 1000. Modules subordinate to these are numbered by hundreds or tens. Incidentally, for small programs like the

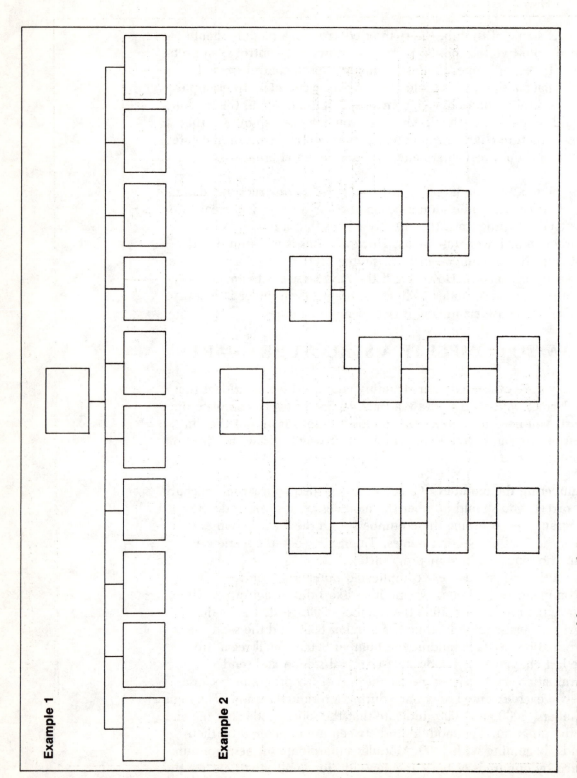

Figure 7-7 Questionable control spans

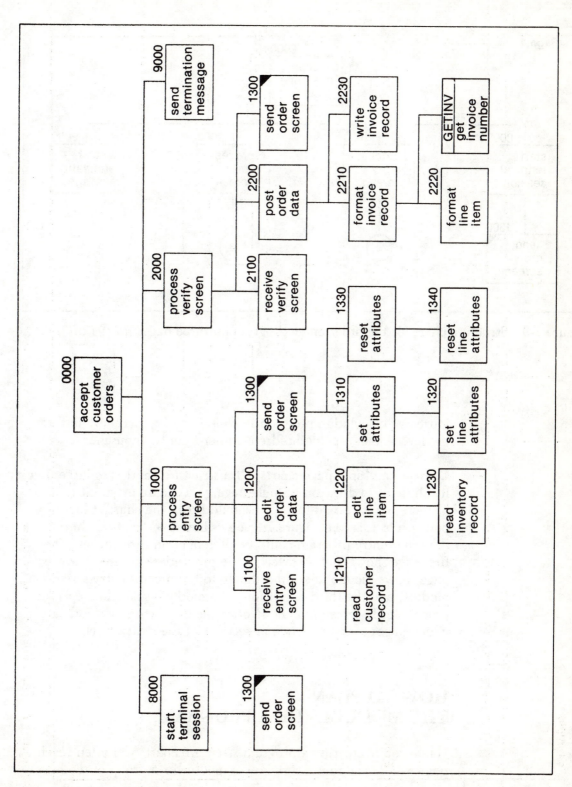

Figure 7-8   Complete structure chart for the order-entry program

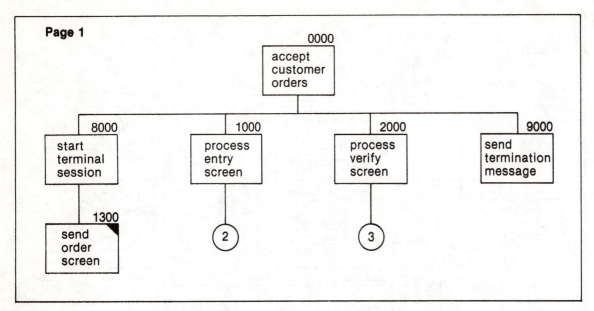

Figure 7-9 Structure chart for the order-entry program on three pages (part 1 of 3)

mortgage-calculation program in chapter 6, I sometimes number the level-1 modules by hundreds rather than by thousands.

Drawing multiple-page charts If a structure chart is so large that it's difficult to draw on a single page, you should extend it to two or more pages. To do this, you should break the chart at logical points. For example, figure 7-9 shows how the structure chart for the order-entry program could be presented on three pages. The first page shows the top levels of the program structure. The second page shows the modules subordinate to the process-entry-screen module, and the third page shows the modules subordinate to the process-verify-screen module. Notice the connectors that indicate which pages contain particular sections of the structure chart.

HOW TO PLAN
THE MODULES OF A PROGRAM

While you're creating a program structure chart, you often reach a point where you're not sure how a module or a group of modules

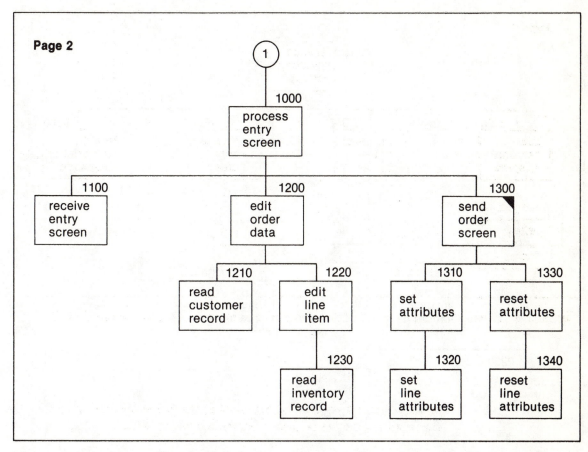

Figure 7-9   Structure chart for the order-entry program on three pages (part 2 of 3)

will work. When that happens, I recommend you use a couple of tools I find particularly useful: pseudocode and screen flow diagrams.

Using pseudocode to understand a module   If you're having trouble deciding whether you can code a module, I suggest you write out the logic required by the module in a shorthand notation called *pseudocode*. For example, figure 7-10 shows the pseudocode for the process-entry-screen module of the order-entry program. I don't have rules for creating pseudocode—you simply write down what needs to be done. Usually, pseudocode looks a lot like COBOL because most of us are familiar with it. You don't have to write COBOL here, but there's no reason to avoid writing it, either. Whatever is easiest for you is best.

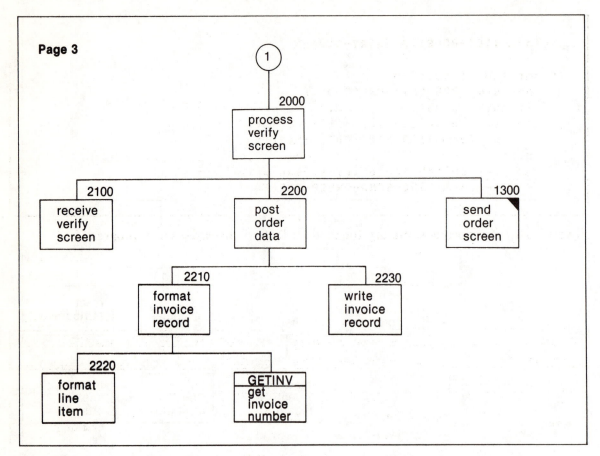

Figure 7-9 Structure chart for the order-entry program on three pages (part 3 of 3)

Remember that pseudocode is only a tool. I do *not* recommend that you create pseudocode for every program module. Instead, use pseudocode only when you're having trouble understanding the function of a particular module. In addition, I do *not* recommend that you maintain pseudocode as program documentation. If your code isn't clear enough to explain what your program does, you'd better change the code.

Some structured design systems have a formalized method of recording module processing requirements. One technique is IBM's *HIPO* (which stands for *Hierarchical Input-Processing-Output*). Figure 7-11 illustrates one version of a HIPO diagram. As you can see, the diagram lists all inputs and outputs for the module and its processing steps. In my opinion, though, HIPO documentation, even with simpler graphics, is mostly a waste of time.

```
perform 1100-RECEIVE-ENTRY-SCREEN.

if not end of session
    perform 1200-EDIT-ORDER-DATA
    if data is valid
        set up switch for verify screen
        perform 1300-SEND-ORDER-SCREEN
    else
        set switch for entry-screen with errors
        perform 1300-SEND-ORDER-SCREEN.
```

Figure 7-10   Pseudocode summary for module 1000 of the order-entry program

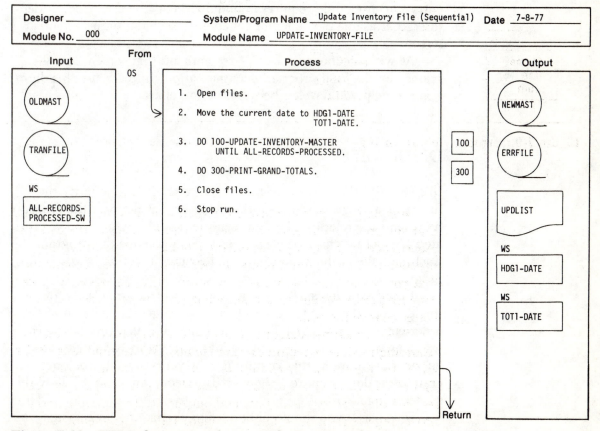

Figure 7-11   HIPO diagram with an emphasis on graphics

Using a screen flow diagram   If you're having trouble creating or understanding the level-1 modules of a program, I suggest you create a *screen flow diagram*, such as the one in figure 7-12. Here, I created a large box for each screen used by the order-entry program. (Even though they use the same map, I consider the entry screen and the verify screen to be two separate screens because they have different functions.) The smaller boxes indicate processing routines. The arrows indicate the flow from one screen or process to another. For example, if the "edit data" function detects errors, the order-entry screen is displayed. In figure 7-12, the bold arrows indicate the "normal" flow through the program (no errors or special conditions encountered).

It's relatively easy to create the level-1 modules of the structure chart from a diagram like this. After you've drawn the start-terminal-session and send-termination-message modules, you simply add one module for each screen on the screen flow diagram. In addition, the screen flow diagram can help you identify the functions at level-2 and below. For example, I know that the process-entry-screen-module requires a module to edit the data since I identified that as one of the major functions associated with the entry screen.

As with pseudocode, I don't recommend that screen flow diagrams become final program documentation. Instead, use this diagram to help you develop better structure charts.

DISCUSSION

In summary, the purpose of the structure chart is to identify the functions a program requires, the modules that perform those functions, and the relationships between the modules. Once you've created a structure chart, you use it as a guide to code the program. Each module on the structure chart becomes a section in your program.

In my experience, I've found that most structure charts for single-screen data-entry programs follow the general pattern of the order-entry program presented in this chapter. As a result, you can use the structure chart in figure 7-5 as a model for all single-screen data-entry programs that require a sight-verify screen. For programs that don't require a sight-verify screen, you should follow the model in figure 7-4.

In general, you should only have to change the processing modules to adapt this structure to any single-screen data-entry pro-

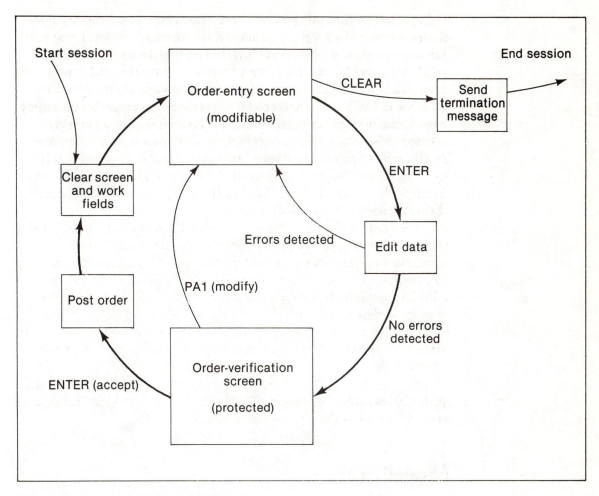

Figure 7-12   Screen flow of the order-entry program

gram. Specifically, you'll have to change the edit module so it reflects the editing requirements of your program. And you'll have to change the post module so it reflects the processing requirements of your program. Still, the same program design, and even much of the code, can be used again and again.

If you've had much experience with other structured design methodologies, you may object to my use of module 8000-START-TERMINAL-SESSION because it's a temporal module. (A *temporal* module is one that's required because of time-related factors, whereas a *functional* module is one that's required because of program function.) Quite frankly, you're right. Unfortunately, pseudo-conversational programming requires that you do special processing for the first-time condition. So there's no way around the temporal module. Still, I don't think using a start-terminal-session module makes your program any less readable or understandable.

At this point, you might not be ready to create your own structure charts for CICS programs. So, after chapter 8 presents some additional CICS elements, chapter 9 presents a sample CICS application, including four complete CICS programs. After you've studied these examples, you should be able to design a wide variety of CICS programs using these techniques.

Terminology

structured program design
program structure chart
structure chart
common module
top-down design
subordination
span of control
pseudocode
HIPO
Hierarchical Input-Processing-Output
screen flow diagram

Objectives

1. Describe how a structure chart is created.

2. Explain how you can tell when a module is *functional*.

3. List and describe seven characteristics you should analyze when you evaluate a structure chart.

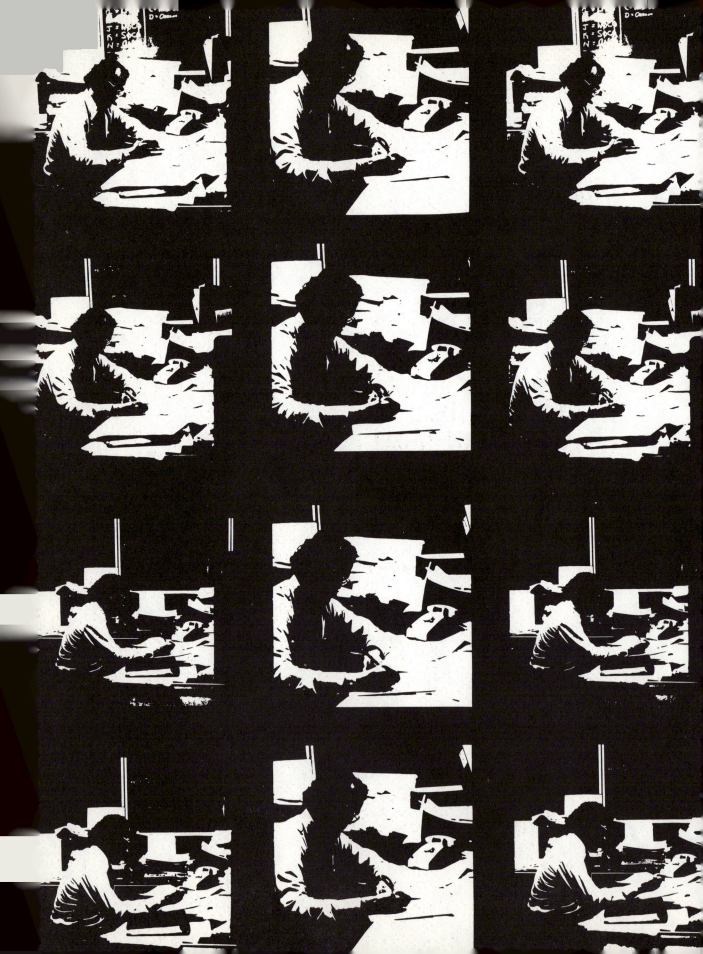

Chapter 8

Expanding
the basic subset
of command-level CICS

In this chapter, I expand the basic CICS subset I presented in
chapter 6. This chapter is divided into two topics. In topic 1, I present a variety of common CICS elements and programming techniques. Then, in topic 2, I present the basic CICS file-handling
commands.

Topic 1   Additional CICS elements

Chapter 6 presented a basic subset of CICS command-level
COBOL. Now, you'll build on that base with some additional
CICS elements and programming techniques. In this topic, you'll
learn how to process CICS exceptional conditions, pass data from
one program to the next using the communication area, use CICS
program control commands, and access fields in the Execute
Interface Block and other CICS areas.

How to handle CICS exceptional conditions

Whenever CICS encounters an unusual or exceptional situation, an
exceptional condition (or just *condition*) is raised. Each condition
has a name. For example, if you try to send a map that's too big for
the terminal, the INVMPSZ (invalid map size) condition is raised.
Almost all of the exceptional conditions abnormally terminate your
task, although a few of them are ignored.

Since most exceptional conditions indicate serious errors,
abnormal termination is appropriate. However, some of the exceptional conditions don't represent errors, but rather conditions you'd
expect during routine processing. If, for example, your program
attempts to read a keyed record that doesn't exist, the NOTFND
condition is raised and the task is terminated. Normally, however,
you don't want a task to terminate just because a record wasn't
found. Instead, you want your program to inform the operator of
the error so he can correct it.

You use the HANDLE CONDITION command, shown in
figure 8-1, to specify what actions your program should take when
certain exceptional conditions are raised. As you can see, the
HANDLE CONDITION command is similar in format to the
HANDLE AID command. Its operation is similar, too. Like the
HANDLE AID command, the HANDLE CONDITION command

The HANDLE CONDITION command

```
EXEC CICS
    HANDLE CONDITION condition-name(procedure-name)...
END-EXEC
```

Explanation

condition-name	The name of a CICS exceptional condition. Up to 12 condition-names may be specified in a single command. More than 12 options may be handled by multiple HANDLE CONDITION commands. The special condition-name ERROR traps all exceptional conditions not otherwise listed.
procedure-name	A paragraph or section name. Control is passed to the procedure-name when the specified condition occurs. If procedure-name is omitted, the effect of any previous HANDLE CONDITION command for the condition is nullified.

Figure 8-1   The HANDLE CONDITION command

specifies a procedure-name (a paragraph or section name) that's given control if the condition is raised. For example, the HANDLE CONDITION command:

```
EXEC CICS
    HANDLE CONDITION NOTFND(210-NOTFND)
END-EXEC.
```

passes control immediately to 210-NOTFND if the NOTFND condition is raised. Note that 210-NOTFND is *not* given control when the HANDLE CONDITION command is executed, but only when the NOTFND condition is raised. In effect, a GO TO is done to 210-NOTFND from whatever part of the program is executing when the NOTFND condition is raised.

Condition	Related CICS command	Caused by
DUPREC	WRITE	The record already exists.
MAPFAIL	RECEIVE MAP	No data was sent by the operator.
NOSPACE	WRITE	The data set does not have enough allocated space to add the record.
NOTOPEN	READ WRITE	The data set is not open.
NOTFND	READ	The requested record is not in the file.
PGMIDERR	LINK XCTL	The requested program is not in the Processing Program Table.

Figure 8-2   Common conditions for the HANDLE CONDITION command

The IBM manual lists 48 conditions the HANDLE CONDITION command can trap. Usually, though, you're only concerned with a few. Figure 8-2 lists the most common exceptional conditions you can specify in a HANDLE CONDITION command.

The MAPFAIL condition is raised when you issue a RECEIVE MAP command but no data was sent from the terminal to your program. This can happen for two reasons: (1) the operator doesn't enter any data, or (2) the operator uses a PA key or the CLEAR key. Rather than code a HANDLE CONDITION command for the MAPFAIL condition, I recommend you provide for it by: (1) issuing a HANDLE AID command to process the PA and CLEAR keys and (2) including in the mapset a one-byte DUMMY field with FSET specified so at least one byte of data is sent to the program when the operator presses the ENTER key or a PF key.

A single HANDLE CONDITION command can specify actions for up to 12 exceptional conditions. For example, the command:

```
EXEC CICS
    HANDLE CONDITION DUPREC(310-DUPREC)
                     NOSPACE(310-NOSPACE)
                     NOTOPEN(310-NOTOPEN)
END-EXEC.
```

handles three conditions: DUPREC, NOSPACE, and NOTOPEN.

You can nullify the effect of a HANDLE CONDITION command by listing the condition name without a paragraph or section name. For example:

```
EXEC CICS
    HANDLE CONDITION NOSPACE
END-EXEC.
```

reverses the effect of any previous HANDLE CONDITION command for the NOSPACE condition. As a result, if the NOSPACE condition is raised after the execution of this command, the task is terminated.

You can use a special condition-name, ERROR, to trap any errors not specifically named in a HANDLE CONDITION command. The routine you specify for the ERROR condition will be invoked for *any* exceptional condition that isn't specifically handled. For example, suppose this command is issued:

```
EXEC CICS
    HANDLE CONDITION DUPKEY(310-DUPKEY)
                     NOTOPEN(310-NOTOPEN)
                     ERROR(310-ERROR)
END-EXEC.
```

Then, if the NOSPACE condition is raised, control transfers to 310-ERROR since I coded ERROR, but not NOSPACE. However, the DUPKEY or NOTOPEN conditions are processed by their respective error-handling routines.

In general, I do *not* recommend that you code ERROR on the HANDLE CONDITION command. Any error you can correct requires its own error-handling routine. For all other errors, it's best to let the system terminate the task. So don't bother with the ERROR condition.

How to use the communication area

In chapter 6, I showed you how to evaluate the length of the communication area to identify the first execution of a program in a terminal session. In that example, I didn't use the communication area to pass data between executions of the program—I just passed a one-byte dummy field so that the length of the communication area would not be zero.

In many cases, however, you need to keep data between program executions. For example, if a program requires several screens to gather data for a single transaction, it must save data from each screen so it can format the transaction record after the last screen is processed. Similarly, a program that accumulates control totals (such as a count of the number of transactions entered) must pass the totals from one execution to the next.

Although you can use several methods for saving data from one execution of a program to the next, the easiest way is to use the communication area. In brief, any data you place in the communication area is available to the next execution of the program.

In general, you should define the communication area with its fields in the Working-Storage Section something like this:

```
01  COMMUNICATION-AREA.
*
    05  CA-PROCESS-FLAG            PIC X.
        88  PROCESS-ENTRY-SCREEN              VALUE '1'.
        88  PROCESS-VERIFY-SCREEN             VALUE '2'.
    05  CA-TRANSACTIONS-ENTERED   PIC S9(5) COMP-3.
```

Here, I defined two fields in the communication area: a one-byte flag used to control the processing done by the next program execution and a five-digit count of the number of transactions processed. The total length of the COMMUNICATION-AREA is four bytes: one for CA-PROCESS-FLAG and three for CA-TRANSACTIONS-ENTERED.

Next, you define DFHCOMMAREA in the Linkage Section so it has the same length as the working storage COMMUNICATION-AREA field. In this case, I'd code:

```
01  DFHCOMMAREA       PIC X(4).
```

Notice that I didn't define the individual fields of DFHCOMMAREA. As you'll see in a moment, you move DFHCOMMAREA to COMMUNICATION-AREA to access the individual fields of the communication area.

It's important you realize that these two fields define two distinct areas of storage. For any given execution of your program except the first, the working storage area represents storage freshly allocated for your program, while the Linkage Section area represents storage saved from the *previous* execution of the program. Each time your program ends, the storage held by DFHCOMMAREA in the Linkage Section is released, and the contents of the working storage definition of the communication area are saved for the Linkage Section of the next execution of the program. (The first time your program is executed, the Linkage Section DFHCOMMAREA doesn't exist.)

I don't recommend you define the fields that make up DFHCOMMAREA in the Linkage Section. Instead, to access the data saved by the previous execution of your program, you should move it to the newly allocated storage defined in the Working-Storage Section. As a result, your Procedure Division should begin with these lines:

```
IF EIBCALEN = ZERO
    PERFORM 8000-START-TERMINAL-SESSION
ELSE
    MOVE DFHCOMMAREA TO COMMUNICATION-AREA
        .
        .
        .
```

Here, EIBCALEN is tested for zero to see if this is the first time the program is executed. If it is, 8000-START-TERMINAL-SESSION is executed. Otherwise, DFHCOMMAREA (in the Linkage Section) is moved to COMMUNICATION-AREA (in the Working-Storage Section). Then, the program can access the individual fields in COMMUNICATION-AREA in subsequent statements.

When you use the communication area, be sure you specify its correct length on the RETURN command. For example, the RETURN command for the communication area I just described should look like this:

```
EXEC CICS
    RETURN TRANSID('TRN1')
           COMMAREA(COMMUNICATION-AREA)
           LENGTH(4)
END-EXEC.
```

If you specify an incorrect length, your program won't operate properly.

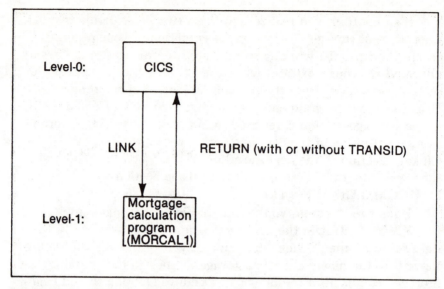

Figure 8-3   The mortgage-calculation program: a simple example of program control

How to use program control commands

Program control commands control the execution of programs within a task. The mortgage-calculation application in chapter 6 illustrates the simplest case of program control. It's always invoked by CICS, and it always ends by passing control back to CICS. Other applications, however, can require that several programs execute within a single task. The CICS commands you use to implement more complicated multi-program applications are RETURN, LINK, and XCTL. You've already seen RETURN, and LINK and XCTL are easy to learn.

The LINK command and logical levels   Figure 8-3 illustrates the logical levels for the mortgage-calculation application. There's nothing here that should surprise you. CICS, at level-0, invokes the mortgage-calculation program (MORCAL1), at level-1, by linking to it.

When the mortgage-calculation program terminates, it issues a RETURN command to pass control back to CICS. The RETURN command may or may not contain the TRANSID option. If it does, the transaction identifier it specifies is invoked by CICS the next time the operator presses an AID key at the terminal. If the RETURN command doesn't include the TRANSID option, CICS

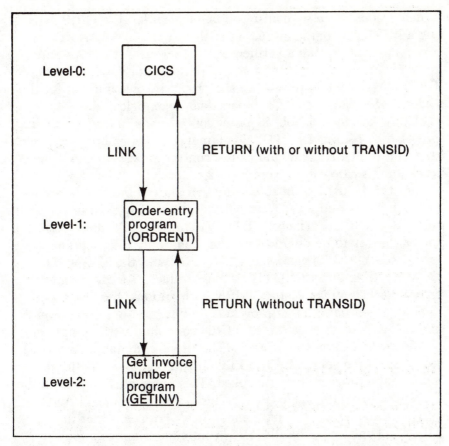

Figure 8-4   The order-entry application: a more complicated
example of program control

ends the terminal session. Regardless of whether the RETURN command includes the TRANSID option, it causes control to be passed up one logical level (in this case, back to CICS).

Just as CICS loads and executes the mortgage-calculation program subordinate to it in logical level-1, your application programs can use the LINK command to invoke programs subordinate to them. For example, look back to the specifications for the order-entry application in figure 7-1. The application actually uses two programs: the order-entry program itself (ORDRENT) and a subordinate program that retrieves invoice numbers from a data set (GETINV). To invoke GETINV, ORDRENT issues a LINK command.

Figure 8-4 illustrates the logical levels for the order-entry application. The order-entry program (ORDRENT) is invoked at logical level-1 by CICS. That's just like the mortgage-calculation program.

When it ends, it passes control up one logical level to CICS by issuing a RETURN command, either with or without TRANSID.

As part of posting a verified order, however, the order-entry program issues a LINK command to pass control down one level to GETINV (at level-2) to retrieve the proper invoice number for the order. LINK causes control to pass *down* one logical level. After GETINV has done its job, it passes control back to the order-entry program by issuing a RETURN command. Here again you can see that the RETURN command causes control to pass *up* one logical level. In this case, that's from level-2 to level-1.

At this point, I want to be sure you understand the difference between a task and a program within a task. The programs in figure 8-4 (ORDRENT and GETINV) are parts of a single task. For the entire task to be pseudo-conversational, only the program at level-1 (ORDRENT) can issue a RETURN with the TRANSID, COMMAREA, and LENGTH options. In fact, if a program at level-2 (or below) issues a RETURN with options, the task terminates abnormally. So in programs that execute in logical level-2 and below, always code the RETURN command with no options.

Figure 8-5 gives the format of the LINK command. As you can see, it has three operands. The PROGRAM operand supplies the name of the program being invoked. This name must appear in the Processing Program Table (PPT). This is similar to the TRANSID option on the RETURN command. The difference is that the TRANSID option on the RETURN command requires a four-character transaction-identifier, but the PROGRAM operand on the LINK command requires an eight-character program name. Also, you can omit TRANSID on the RETURN command, but PROGRAM is required on the LINK command.

The COMMAREA and LENGTH operands work the same way for the LINK command as they do for the RETURN command. The data in the Working-Storage Section communication area is passed to the linked program's Linkage Section DFHCOMMAREA.

If the program specified in the LINK command doesn't exist, the PGMIDERR condition is raised. Since an operator can disable programs in a CICS system, I recommend you always code a HANDLE CONDITION command for the PGMIDERR condition before you code a LINK command.

The most common use for LINK is to invoke subprograms. In figure 8-4, a LINK command invokes a subprogram to retrieve an invoice number. This example illustrates the parallel between GETINV invoked by the LINK command and a traditional COBOL batch subprogram invoked by a CALL statement.

At this point, you're probably wondering why GETINV isn't invoked by a CALL statement to begin with. That's because it

---

The LINK command

```
EXEC CICS
    LINK PROGRAM(alphanumeric-data-value)
        [COMMAREA(data-name)
        [LENGTH(numeric-data-value)]
END-EXEC
```

Explanation

PROGRAM   The name of the program to be linked. This name must appear in the Processing Program Table (PPT).

COMMAREA   The name of the communication area that will be passed to the program.

LENGTH   The length of the communication area. May be a numeric literal or a data-name.

Figure 8-5   The LINK command

---

requires the use of CICS file-handling commands to do its job. If a program uses any CICS commands, you cannot invoke it using the CALL statement; you must issue a LINK command instead. On the other hand, if a subprogram doesn't require any CICS services, then you can use the CALL statement to invoke it. But because of complications the Linkage Editor introduces, it's usually easier to include source code for commonly used routines directly in your programs. (I suggest you create COPY books that contain sub-routine source code.)

In general, using the LINK command is an inefficient way to invoke another program. That's because while the invoked program is executing, the program that issued the LINK still occupies main storage. It has to remain in storage so control can be passed back to it when the invoked program terminates.

In many applications, however, a program doesn't need to return to the program that invoked it. For example, in a menu application, you want to transfer control to the program the operator selected and, perhaps, never return to the menu program. In this case, a LINK command would be inappropriate. In fact, if

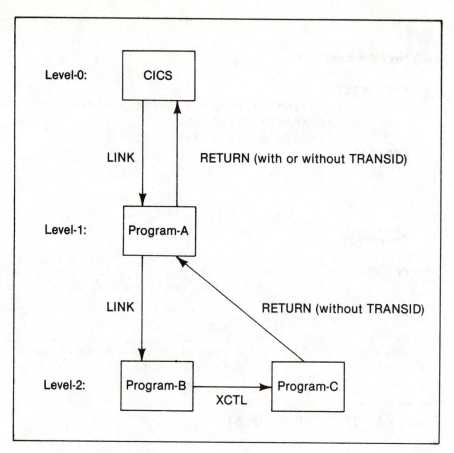

Figure 8-6   Operation of the XCTL command

the program selected by the operator is pseudo-conversational, a LINK command would be invalid since only a program at level-1 can issue a RETURN command with the TRANSID option. In this case, you use the XCTL command instead.

The XCTL command   Unlike LINK, the XCTL command (pronounced X-control) transfers control to another program *without* setting up a return mechanism. As a result, control doesn't return to the program that issues an XCTL command. The critical distinction between LINK and XCTL is that while the LINK command transfers control to a program at the *next lower* logical level, the XCTL command transfers control to a program at the *same* logical level.

To illustrate, consider figure 8-6. Here, CICS invokes program-A at level-1. Next, program-A issues a LINK command to

---

The XCTL command

```
EXEC CICS
     XCTL PROGRAM(alphanumeric-data-value)
         ⌈COMMAREA(data-name)        ⌉
         ⌊LENGTH(numeric-data-value)⌋
END-EXEC
```

Explanation

PROGRAM	The name of the program to be invoked. This name must appear in the Processing Program Table (PPT).
COMMAREA	The name of the communication area that will be passed to the program.
LENGTH	The length of the communication area. May be a numeric literal or a data-name.

Figure 8-7   The XCTL command

program-B at level-2. Then, program-B issues an XCTL command to invoke program-C at the same level. When program-C issues a RETURN command (without the TRANSID option), control is returned to the next higher level. So, execution continues with the statement in program-A after the LINK command that invoked program-B.

The XCTL command, shown in figure 8-7, is similar in format to the LINK command. Like the LINK and RETURN commands, the XCTL command allows you to pass data using the COMMAREA and LENGTH options. Again, the program that XCTL invokes receives the data in DFHCOMMAREA. If the program specified in the XCTL command doesn't exist, the PGMIDERR condition is raised. So, as with the LINK command, I recommend you always code a HANDLE CONDITION command for the PGMIDERR condition whenever you use an XCTL command.

```
01    DFHEIBLK.
02      EIBTIME  PIC S9(7) COMP-3.
02      EIBDATE  PIC S9(7) COMP-3.
02      EIBTRNID PIC X(4).
02      EIBTASKN PIC S9(7) COMP-3.
02      EIBTRMID PIC X(4).
02      DFHEIGDI COMP PIC S9(4).
02      EIBCPOSN COMP PIC S9(4).
02      EIBCALEN COMP PIC S9(4).
02      EIBAID   PIC X(1).
02      EIBFN    PIC X(2).
02      EIBRCODE PIC X(6).
02      EIBDS    PIC X(8).
02      EIBREQID PIC X(8).
02      EIBRSRCE PIC X(8).
02      EIBSYNC  PIC X(1).
02      EIBFREE  PIC X(1).
02      EIBRECV  PIC X(1).
02      EIBFIL02 PIC X(1).
02      EIBATT   PIC X(1).
02      EIBEOC   PIC X(1).
02      EIBFMH   PIC X(1).
02      EIBCOMPL PIC X(1).
02      EIBSIG   PIC X(1).
02      EIBCONF  PIC X(1).
02      EIBERR   PIC X(1).
02      EIBERRCD PIC X(4).
02      EIBSYNRB PIC X(1).
02      EIBNODAT PIC X(1).
```

Figure 8-8   Fields in the Execute Interface Block

How to use the fields in the Execute Interface Block

As I explained in chapter 6, the Execute Interface Block is a CICS area that contains information related to the current task. Figure 8-8 shows the fields contained in the Execute Interface Block. (This is the code the command-level translator automatically inserts into your programs' Linkage Sections.) The highlighted fields are the ones you're likely to use in coding and debugging your programs. Some of these fields are initialized when the task is started; others are updated each time certain CICS commands are executed. You already know how to use EIBCALEN; now, I want to explain how to use some of the other fields.

EIBTIME   EIBTIME contains the time of day your task was started. The time is stored as a seven-digit packed decimal number in the form 0HHMMSS (one leading zero followed by two-digit hours, minutes, and seconds). This assumes a 24-hour clock, so 2:00 p.m. is hour 14. As a result, 38 seconds after 2:41 p.m. is stored as 0144138. Midnight is stored as 0000000; one second before midnight is 0235959.

   You probably won't use EIBTIME often. Since EIBTIME indicates the time the task was started, not the actual current time, it has little use in time-critical applications.

EIBDATE   EIBDATE contains the date the task was started. The format of EIBDATE is 00YYDDD, where DDD represents the three digits that indicate what number day in the year it is. Thus, July 1, 1983 is stored as 0083182 (the 182nd day of 1983).

   Although the YYDDD format is useful for date comparisons, it's inappropriate for display purposes. As a result, if you want to display the current date, you can first convert EIBDATE into the standard form MM/DD/YY. You can do this several ways. One is to place the conversion routine source code in a COPY book. Then, you can include that code in your program when appropriate.

   The usual way is to convert the date once at the start of each day, and place the converted date in a CICS work area that's accessible to all programs. In a few moments, I'll show you how to use CICS work areas.

   Under DOS/VSE, you can avoid the date-conversion problem altogether by using the special register CURRENT-DATE rather than EIBDATE. CURRENT-DATE, which is already stored in the form MM/DD/YY, can be used as a sending field in a MOVE statement. I don't recommend you use CURRENT-DATE, however, because it's invalid when running CICS on an OS/VS system.

EIBTRNID   EIBTRNID contains the transaction identifier that started the current task. One of the common uses of EIBTRNID is to determine how your program was started. For example, suppose you want to insure that a program is invoked only from a menu. In other words, you don't want the program to be started by entering a transaction identifier at a terminal. (Remember that a task is started by a single transaction identifier, even though it may consist

```
   8000-START-TERMINAL-SESSION.
*
      IF EIBTRNID NOT = 'MENU'
          EXEC CICS
              RETURN
          END-EXEC.
      .
      .
      .
```

Figure 8-9   Using EIBTRNID to insure that a program is started from a menu

of several different programs.) Figure 8-9 shows a simple test you could place in the start-terminal-session module to check this. Here, if EIBTRNID is anything other than MENU (the transaction identifier that starts the menu program), a RETURN command is issued to terminate the task.

EIBTRMID   This field supplies the name of the terminal running the task. The terminal name that appears in EIBTRMID isn't a physical device type like 3270-2, but rather a symbolic name assigned to a terminal to meet an installation's specific requirements. (An example of a terminal name is H400.) These names are used primarily for security purposes. For example, if you want to restrict a program to certain terminals, you could test EIBTRMID to make sure the terminal is eligible to run the task. If not, your program would issue a RETURN command to terminate the task.

EIBCPOSN   This field supplies the screen position of the cursor. The cursor position is a number from 0 to 1919, indicating the cursor's displacement on the screen. To convert this to line/column format, simply divide by 80 (for terminals with 80-character lines). The integer portion of the answer plus 1 is the line number; the remainder plus 1 is the column number. For example, cursor position 255 is line 4, column 16 (255/80 = 3, remainder 15). EIBCPOSN is automatically updated after any RECEIVE command.

EIBAID   EIBAID is a one-character field that indicates which attention key was used for the last RECEIVE command. Although you can use EIBAID rather than a HANDLE AID command to detect special function keys, I prefer to use the HANDLE AID command.

EIB fields used for debugging   Three of the Execute Interface Block's fields are particularly useful when debugging a command-level CICS program: EIBFN, EIBRCODE, and EIBDS. EIBFN indicates which CICS command was executed last, and EIBRCODE indicates that command's completion status. The Application Programmer's Reference manual lists possible values for these fields. EIBDS contains the name of the data set processed by the last file-control command. EIBDS is normally used for debugging, although you may occasionally access EIBDS in a file-control error-processing routine.

The rest of the fields in the Execute Interface Block are seldom-used, so I won't describe them here. You can find a complete explanation of them in the Application Programmer's Reference manual.

How to access CICS areas

Command-level COBOL allows you to access areas of storage that are owned by CICS rather than by your application program. Some CICS areas are provided automatically, and others must be set up explicitly. CICS automatically provides four such areas: the *CSA (Common System Area)*, the *TCTUA (Terminal Control Table User Area), the TWA (Transaction Work Area)*, and the *CWA (Common Work Area)*. You'll hear and read about the first three of these areas, but they're largely holdovers from macro-level CICS and are seldom-used in command-level programming. However, you will use the fourth, the CWA.

The CWA is an area of storage that's available to all tasks in a CICS system. Typically, the CWA is used to store limited amounts of information that might be useful to many or all programs in an installation. For example, a typical CWA might contain two fields: the current date already converted to the form MM/DD/YY (that way each program doesn't have to do the conversion), and the company name (that way, you can install the software for another company by changing only the company name in the CWA). The CWA might also contain the day of the week, system start-up time, job name, and so on; its actual contents vary from installation to installation.

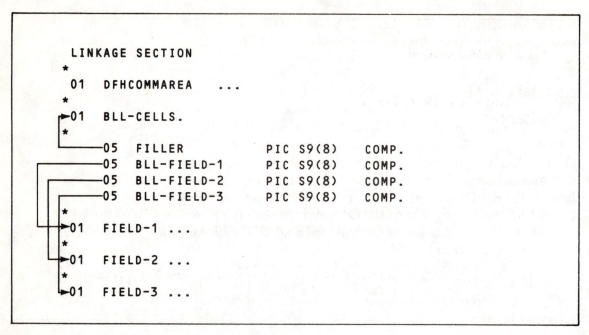

```
      LINKAGE SECTION
  *
    01   DFHCOMMAREA    ...
  *
  01  BLL-CELLS.
  *
        05   FILLER           PIC  S9(8)    COMP.
        05   BLL-FIELD-1      PIC  S9(8)    COMP.
        05   BLL-FIELD-2      PIC  S9(8)    COMP.
        05   BLL-FIELD-3      PIC  S9(8)    COMP.
  *
  01  FIELD-1 ...
  *
  01  FIELD-2 ...
  *
  01  FIELD-3 ...
```

Figure 8-10   BLL cells in the Linkage Section

Since these areas are defined outside your program, you must define them in the Linkage Section rather than in the Working-Storage Section. When CICS loads and executes your program, it expects to find two fields defined in the Linkage Section: the Execute Interface Block and DFHCOMMAREA. As a result, CICS automatically establishes *addressability* to these two fields. However, if you define any other field in the Linkage Section (such as the CWA), you must establish addressability to it yourself. If you don't, your program will abend with an addressing exception when you try to access the field.

To establish addressability to a field in the Linkage Section, you use a convention called *Base Locator for Linkage* (or *BLL*). Figure 8-10 illustrates this convention. Quite simply, you must define an 01-level item in the Linkage Section following DFHCOMMAREA. In figure 8-10, I called this item BLL-CELLS, but the name doesn't matter. Each field in BLL-CELLS is a pointer that stores the address of a Linkage Section field. These pointers must be defined as PIC S9(8) COMP. The first pointer points to the BLL-CELLS item itself. Then, each subsequent pointer points to an 01-level item that follows in the Linkage Section. In figure 8-10, the pointer named BLL-FIELD-1 is used to

---

The ADDRESS command

```
EXEC CICS
     ADDRESS CWA(pointer)
END-EXEC
```

Explanation

CWA   Establishes addressability to the Common Work Area, a user-
                            defined storage area common to all tasks in a CICS system.

Note: The ADDRESS command can also be used to establish addressability to other
        CICS areas. See the IBM manual for details.

Figure 8-11   The ADDRESS command

establish addressability to FIELD-1. Similarly, BLL-FIELD-2 is
used for FIELD-2, and BLL-FIELD-3 is used for FIELD-3.

Remember that the names of the BLL cells don't matter. What
does matter is the order in which you code them. Within the BLL-
CELLS group, the first pointer points to itself. The second pointer
points to the first subsequent 01 item, the third pointer points to
the second subsequent 01 item, and so on.

Coding the BLL cells in the Linkage Section defines the
pointers that will be used to address fields in the Linkage Section.
However, before you can use any of these fields, you must load the
pointers with the correct address. To do this, you use the
ADDRESS command, shown in figure 8-11. The ADDRESS command simply loads the address of the named field into the specified
BLL cell. For example, if you code this ADDRESS command:

```
EXEC CICS
     ADDRESS CWA(BLL-CWA)
END-EXEC.
```

the address of the CWA is placed in BLL-CWA. Then, the fields in
the CWA can be accessed by your program.

```
    LINKAGE SECTION.
*
 01   DFHCOMMAREA                PIC X.
*
 01   BLL-CELLS.
*
      05   FILLER                PIC S9(8)    COMP.
      05   BLL-CWA               PIC S9(8)    COMP.
*
 01   COMMON-WORK-AREA.
*
      05   CWA-CURRENT-DATE      PIC X(8).
      05   CWA-COMPANY-NAME      PIC X(30).
*
 PROCEDURE DIVISION.
*
 000-PROCESS-CUSTOMER-INQUIRY.
*
      EXEC CICS
          ADDRESS CWA(BLL-CWA)
      END-EXEC.
          .
          .
          .
```

Figure 8-12   Addressing the Common Work Area

To illustrate, consider figure 8-12. This figure shows how to access a CWA that contains two fields: the current date (MM/DD/YY) and the company name (30 characters). Here, BLL-CWA is the name of the pointer that will be used for COMMON-WORK-AREA. When the ADDRESS command is issued, the fields in COMMON-WORK-AREA are accessible, so the program can process CWA-CURRENT-DATE and CWA-COMPANY-NAME.

Besides addressing CICS areas like the CWA, the BLL mechanism can be used for two other types of storage areas: (1) pre-defined constant tables, and (2) buffers used for locate-mode I/O. A CICS *constant table* is an area of storage that contains values for a commonly used table. Rather than code the table in the Working-Storage Section of each program, the table is loaded into storage once and defined in each program in the Linkage Section. You'll learn how to create and access constant tables in *CICS for the COBOL Programmer, Part 2.*

Locate-mode I/O is an I/O technique that defines I/O areas in the Linkage Section rather than in working storage. When you use locate-mode I/O, your program processes data while it's still in a CICS buffer. Locate-mode I/O is used in some installations. Although locate-mode I/O is a bit more efficient, *move-mode I/O* is both safer and easier to use. As a result, I don't cover locate-mode I/O in this book. In the next topic, I'll present basic CICS commands that allow your programs to do move-mode file I/O.

Discussion

As you begin to develop command-level COBOL programs, you'll find many occasions to use the CICS elements and programming techniques presented in this topic. In the next topic, I present basic file-handling commands that, combined with the materials you've already learned, will enable you to code a wide variety of CICS application programs.

Terminology

exceptional condition
condition
CSA
Common System Area
TCTUA
Terminal Control Table User Area
TWA
Transaction Work Area
CWA
Common Work Area
addressability
Base Locator for Linkage
BLL
constant table
locate-mode I/O
move-mode I/O

Objective

Apply the CICS elements described in this topic to appropriate aspects of programming problems.

Topic 2 CICS file-control commands

CICS provides file-handling commands to perform all basic file-manipulation operations, including random or sequential read, write, rewrite, and delete. You can use these commands on ISAM, BDAM, and VSAM files. In this topic, I show you how to process VSAM files randomly. The coding for ISAM files is the same as it is for VSAM keyed files, and BDAM files are rarely used. (*Part 2, An Advanced Course*, presents the coding requirements for sequential file processing.)

To code file-control commands for VSAM files, it isn't critical that you have a solid understanding of how VSAM files are organized, as long as you understand the idea of an indexed file. As a result, I'm not going to present any conceptual background on VSAM file organization in this topic. If you desire this background, or if you need to use the VSAM utility (IDCAMS), I recommend my book *VSAM for the COBOL Programmer*, available from Mike Murach & Associates.

One thing you should realize when you process a VSAM file under CICS is that CICS does *not* allow null VSAM files to be processed. A null VSAM file is one that has never contained a record. The easiest way to ensure that a VSAM file isn't null is to write a standard batch COBOL program that opens the VSAM for output, writes a record, deletes it, and closes the file. Then, the file can be processed by CICS. This program should be run immediately after the VSAM data set is defined.

The READ command

The READ command, shown in figure 8-13, retrieves a record from a file. In its simplest form, you code the READ command like this:

```
EXEC CICS
    READ DATASET('CUSTMAST')
        INTO(CUSTOMER-MASTER-RECORD)
        RIDFLD(CM-CUSTOMER-NUMBER)
END-EXEC.
```

The READ command

```
EXEC CICS
     READ DATASET(alphanumeric-data-value)
          INTO(data-name)
          RIDFLD(data-name)
         [RRN]
         [UPDATE]
END-EXEC
```

Explanation

DATASET	The file-name from the File Control Table. Usually specified as a literal string in quotes.
INTO	The area that will contain the record being read.
RIDFLD	The field identifying the record. For VSAM keyed files (KSDS), the value is the key of the record. For relative-record files (RRDS), the value is the relative-record number.
RRN	RRN must be coded if the file is a relative-record VSAM file (RRDS).
UPDATE	Specifies that you intend to update the record with a REWRITE or a DELETE command.

Figure 8-13   The READ command

Here, a record is read from a VSAM key-sequenced file named CUSTMAST and placed in a working storage field named CUSTOMER-MASTER-RECORD. The RIDFLD parameter supplies the value of the key used for the retrieval. So, if CM-CUSTOMER-NUMBER has a value of 10567, the record with key 10567 is read.

What happens if the requested record isn't in the file? In COBOL, you specify an INVALID KEY clause on the READ statement to process the record-not-found condition. In CICS, the NOTFND condition is raised if the record isn't found. As a result, you should code a HANDLE CONDITION command for the NOTFND condition along with a READ statement. If you don't, the NOTFND condition causes the program to terminate.

```
 210-READ-ACCOUNT-RECORD SECTION.
*
     EXEC CICS
         HANDLE CONDITION NOTFND(210-NOTFND)
     END-EXEC.
     EXEC CICS
         READ DATASET('ACCOUNT')
             INTO(ACCOUNT-RECORD)
             RIDFLD(AR-ACCOUNT-NUMBER)
     END-EXEC.
     MOVE 'Y' TO RECORD-FOUND-SW.
     GO TO 210-EXIT.
*
 210-NOTFND.
*
     MOVE 'N' TO RECORD-FOUND-SW.
*
 210-EXIT.
*
     EXIT.
```

Figure 8-14   Typical coding for a read module

Figure 8-14 shows the coding for a typical read module. In the error routine for the NOTFND condition, a switch is set to indicate that the record doesn't exist. I recommend you use a switch like this, rather than place processing logic right in the error routine. That way, you'll keep your read modules simple.

Incidentally, in a CICS READ command, the record key field identified by the RIDFLD parameter doesn't necessarily have to be a part of the record area specified in the INTO parameter. If you wish, you can specify a separate working storage field for the RIDFLD parameter. Usually, though, it's easiest to use the key field in the record description for the record key.

To read a record from a relative-record file, you specify RRN on the READ command. Then, the RIDFLD value represents the number of the record you wish to retrieve. For example, if the RIDFLD value is 1, the first record is returned; if it's 2, the second record is returned; and so on. You define the record number field as a fullword binary item, like this:

```
01   INVMAST-RRN          PIC S9(8)   COMP.
```

Since most files processed by CICS are key-sequenced VSAM files, you won't code the RRN option often.

If you intend to update the record read by a READ command, you must specify the UPDATE option. The UPDATE option causes the requested record to be reserved by your task until you issue a REWRITE, DELETE, or UNLOCK command (actually, for a VSAM file, the entire control interval containing the record is held). Coding the READ command with the UPDATE option insures that no other task can modify the record while your task is updating it. You'll see in a moment how the REWRITE, DELETE, and UNLOCK commands are used.

If your application requires that your program update more than one record in a single file, I recommend you code the CICS commands in this sequence:

```
READ/UPDATE record 1
REWRITE record 1
READ/UPDATE record 2
REWRITE record 2
```

In other words, don't issue a series of READ with UPDATE commands on the same file without intervening REWRITE, DELETE, or UNLOCK commands.

The WRITE command

The WRITE command, shown in figure 8-15, adds a record to a file. As you can see, the WRITE command is similar in format to the READ command. The DATASET operand indicates the name of the data set, the FROM option names the output record to be written, and RIDFLD provides the record's key value. Again, the RIDFLD can be a part of the record or a separate field defined in the Working-Storage Section. For a relative-record file, you must code RRN and define the record number field as a fullword binary item.

The WRITE command


```
EXEC CICS
     WRITE DATASET(alphanumeric-data-value)
           FROM(data-name)
           RIDFLD(data-name)
          [RRN]
END-EXEC
```


Explanation

DATASET	The file-name from the File Control Table. Usually specified as a literal string in quotes.
FROM	The record to be written.
RIDFLD	The field identifying the record. For VSAM keyed files (KSDS), the value is the key of the record. For relative-record files (RRDS), the value is the relative-record number.
RRN	RRN must be coded if the file is a relative-record VSAM file (RRDS).

Figure 8-15 The WRITE command

Figure 8-16 shows a typical write module. Here, the HANDLE CONDITION command sets up an error routine for the DUPREC condition. If a WRITE command attempts to add a record with a key that already exists, the DUPREC condition is raised. As a result, the HANDLE CONDITION command serves the same function as the INVALID KEY clause on a standard COBOL WRITE statement. Again, notice that all I do in the error routine is set a switch. I prefer not to place complicated logic in a write module. That way, my write modules are both simple and reusable.

The REWRITE command

The REWRITE command, shown in figure 8-17, updates a record in a file. Before you issue a REWRITE command, you must first issue a READ command with the UPDATE option.

```
    510-WRITE-ACCOUNT-RECORD SECTION.
*
        EXEC CICS
            HANDLE CONDITION DUPREC(510-DUPREC)
        END-EXEC.
        EXEC CICS
            WRITE DATASET('ACCOUNT')
                  FROM(ACCOUNT-RECORD)
                  RIDFLD(AR-ACCOUNT-NUMBER)
        END-EXEC.
        MOVE 'N' TO RECORD-EXISTS-SW.
        GO TO 510-EXIT.
*
    510-DUPREC.
*
        MOVE 'Y' TO RECORD-EXISTS-SW.
*
    510-EXIT.
*
        EXIT.
```

Figure 8-16 Typical coding for a write module

To illustrate, figure 8-18 shows a typical update module that includes both a READ with UPDATE command and a REWRITE command. This module is performed after the operator has entered the required modifications and the new record has been formatted in the field NEW-ACCOUNT-RECORD. (The previous execution of the program issued a READ command that retrieved the original record and displayed it for modification.) The HANDLE CONDITION command in figure 8-18 sets up error processing for the NOTFND condition that may occur for the READ command. Then, the READ command obtains the record so the REWRITE command can update it. Once the REWRITE command is executed, the effect of the UPDATE option ends and other tasks can access the record. In figure 8-18, the READ and REWRITE commands specify different record areas. If they specified the same area, the module would simply read and rewrite the same data, without incorporating changes the operator made.

```
The REWRITE command

EXEC CICS
     REWRITE DATASET(alphanumeric-data-value)
             FROM(data-name)
END-EXEC
```

Explanation

DATASET   The file-name from the File Control Table. Usually specified as
                           a literal string in quotes.

FROM   The area containing the record to be written.

Note: The record must be previously read with a READ command with the UPDATE option.

Figure 8-17   The REWRITE command

Notice in this example that I didn't code the READ and
REWRITE commands in separate modules. That's because you can
consider the READ (with the UPDATE option) and REWRITE
combination as a single function: update the customer record. The
only reason I'd code them in separate modules is if the same READ
command is needed at more than one point in the program.

The DELETE command

The DELETE command, shown in figure 8-19, deletes a record
from a VSAM file (the DELETE command is invalid for ISAM or
BDAM files). You can use the DELETE command in two ways.
The first is to issue a READ command with the UPDATE option
and then to issue a DELETE command like this:

```
EXEC CICS
     DELETE DATASET('CUSTMAST')
END-EXEC.
```

Since the READ command identified the record, the RIDFLD
option on this DELETE command is unnecessary.

```
    340-UPDATE-ACCOUNT-RECORD SECTION.
*
        EXEC CICS
            HANDLE CONDITION NOTFND(340-NOTFND)
        END-EXEC.
        EXEC CICS
            READ DATASET('ACCOUNT')
                INTO(ACCOUNT-RECORD)
                RIDFLD(AR-ACCOUNT-NUMBER)
                UPDATE
        END-EXEC.
        MOVE 'Y' TO RECORD-FOUND-SW.
        EXEC CICS
            REWRITE DATASET('ACCOUNT')
                    FROM(NEW-ACCOUNT-RECORD)
        END-EXEC.
        GO TO 340-EXIT.
*
    340-NOTFND.
*
        MOVE 'N' TO RECORD-FOUND-SW.
*
    340-EXIT.
*
        EXIT.
```

Figure 8-18 Typical coding for an update module

The second way to use the DELETE command is to code the RIDFLD option on the DELETE command, as in the typical delete module shown in figure 8-20. Here, a HANDLE CONDITION command processes the NOTFND condition. Then, a DELETE command deletes the record identified by AR-ACCOUNT-NUMBER.

The UNLOCK command

If you issue a READ UPDATE command with the update option for a record and then discover that the record doesn't need to be

---

The DELETE command

```
EXEC CICS
     DELETE DATASET(alphanumeric-data-value)
           [RIDFLD(data-name)]
           [RRN]
END-EXEC
```

Explanation

DATASET	The file-name from the File Control Table. Usually specified as a literal string in quotes.
RIDFLD	The field identifying the record to be deleted. Required only if the record is not previously read by a READ command with the UPDATE option.
RRN	RRN must be coded if the file is a relative-record VSAM file (RRDS) and the RIDFLD option is coded.

Figure 8-19   The DELETE command

updated or deleted, you can release the record to other tasks by issuing an UNLOCK command, like this:

```
EXEC CICS
     UNLOCK DATASET('CUSTMAST')
END-EXEC.
```

Figure 8-21 gives the format for the UNLOCK command. Since any records held by the UPDATE option are released when your task is terminated anyway, you normally don't use the UNLOCK command. However, if your program does considerable processing before terminating, an UNLOCK command may be appropriate.

```
   360-DELETE-ACCOUNT-RECORD SECTION.
*
    EXEC CICS
        HANDLE CONDITION NOTFND(360-NOTFND)
    END-EXEC.
    EXEC CICS
        DELETE DATASET('ACCOUNT')
               RIDFLD(AR-ACCOUNT-NUMBER)
    END-EXEC.
    MOVE 'Y' TO RECORD-FOUND-SW.
    GO TO 360-EXIT.
*
  360-NOTFND.
*
    MOVE 'N' TO RECORD-FOUND-SW.
*
  360-EXIT.
*
    EXIT.
```

Figure 8-20   Typical coding for a delete module

```
The UNLOCK command

EXEC CICS
     UNLOCK DATASET(alphanumeric-data-value)
END-EXEC


Explanation

DATASET                    The file-name from the File Control Table. Usually specified as
                           a literal string in quotes.
```

Figure 8-21   The UNLOCK command

Condition	Cause
DSIDERR	The data set isn't defined in the FCT.
ILLOGIC	A VSAM error has occurred.
INVREQ	The I/O request is invalid.
IOERR	An I/O error has occurred.
LENGERR	A length error has occurred.
NOSPACE	There is not enough space to complete the operation.
NOTOPEN	The data set is not open.

Figure 8-22   File-control exceptional conditions

File-control exceptional conditions

Besides the NOTFND and DUPREC conditions I've already mentioned, CICS file-control commands can lead to a number of other exceptional conditions. Figure 8-22 summarizes these conditions. How they're handled varies from shop to shop. So, you should find out what your shop's standards are and follow them.

Discussion

In this topic, I briefly presented the formats of the basic CICS file-control commands. If you understand how standard COBOL file-handling statements work, you should have no trouble understanding the CICS file-control elements presented in this topic. In the next topic, you'll see several complete program examples that use CICS file-control features extensively.

Of course, there are many other CICS file-handling features I haven't covered here, including alternate index files and file browsing. These topics will be covered in the second book of this series.

Objective

Given the specifications for a CICS program involving the file-control commands presented in this topic, code a workable solution.

Chapter 9

A sample CICS application

Now that you've learned a basic subset of CICS commands and programming techniques, you're ready to analyze several model programs. The two topics of this chapter present an invoicing system, an application implemented in command-level CICS. Topic 1 describes the system design background you need to understand the invoicing application, and topic 2 presents four model COBOL programs from it: a menu, a data-entry program, a maintenance program, and a subprogram that does no terminal I/O.

Topic 1   An overview
of the invoicing application

This topic presents a brief overview of a menu-driven invoicing application. I simplified this application to make it easier for you to understand. Nevertheless, it illustrates how the CICS elements this book presents work together.

System design for the invoicing application

Figure 9-1 is a *data flow diagram* (or *DFD*) for the invoicing application. Quite simply, a data flow diagram shows the relationships between *processes* (or programs), indicated by circles, and *data stores* (or files), indicated by parallel lines. The link between a process and a data store, called a *data flow*, is indicated by an arrow.

If you're not familiar with data flow diagrams, I recommend you read *How to Design and Develop Business Systems* by Steve Eckols, available from Mike Murach & Associates. But even if you don't know how to create data flow diagrams, I think you'll find that figure 9-1 is a good overview of the invoicing application.

The key program in this application is the order-entry program. It accepts orders from an operator and writes them to an invoice file, using three other files for reference information: inventory, customers, and invoice control. Once the order-entry program has added orders to the invoice file, the invoicing function prints invoices, moving data from the invoice file to an invoice archive file for retrieval later. The invoicing function also uses the customer and inventory files for reference. The customer-maintenance program allows additions, changes, and deletions for records in the customer file. Finally, the customer-inquiry function displays data stored in the customer and invoice archive files.

As I said at the beginning of this topic, I simplified the invoicing application to make it easier for you to understand. As a result, I omitted what would normally be an important part of a production invoicing application: posting sales to accounts receivable. After all, this book is designed to teach you CICS commands and programming techniques, not system design. Even so, I want you to keep in mind that you'd certainly see a connection to accounts receivable (and probably to other subsystems as well) in a real invoicing system.

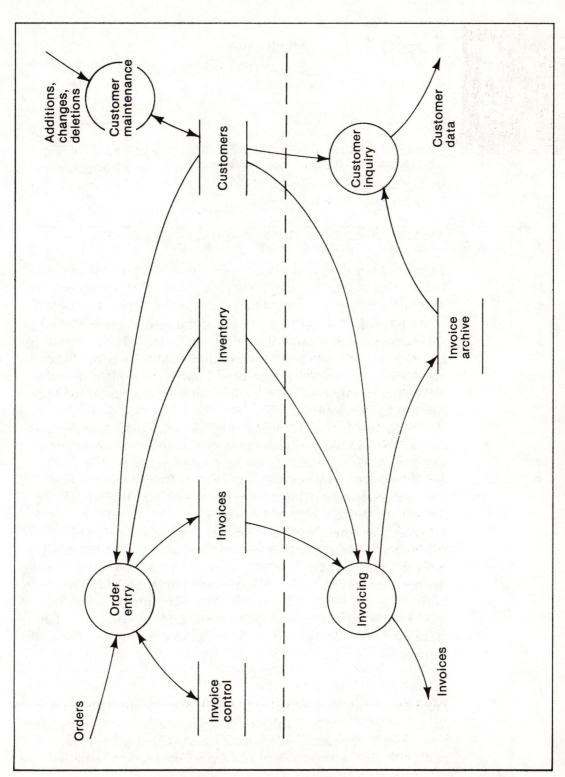

Figure 9-1 Data flow diagram for the invoicing application

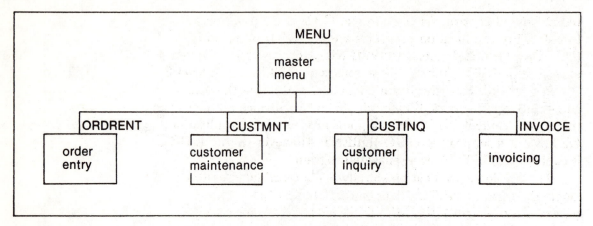

Figure 9-2   System structure chart for the invoicing application

This book illustrates the portion of the invoicing application that's above the horizontal dashed line in figure 9-1. The invoicing and customer-inquiry functions require CICS features you haven't learned yet. In *Part 2: An Advanced Course*, I'll explain those features and present programs that perform both the customer-inquiry and invoicing functions.

Figure 9-2 is the *system structure chart* for the invoicing application. You can use the system structure chart to organize system functions, design a menu structure, plan program development, and document completed systems. *How to Design and Develop Business Systems* describes how to use the system structure chart throughout design and implementation.

I use the system structure chart here to document the invoicing application's menu structure. As you can see in the system structure chart in figure 9-2, the invoicing application has one menu program (named master menu) that invokes programs that perform the four functions in the DFD in figure 9-1. The menu program isn't part of the DFD because its only purpose is to control the functions that make up the application—it doesn't make any changes to the application's files.

Program control in the invoicing application   Figure 9-3 illustrates the relationship between the invoicing application's menu structure and the program control commands each program issues. Here, boxes represent programs, and the arrows connecting the boxes rep-

resent flow of control. As you can see, CICS is the program at
level-0. Three application programs are at level-1: order entry
(ORDRENT), master menu (INVMENU), and customer maintenance (CUSTMNT). Finally, the subprogram GETINV is at level-2.

You should remember from chapters 7 and 8 that the order-
entry program invokes GETINV to retrieve an invoice number from
the invoice control file. From the point of view of the application,
GETINV is a subprogram of ORDRENT. However, as far as CICS
is concerned, GETINV is a separate program.

The invoicing application starts when a terminal operator
enters the trans-id MENU. That causes CICS to LINK to the
master-menu program INVMENU. When the operator makes a
selection, the master-menu program issues an XCTL command to
transfer control to the order-entry program (ORDRENT) or to the
customer-maintenance program (CUSTMNT). For simplicity, figure
9-3 illustrates only the programs I discuss in the next topic; I omitted the invoicing and customer-inquiry programs. At any rate, the
master-menu program issues XCTL commands to pass control to
the application programs.

Control returns to the master-menu program in two ways. The
customer-maintenance program transfers control back to the menu by
issuing an XCTL command that specifies PROGRAM('INVMENU').
In contrast, the order-entry program issues a RETURN command
with TRANSID('MENU') specified. That's because the order-
entry program displays a termination message before returning to
the menu, but the customer-maintenance program doesn't.

Also, notice that the order-entry program issues a LINK command to GETINV. GETINV, in turn, passes control back to the
order-entry program by issuing a RETURN command.

Program control in the invoicing application is complicated
because all of its programs (except the subprogram GETINV) are
pseudo-conversational. Consider, for example, what this forces the
order-entry program to do. As you've just seen, when the operator
ends a pseudo-conversational order-entry session, control passes
back to the menu because ORDRENT issues the command
RETURN TRANSID('MENU'). But during a pseudo-
conversational order-entry session, ORDRENT must end and be
restarted over and over. To make this possible, ORDRENT ends by
issuing the command RETURN TRANSID('ORD1'). This command passes control back to CICS, and the task ends. The next
time the operator presses an AID key, CICS uses the trans-id ORD1
to reload and execute ORDRENT directly, without going through
the master-menu program. As you can see in figure 9-3, the

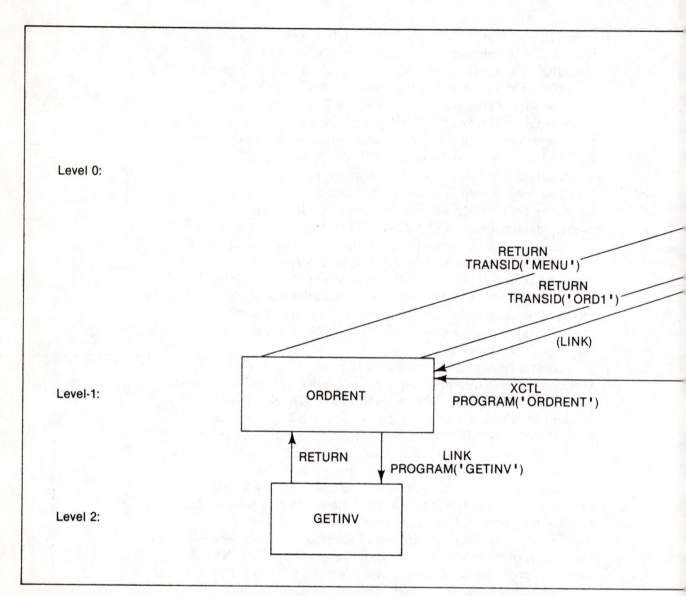

Figure 9-3   Program control in the invoicing application

customer-maintenance program works the same way. It ends during a pseudo-conversational session by issuing the command
RETURN TRANSID('MNT1').

Data sets in the invoicing application   As you can see in the DFD
in figure 9-1, the part of the invoicing application I illustrate in this

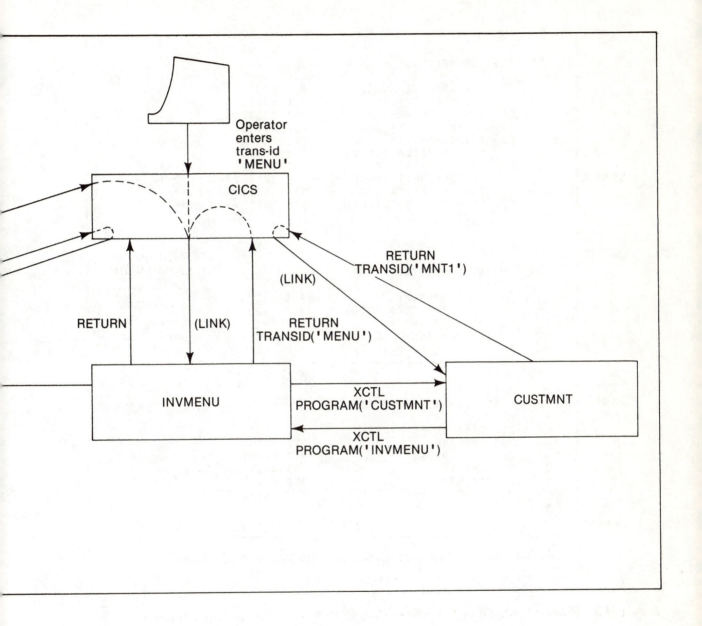

book uses four data sets: invoice control (INVCTL), invoices
(INVOICE), inventory (INVMAST), and customers (CUSTMAST).
I created a COPY book for the record layout for each of these files,
except for INVCTL. Since only one of the programs in the invoicing application (order entry) uses INVCTL, there was no point in
creating a separate COPY book for it.

```
01   INVOICE-RECORD.
*
     05   INV-INVOICE-NUMBER        PIC 9(5).
     05   INV-INVOICE-DATE          PIC 9(6).
     05   INV-CUSTOMER-NUMBER       PIC X(5).
     05   INV-PO-NUMBER             PIC X(10).
     05   INV-LINE-ITEM             OCCURS 10.
          10   INV-ITEM-NUMBER      PIC X(5).
          10   INV-QUANTITY         PIC S9(5)      COMP-3.
          10   INV-UNIT-PRICE       PIC S9(5)V99   COMP-3.
          10   INV-EXTENSION        PIC S9(5)V99   COMP-3.
     05   INV-INVOICE-TOTAL         PIC S9(5)V99   COMP-3.
*


01   INVENTORY-MASTER-RECORD.
*
     05   IM-ITEM-NUMBER            PIC X(5).
     05   IM-ITEM-DESCRIPTION       PIC X(20).
     05   IM-UNIT-PRICE             PIC S9(5)V99   COMP-3.
     05   IM-ON-HAND-QUANTITY       PIC S9(5)      COMP-3.
*


01   CUSTOMER-MASTER-RECORD.
*
     05   CM-CUSTOMER-NUMBER        PIC X(5).
     05   CM-NAME                   PIC X(30).
     05   CM-ADDRESS                PIC X(30).
     05   CM-CITY                   PIC X(21).
     05   CM-STATE                  PIC XX.
     05   CM-ZIP-CODE               PIC X(5).
*
```

Figure 9-4   Record layouts for the data files in the invoicing application

Figure 9-4 shows the COPY books for the other three data-file record layouts. These record layouts are simplified; in a production system, they'd probably be more complicated. For example, the customer master file would probably contain sales history data, and the invoice file would probably include shipping information as well as freight and sales tax charges. In addition, alternate-index relationships might exist between the files. For example, the customer-number field might be an alternate index for the invoice file. Still, the simplified record formats shown in figure 9-4 are adequate for the model programs this chapter presents.

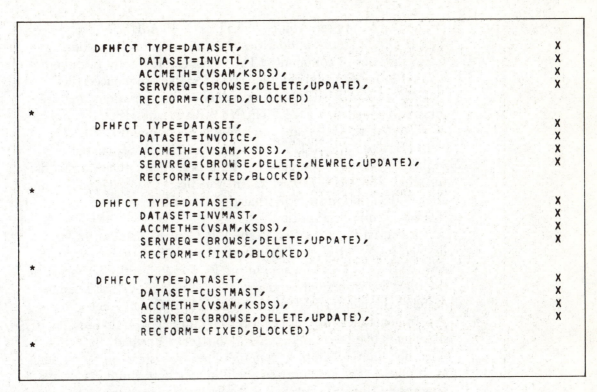

```
        DFHFCT TYPE=DATASET,                                    X
               DATASET=INVCTL,                                  X
               ACCMETH=(VSAM,KSDS),                             X
               SERVREQ=(BROWSE,DELETE,UPDATE),                  X
               RECFORM=(FIXED,BLOCKED)
    *
        DFHFCT TYPE=DATASET,                                    X
               DATASET=INVOICE,                                 X
               ACCMETH=(VSAM,KSDS),                             X
               SERVREQ=(BROWSE,DELETE,NEWREC,UPDATE),           X
               RECFORM=(FIXED,BLOCKED)
    *
        DFHFCT TYPE=DATASET,                                    X
               DATASET=INVMAST,                                 X
               ACCMETH=(VSAM,KSDS),                             X
               SERVREQ=(BROWSE,DELETE,UPDATE),                  X
               RECFORM=(FIXED,BLOCKED)
    *
        DFHFCT TYPE=DATASET,                                    X
               DATASET=CUSTMAST,                                X
               ACCMETH=(VSAM,KSDS),                             X
               SERVREQ=(BROWSE,DELETE,UPDATE),                  X
               RECFORM=(FIXED,BLOCKED)
    *
```

Figure 9-5   File Control Table entries for the invoicing application

CICS table entries for the invoicing application

For an application like this to work, the CICS tables must contain
definitions of the system's files, programs, and transactions. In most
installations, systems programmers change the CICS tables when
new programs are developed or old ones are modified. When a systems programmer changes a CICS table, he codes and assembles an
assembler language program that uses macro instructions much like
those that define a BMS mapset.

As an application programmer, you probably won't update
CICS tables yourself. Nevertheless, you need to be able to supply
the systems programmers with the information they need to keep
the tables up-to-date. Figures 9-5 through 9-7 are the table entries
for the invoicing system you'd need to describe to the systems
programmers.

File Control Table entries   Figure 9-5 shows the File Control
Table (FCT) entries required for the portion of the invoicing application this chapter illustrates. As you can see, one DFHFCT macro

defines each data set. You code TYPE = DATASET for each entry.
The DATASET option identifies the data set name you code in
CICS file-control commands. The ACCMETH option in these
examples specifies that the files are VSAM key-sequenced files
(KSDS). The SERVREQ option indicates the operations that are
allowed for the files. DELETE, NEWREC, and UPDATE indicate,
respectively, that you can issue the CICS commands DELETE,
WRITE, and REWRITE on the data set. BROWSE enables
sequential access to the data set. I'll explain the CICS commands
for sequential access in *Part 2: An Advanced Course*. Finally, the
RECFORM option specifies that the data sets have fixed and
blocked record organization.

Each data set specified in the File Control Table must be
defined in the job stream that starts the CICS system. On an OS
system, the DATASET name in the FCT matches the DSNAME in
the file's DD statement; under DOS, the FCT DATASET name
matches the name specified in the file's DLBL statement.

In general, as an application programmer, you do *not* add JCL
statements like these to the CICS job stream. Instead, the CICS
JCL, like the CICS tables, is maintained by systems programmers. I
mention the JCL here only so you'll have a better understanding of
how the FCT entries relate CICS files to the operating system.

Processing Program Table entries   Figure 9-6 shows the Processing
Program Table (PPT) entries for the invoicing application. You
must code an entry for each program in the system, regardless of
the level at which it's invoked. That includes mapsets as well as
application programs. TYPE = ENTRY is coded for each macro.
The PROGRAM option identifies the CICS program name, and the
PGMLANG option specifies its language. If you omit the
PGMLANG option, assembler is assumed. That's why I didn't code
PGMLANG on the macros that define mapsets.

Program Control Table entries   Figure 9-7 shows the Program
Control Table (PCT) entries that define the trans-ids the invoicing
application examples in this chapter use. Again, TYPE = ENTRY is
always coded. Then, the TRANSID option specifies the transaction
identifier used to invoke a task. Finally, the PROGRAM option
specifies the program associated with the trans-id. Figure 9-7
defines three trans-ids: MENU, ORD1, and MNT1 for, respectively, the menu, order-entry, and customer-maintenance programs. Remember that the trans-ids ORD1 and MNT1 are required
for the order-entry and customer-maintenance programs to be
pseudo-conversational.

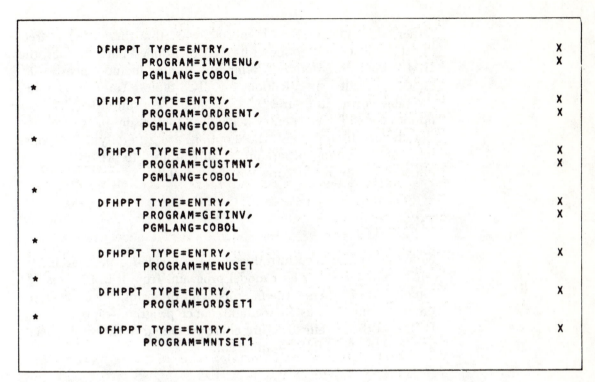

```
           DFHPPT TYPE=ENTRY,                                    X
                  PROGRAM=INVMENU,                               X
                  PGMLANG=COBOL
  *
           DFHPPT TYPE=ENTRY,                                    X
                  PROGRAM=ORDRENT,                               X
                  PGMLANG=COBOL
  *
           DFHPPT TYPE=ENTRY,                                    X
                  PROGRAM=CUSTMNT,                               X
                  PGMLANG=COBOL
  *
           DFHPPT TYPE=ENTRY,                                    X
                  PROGRAM=GETINV,                                X
                  PGMLANG=COBOL
  *
           DFHPPT TYPE=ENTRY,                                    X
                  PROGRAM=MENUSET
  *
           DFHPPT TYPE=ENTRY,                                    X
                  PROGRAM=ORDSET1
  *
           DFHPPT TYPE=ENTRY,                                    X
                  PROGRAM=MNTSET1
```

Figure 9-6   Processing Program Table entries for the invoicing application

```
           DFHPCT TYPE=ENTRY,                                    X
                  TRANSID=MENU,                                  X
                  PROGRAM=INVMENU
  *
           DFHPCT TYPE=ENTRY,                                    X
                  TRANSID=ORD1,                                  X
                  PROGRAM=ORDRENT
  *
           DFHPCT TYPE=ENTRY,                                    X
                  TRANSID=MNT1,                                  X
                  PROGRAM=CUSTMNT
```

Figure 9-7   Program Control Table entries for the invoicing application

Other table entries   You should be aware that there are hundreds of table entries and options I haven't mentioned here. In fact, the IBM *System Programmer's Reference Manual* includes nearly 300 pages of detailed specifications for CICS tables. You can see that the table entries in figures 9-5 through 9-7 are simplified. The exact options coded for each entry depend on factors unique to your installation. In any event, those options are generally the responsibility of the systems programmer; all you need to provide is the information given in figures 9-5 through 9-7.

Discussion

Now that you've been introduced to the invoicing application, you're ready to study four model programs from it in the next topic. Three of them—the master-menu program, the order-entry program, and the customer-maintenance program—appear in the DFD and the system structure chart presented in this topic. The fourth is the GETINV subprogram.

Terminology

data flow diagram
DFD
process
data store
data flow
system structure chart

Objectives

1. Describe the sample invoicing system presented in this topic.

2. Explain the CICS table entries required to support this application.

Topic 2   Four model programs

In the last topic, you saw an overview of a simple invoicing application. In this topic, I present four programs from that application: the master-menu program, the customer-maintenance program, the order-entry program, and the GETINV subprogram. These programs illustrate most of the CICS commands and programming techniques I've described in this book, and they're good models for many application programs you'll be called upon to write.

For each program (except GETINV), I've included a screen layout, a structure chart, the mapset listing, a listing of the symbolic map I created, and the source listing. For GETINV, I only included the source listing since the program doesn't use a map and has only one module. As you read the source listings, you may need to refer to the record descriptions in figure 9-4 of the last topic.

When you study these programs, don't get discouraged if you don't understand every line of code immediately. These programs combine many CICS and COBOL elements that are new to you, so it's natural that you'll need to read through them more than once to understand them. Each time you read through one of these model programs, the CICS and COBOL elements it illustrates will become clearer.

One of the best ways to study these programs is to read each of them a couple of times to get a general idea of how they work. Then, design and code your own CICS programs using one or more of these model programs for guidance. By experimenting with the CICS commands and the related COBOL statements, you'll rapidly come to understand how they work.

The master-menu program

Figures 9-8 through 9-12 present the master-menu program. The screen layout in figure 9-8 shows that the program asks the operator to select one of four functions: order entry, customer maintenance, customer inquiry, or invoicing. When the operator has made a selection (by entering the number 1, 2, 3, or 4), the master-menu program issues an XCTL command to load and execute the correct program. If the operator presses the clear key, the master-menu program terminates without branching to another program.

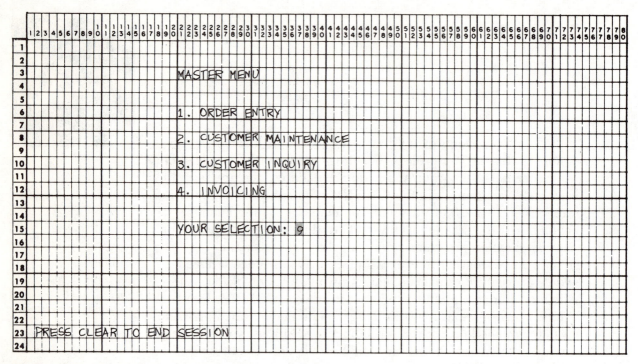

Figure 9-8   Screen layout for the master-menu program

Figure 9-9 presents the structure chart for this program. Here, module 100 is the main processing module. As you can see, it controls subordinate modules to receive the menu screen, edit the selection, and branch to the selected program. If the selection is invalid, module 140 is invoked to redisplay the menu screen with an error message.

Figure 9-10 presents the mapset listing for the master-menu program, and figure 9-11 presents the symbolic map I created. Since the operator message on line 23 never changes for this program, I coded it with an INITIAL value and didn't include it in the symbolic map.

Figure 9-12 presents the source code for the master-menu program. Module 000 should present nothing new to you. It controls the pseudo-conversational logic of the program.

In module 100, a PERFORM statement invokes module 110 to receive the menu map. Then, if the operator doesn't press the clear key, module 120 edits the selection. If the selection is valid, module 130 branches to the correct program; otherwise, module 140 sends the menu map back to the terminal with an error message.

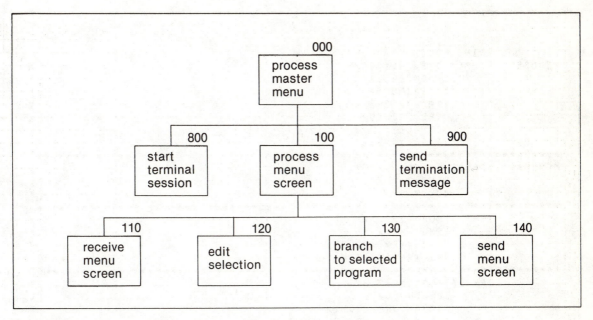

Figure 9-9   Structure chart for the master-menu program

In module 120, a working storage field named WS-PROGRAM-NAME is set to the correct program name for the function the operator selects. Then, module 130 issues an XCTL command to branch to the program specified in WS-PROGRAM-NAME. As a result, control never returns to the master-menu program from module 130.

From the point of view of structured programming, you might object to the XCTL command in module 130. After all, one of the basic principles of structured programming is that every module has one and only one exit point. Wouldn't it be better to code the XCTL command in module 000, thus maintaining the structural integrity of the program?

This is a valid objection. However, I still think it's best to code the XCTL command in module 130. If you code the XCTL command in module 000, you have to test for the PGMIDERR condition there as well. And that means you have to code a HANDLE CONDITION command and an error routine in module 000. In addition, you have to perform module 140 from module 000 so that an error message is sent to the terminal if the PGMIDERR condition does occur. In short, if you code the XCTL command in module 000, that module becomes overly complicated. So in this case, it's best to compromise strict adherence to the rules of structured programming for the sake of program clarity and simplicity.

```
           PRINT NOGEN
MENUSET    DFHMSD TYPE=&SYSPARM,                                          X
                  LANG=COBOL,                                            X
                  MODE=INOUT,                                            X
                  TERM=3270-2,                                           X
                  CTRL=FREEKB,                                           X
                  STORAGE=AUTO,                                          X
                  TIOAPFX=YES
***********************************************************************
MENUMAP    DFHMDI SIZE=(24,80),                                          X
                  LINE=1,                                               X
                  COLUMN=1
***********************************************************************
           DFHMDF POS=(3,20),                                            X
                  LENGTH=11,                                            X
                  ATTRB=(BRT,PROT),                                     X
                  INITIAL='MASTER MENU'
***********************************************************************
           DFHMDF POS=(6,20),                                            X
                  LENGTH=14,                                            X
                  ATTRB=(BRT,PROT),                                     X
                  INITIAL='1. ORDER ENTRY'
***********************************************************************
           DFHMDF POS=(8,20),                                            X
                  LENGTH=23,                                            X
                  ATTRB=(BRT,PROT),                                     X
                  INITIAL='2. CUSTOMER MAINTENANCE'
***********************************************************************
           DFHMDF POS=(10,20),                                           X
                  LENGTH=19,                                            X
                  ATTRB=(BRT,PROT),                                     X
                  INITIAL='3. CUSTOMER INQUIRY'
***********************************************************************
           DFHMDF POS=(12,20),                                           X
                  LENGTH=12,                                            X
                  ATTRB=(BRT,PROT),                                     X
                  INITIAL='4. INVOICING'
***********************************************************************
           DFHMDF POS=(15,20),                                           X
                  LENGTH=15,                                            X
                  ATTRB=(BRT,PROT),                                     X
                  INITIAL='YOUR SELECTION:'
SELECT     DFHMDF POS=(15,36),                                           X
                  LENGTH=1,                                             X
                  ATTRB=(UNPROT,NUM)
           DFHMDF POS=(15,38),                                           X
                  LENGTH=1,                                             X
                  ATTRB=PROT
***********************************************************************
```

Figure 9-10   Mapset listing for the master-menu program (part 1 of 2)

```
          DFHMDF POS=(23,1),                                              X
                 LENGTH=26,                                               X
                 ATTRB=(BRT,PROT),                                        X
                 INITIAL='PRESS CLEAR TO END SESSION'
ERROR     DFHMDF POS=(24,1),                                              X
                 LENGTH=77,                                               X
                 ATTRB=(BRT,PROT)
DUMMY     DFHMDF POS=(24,79),                                             X
                 LENGTH=1,                                                X
                 ATTRB=(DRK,PROT,FSET),                                   X
                 INITIAL=' '
**********************************************************************
          DFHMSD TYPE=FINAL
          END
```

Figure 9-10   Mapset listing for the master-menu program (part 2 of 2)

```
   01   MENU-MAP.
   *
       05   FILLER                      PIC X(12).
   *
       05   MM-L-SELECTION              PIC S9(4)     COMP.
       05   MM-A-SELECTION              PIC X.
       05   MM-D-SELECTION              PIC 9.
   *
       05   MM-L-ERROR-MESSAGE          PIC S9(4)     COMP.
       05   MM-A-ERROR-MESSAGE          PIC X.
       05   MM-D-ERROR-MESSAGE          PIC X(77).
   *
       05   MM-L-DUMMY                  PIC S9(4)     COMP.
       05   MM-A-DUMMY                  PIC X.
       05   MM-D-DUMMY                  PIC X.
```

Figure 9-11   Programmer-generated symbolic map for the master-menu program

```
     IDENTIFICATION DIVISION.
*
 PROGRAM-ID.    INVMENU.
*AUTHOR.         DOUG LOWE.
*DATE.           OCTOBER 14, 1983.
*NOTES.          THIS PROGRAM DISPLAYS A MENU, ACCEPTS AND EDITS
*                AN OPERATOR SELECTION, AND BRANCHES TO THE
*                CORRECT PROGRAM BASED ON THE OPERATOR SELECTION.
*
 ENVIRONMENT DIVISION.
*
 DATA DIVISION.
*
 WORKING-STORAGE SECTION.
*
 01  SWITCHES.
*
     05  END-SESSION-SW          PIC X      VALUE 'N'.
         88  END-SESSION                    VALUE 'Y'.
     05  VALID-DATA-SW           PIC X      VALUE 'Y'.
         88  VALID-DATA                     VALUE 'Y'.
*
 01  WORK-FIELDS.
*
     05  WS-PROGRAM-NAME         PIC X(8)  VALUE SPACE.
*
 01  END-OF-SESSION-MESSAGE      PIC X(13) VALUE 'SESSION ENDED'.
*
 01  COMMUNICATION-AREA          PIC X.
*
 COPY MENUSET.
*
 LINKAGE SECTION.
*
 01  DFHCOMMAREA                 PIC X.
*
 PROCEDURE DIVISION.
*
 000-PROCESS-MASTER-MENU SECTION.
*
     IF EIBCALEN = ZERO
         PERFORM 800-START-TERMINAL-SESSION
     ELSE
         PERFORM 100-PROCESS-MENU-SCREEN.
     IF END-SESSION
         PERFORM 900-SEND-TERMINATION-MESSAGE
         EXEC CICS
             RETURN
         END-EXEC
     ELSE
         EXEC CICS
             RETURN TRANSID('MENU')
                    COMMAREA(COMMUNICATION-AREA)
                    LENGTH(1)
         END-EXEC.
```

Figure 9-12   Source listing for the master-menu program (part 1 of 3)

```
/
 100-PROCESS-MENU-SCREEN SECTION.
*
     PERFORM 110-RECEIVE-MENU-SCREEN.
     IF NOT END-SESSION
         IF VALID-DATA
             PERFORM 120-EDIT-SELECTION
             IF VALID-DATA
                 PERFORM 130-BRANCH-TO-SELECTED-PROGRAM.
     IF NOT END-SESSION
         PERFORM 140-SEND-MENU-SCREEN.
*
 110-RECEIVE-MENU-SCREEN SECTION.
*
     EXEC CICS
         HANDLE AID CLEAR(110-CLEAR-KEY)
                    ANYKEY(110-ANYKEY)
     END-EXEC.
     EXEC CICS
         RECEIVE MAP('MENUMAP')
                 MAPSET('MENUSET')
                 INTO(MENU-MAP)
     END-EXEC.
     GO TO 110-EXIT.
*
 110-CLEAR-KEY.
*
     MOVE 'Y' TO END-SESSION-SW.
     GO TO 110-EXIT.
*
 110-ANYKEY.
*
     MOVE 'N' TO VALID-DATA-SW.
     MOVE 'INVALID KEY PRESSED' TO MM-D-ERROR-MESSAGE.
*
 110-EXIT.
*
     EXIT.
*
 120-EDIT-SELECTION SECTION.
*
     IF MM-D-SELECTION NOT NUMERIC
         MOVE 'N' TO VALID-DATA-SW
         MOVE 'INVALID SELECTION' TO MM-D-ERROR-MESSAGE
     ELSE IF MM-D-SELECTION = 1
         MOVE 'ORDRENT' TO WS-PROGRAM-NAME
     ELSE IF MM-D-SELECTION = 2
         MOVE 'CUSTMNT' TO WS-PROGRAM-NAME
     ELSE IF MM-D-SELECTION = 3
         MOVE 'CUSTINQ' TO WS-PROGRAM-NAME
     ELSE IF MM-D-SELECTION = 4
         MOVE 'INVOICE' TO WS-PROGRAM-NAME
     ELSE
         MOVE 'N' TO VALID-DATA-SW
         MOVE 'INVALID SELECTION' TO MM-D-ERROR-MESSAGE.
```

Figure 9-12   Source listing for the master-menu program (part 2 of 3)

```
/
130-BRANCH-TO-SELECTED-PROGRAM SECTION.
*
    EXEC CICS
        HANDLE CONDITION PGMIDERR(130-PGMIDERR)
    END-EXEC.
    EXEC CICS
        XCTL PROGRAM(WS-PROGRAM-NAME)
    END-EXEC.
*
130-PGMIDERR.
*
    MOVE 'N' TO VALID-DATA-SW.
    MOVE 'THAT PROGRAM CANNOT BE FOUND' TO MM-D-ERROR-MESSAGE.
*
130-EXIT.
*
    EXIT.
*
140-SEND-MENU-SCREEN SECTION.
*
    MOVE -1 TO MM-L-SELECTION.
    EXEC CICS
        SEND MAP('MENUMAP')
             MAPSET('MENUSET')
             FROM(MENU-MAP)
             DATAONLY
             CURSOR
    END-EXEC.
*
800-START-TERMINAL-SESSION SECTION.
*
    MOVE LOW-VALUE TO MENU-MAP.
    MOVE -1 TO MM-L-SELECTION.
    EXEC CICS
        SEND MAP('MENUMAP')
             MAPSET('MENUSET')
             FROM(MENU-MAP)
             ERASE
             CURSOR
    END-EXEC.
*
900-SEND-TERMINATION-MESSAGE SECTION.
*
    EXEC CICS
        SEND TEXT FROM(END-OF-SESSION-MESSAGE)
                  LENGTH(13)
                  ERASE
                  FREEKB
    END-EXEC.
```

Figure 9-12   Source listing for the master-menu program (part 3 of 3)

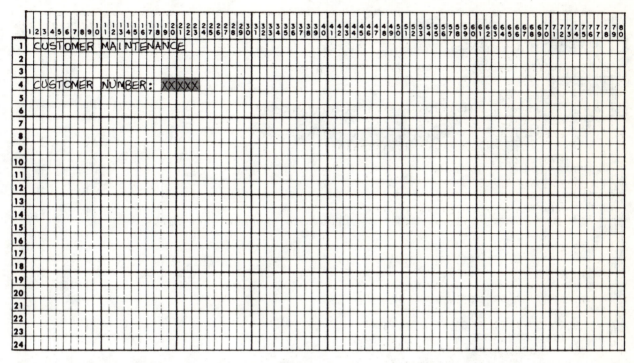

Figure 9-13   Screen layout for the customer-maintenance program (part 1 of 2)

The customer-maintenance program

Figures 9-13 through 9-18 present the customer-maintenance program. As you can see in figure 9-13, the program uses two screens. In the first one, the operator enters a customer number. If a corresponding customer record exists, the program displays the second screen along with the data from the record. Then, the operator can change the data or press PF1 to delete the record. If the record doesn't exist, the program displays the second screen with no initial data, and the operator enters data for the record to be added.

Since the operation of the maintenance program is somewhat complex, I drew the screen flow diagram in figure 9-14 to help me understand it. Here, the bold lines represent the usual flow of control through the program, while the lighter lines represent unusual or exceptional conditions. If you follow the flow of control through this diagram, you should have a good understanding of how the maintenance program works.

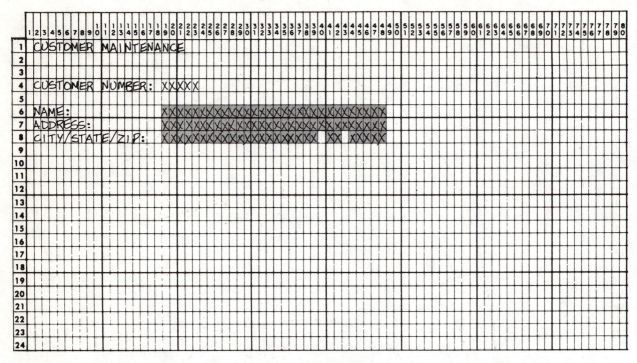

Figure 9-13   Screen layout for the customer-maintenance program (part 2 of 2)

Figure 9-15 presents the structure chart for this program. As you can see, there are three level-1 modules: (1) start terminal session, (2) process key screen, and (3) process customer screen. I chose not to include a send-termination-message module in this program.

Module 1000 controls four subordinate modules to receive the key screen, read the customer record, and send either a customer screen or another key screen (the key screen is sent if the operator doesn't enter a customer number).

Module 2000 controls six modules. First, it invokes module 2100 to receive the customer screen. Then, it invokes one of modules 2200, 2300, or 2400, depending on the maintenance function required (add, change, or delete). Finally, it invokes module 1300 or 1400 to send a customer screen or a key screen to the terminal.

Figure 9-16 is the mapset for this program. I want you to notice two points here. First, this mapset defines two maps: one for the key screen, the other for the customer data screen. Second, I coded the FSET attribute for each unprotected field in the customer data screen. That way, each field is sent to the program, even if the operator enters no data. I could have put the customer

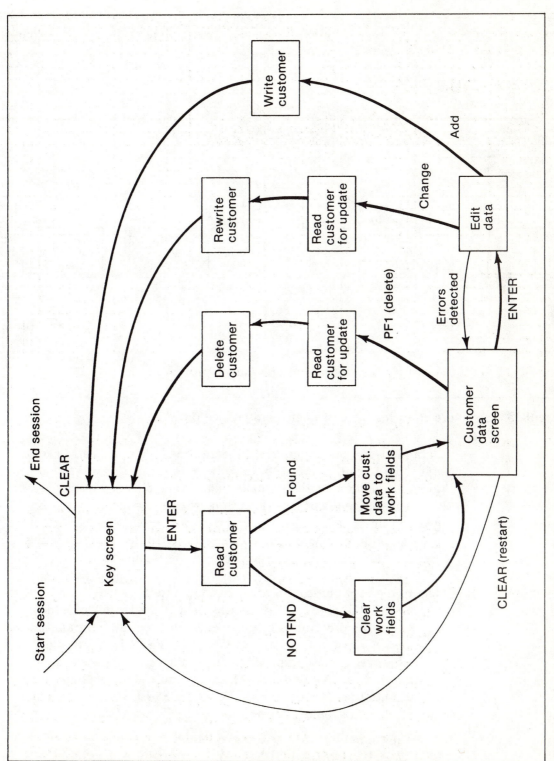

Figure 9-14 Screen flow diagram for the customer-maintenance program

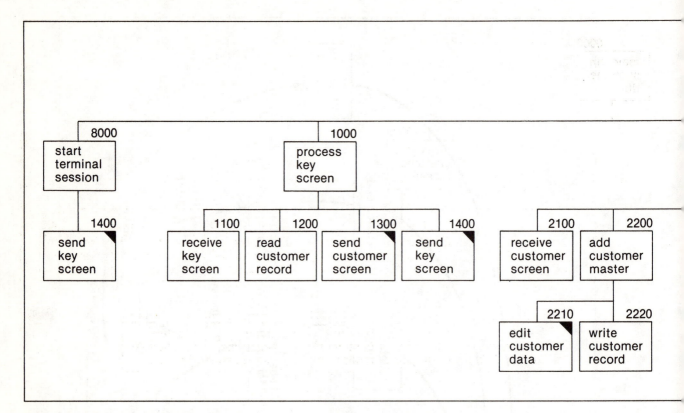

Figure 9-15 Structure chart for the customer-maintenance program

data fields in the communication area, but I chose instead to transmit them from the screen to illustrate how to use this technique. Figure 9-17 presents the symbolic maps I created for this mapset.

The source listing for the customer-maintenance program is given in figure 9-18. If you understand how pseudo-conversational programming works, you should have little trouble understanding this program. Let me point out some of the highlights:

1. In the communication area, I coded a field named CA-PROCESS-FLAG. I use this field to keep track of which screen the program is processing. Each time the program sends the key screen, it moves 1 to CA-PROCESS-FLAG. Similarly, whenever the program sends the customer data screen, it moves 2 to CA-PROCESS-FLAG. Module 0000 evaluates the conditions associated with CA-PROCESS-FLAG to determine whether it should perform module 1000 or 2000.

2. The communication area also contains a switch (CA-CUSTOMER-FOUND-SW) that's used to determine which maintenance function is to be done (add, change, or delete). Module 1200 reads the customer record and sets

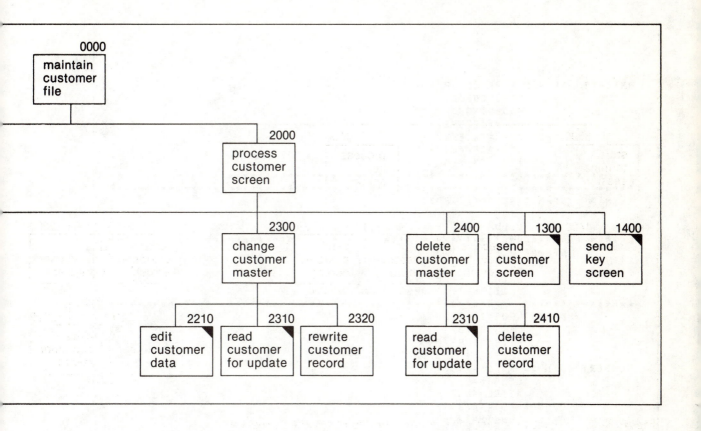

CA-CUSTOMER-FOUND-SW to indicate whether or not the record was found. Module 2000 uses a complex nested IF statement that evaluates the conditions associated with CA-CUSTOMER-FOUND-SW to determine what function to do. It allows a change or delete if the record exists; otherwise, it allows an add.

3. Module 0000 controls the pseudo-conversational logic of the program. It's similar to module 000 of the mortgage-calculation program in chapter 6. However, when the operator signals the end of the customer-maintenance session, module 0000 issues an XCTL command to return control to the master-menu program. This program doesn't need to end with RETURN TRANSID('MENU') because it doesn't display a termination message—it can pass control directly back to the master-menu program.

4. Module 1000 controls the processing of a key screen. Notice that I included a simple edit test in module 1000. I didn't create a separate edit module because the edit is trivial. This program allows any customer number to be entered, as long as it

```
        PRINT NOGEN
MNTSET1 DFHMSD TYPE=&SYSPARM,                                              X
               LANG=COBOL,                                                 X
               MODE=INOUT,                                                 X
               TERM=3270-2,                                                X
               CTRL=FREEKB,                                                X
               STORAGE=AUTO,                                               X
               TIOAPFX=YES
********************************************************************************
********************************************************************************
MNTMAP1 DFHMDI SIZE=(24,80),                                               X
               LINE=1,                                                     X
               COLUMN=1
********************************************************************************
        DFHMDF POS=(1,1),                                                  X
               LENGTH=20,                                                  X
               ATTRB=(BRT,PROT),                                           X
               INITIAL='CUSTOMER MAINTENANCE'
********************************************************************************
        DFHMDF POS=(4,1),                                                  X
               LENGTH=16,                                                  X
               ATTRB=(BRT,PROT),                                           X
               INITIAL='CUSTOMER NUMBER:'
NUMBER1 DFHMDF POS=(4,18),                                                 X
               LENGTH=5,                                                   X
               ATTRB=(UNPROT,IC)
        DFHMDF POS=(4,24),                                                 X
               LENGTH=1,                                                   X
               ATTRB=PROT
********************************************************************************
MESSAG1 DFHMDF POS=(23,1),                                                 X
               LENGTH=79,                                                  X
               ATTRB=(BRT,PROT)
ERROR1  DFHMDF POS=(24,1),                                                 X
               LENGTH=77,                                                  X
               ATTRB=(BRT,PROT)
DUMMY1  DFHMDF POS=(24,79),                                                X
               LENGTH=1,                                                   X
               ATTRB=(DRK,PROT,FSET),                                      X
               INITIAL=' '
********************************************************************************
********************************************************************************
MNTMAP2 DFHMDI SIZE=(24,80),                                               X
               LINE=1,                                                     X
               COLUMN=1
********************************************************************************
        DFHMDF POS=(1,1),                                                  X
               LENGTH=20,                                                  X
               ATTRB=(BRT,PROT),                                           X
               INITIAL='CUSTOMER MAINTENANCE'
********************************************************************************
```

Figure 9-16 Mapset listing for the customer-maintenance program (part 1 of 3)

```
               DFHMDF POS=(4,1),                                           X
                      LENGTH=16,                                           X
                      ATTRB=(BRT,PROT),                                    X
                      INITIAL='CUSTOMER NUMBER:'
NUMBER2        DFHMDF POS=(4,18),                                          X
                      LENGTH=5,                                            X
                      ATTRB=(PROT,FSET)
               DFHMDF POS=(4,24),                                          X
                      LENGTH=1,                                            X
                      ATTRB=PROT
**************************************************************************
               DFHMDF POS=(6,1),                                          X
                      LENGTH=5,                                            X
                      ATTRB=(BRT,PROT),                                    X
                      INITIAL='NAME:'
NAME           DFHMDF POS=(6,18),                                         X
                      LENGTH=30,                                          X
                      ATTRB=(UNPROT,FSET)
               DFHMDF POS=(6,49),                                         X
                      LENGTH=1,                                           X
                      ATTRB=ASKIP
**************************************************************************
               DFHMDF POS=(7,1),                                          X
                      LENGTH=8,                                            X
                      ATTRB=(BRT,PROT),                                    X
                      INITIAL='ADDRESS:'
ADDRESS        DFHMDF POS=(7,18),                                         X
                      LENGTH=30,                                          X
                      ATTRB=(UNPROT,FSET)
               DFHMDF POS=(7,49),                                         X
                      LENGTH=1,                                           X
                      ATTRB=ASKIP
**************************************************************************
               DFHMDF POS=(8,1),                                          X
                      LENGTH=15,                                          X
                      ATTRB=(BRT,PROT),                                   X
                      INITIAL='CITY/STATE/ZIP:'
CITY           DFHMDF POS=(8,18),                                         X
                      LENGTH=21,                                          X
                      ATTRB=(UNPROT,FSET)
STATE          DFHMDF POS=(8,40),                                         X
                      LENGTH=2,                                           X
                      ATTRB=(UNPROT,FSET)
ZIP            DFHMDF POS=(8,43),                                         X
                      LENGTH=5,                                           X
                      ATTRB=(UNPROT,FSET)
               DFHMDF POS=(8,49),                                         X
                      LENGTH=1,                                           X
                      ATTRB=ASKIP
**************************************************************************
```

Figure 9-16   Mapset listing for the customer-maintenance program (part 2 of 3)

```
MESSAG2   DFHMDF POS=(23,1),                                              X
                 LENGTH=79,                                               X
                 ATTRB=(BRT,PROT)
ERROR2    DFHMDF POS=(24,1),                                              X
                 LENGTH=77,                                               X
                 ATTRB=(BRT,PROT)
DUMMY2    DFHMDF POS=(24,79),                                             X
                 LENGTH=1,                                                X
                 ATTRB=(DRK,PROT,FSET),                                   X
                 INITIAL=' '
*********************************************************************************
          DFHMSD TYPE=FINAL
          END
```

Figure 9-16 Mapset listing for the customer-maintenance program (part 3 of 3)

isn't spaces. Other systems may require more rigorous editing of fields. However, that's strictly a COBOL consideration. Regardless of how extensive a program's editing requirements are, the CICS commands and programming techniques required are essentially the same.

5. Module 2200 controls the add function. It first invokes module 2210 to edit the customer data. Here again, the editing requirements are minimal: all the operator has to do is enter something in each field. (In other programs, editing requirements will almost certainly be more extensive.) If the data is valid, module 2200 performs module 2220 to write a record to the customer file. In module 2220, a HANDLE CONDITION command sets up an error routine for the DUPREC condition. Normally, the DUPREC condition won't come up here. The only reason it would is if another operator adds the record between executions of the program.

6. Module 2300 processes the change function. After editing the data, it performs module 2310 to read the customer record for update purposes. Then, it performs module 2320 to rewrite the record.

7. Module 2400 processes the delete function. Here, module 2310 is invoked to read the customer record for update. Then, module 2410 deletes the record.

As you might guess, there are other ways to implement a file-maintenance program. One is to require the operator to indicate which function to perform—add, delete, or change—by using a PF

```
  01   KEY-MAP.
  *
       05   FILLER                     PIC X(12).
  *
       05   KM-L-CUSTOMER-NUMBER       PIC S9(4)   COMP.
       05   KM-A-CUSTOMER-NUMBER       PIC X.
       05   KM-D-CUSTOMER-NUMBER       PIC X(5).
  *
       05   KM-L-OPERATOR-MESSAGE      PIC S9(4)   COMP.
       05   KM-A-OPERATOR-MESSAGE      PIC X.
       05   KM-D-OPERATOR-MESSAGE      PIC X(79).
  *
       05   KM-L-ERROR-MESSAGE         PIC S9(4)   COMP.
       05   KM-A-ERROR-MESSAGE         PIC X.
       05   KM-D-ERROR-MESSAGE         PIC X(77).
  *
       05   KM-L-DUMMY                 PIC S9(4)   COMP.
       05   KM-A-DUMMY                 PIC X.
       05   KM-D-DUMMY                 PIC X.
  *
  01   CUSTOMER-DATA-MAP.
  *
       05   FILLER                     PIC X(12).
  *
       05   CDM-L-CUSTOMER-NUMBER      PIC S9(4)   COMP.
       05   CDM-A-CUSTOMER-NUMBER      PIC X.
       05   CDM-D-CUSTOMER-NUMBER      PIC X(5).
  *
       05   CDM-L-NAME                 PIC S9(4)   COMP.
       05   CDM-A-NAME                 PIC X.
       05   CDM-D-NAME                 PIC X(30).
  *
       05   CDM-L-ADDRESS              PIC S9(4)   COMP.
       05   CDM-A-ADDRESS              PIC X.
       05   CDM-D-ADDRESS              PIC X(30).
  *
       05   CDM-L-CITY                 PIC S9(4)   COMP.
       05   CDM-A-CITY                 PIC X.
       05   CDM-D-CITY                 PIC X(21).
  *
       05   CDM-L-STATE                PIC S9(4)   COMP.
       05   CDM-A-STATE                PIC X.
       05   CDM-D-STATE                PIC XX.
  *
       05   CDM-L-ZIP-CODE             PIC S9(4)   COMP.
       05   CDM-A-ZIP-CODE             PIC X.
       05   CDM-D-ZIP-CODE             PIC X(5).
  *
       05   CDM-L-OPERATOR-MESSAGE     PIC S9(4)   COMP.
       05   CDM-A-OPERATOR-MESSAGE     PIC X.
       05   CDM-D-OPERATOR-MESSAGE     PIC X(79).
```

Figure 9-17   Programmer-generated symbolic map for the customer-maintenance
program (part 1 of 2)

```
*
       05   CDM-L-ERROR-MESSAGE        PIC S9(4)   COMP.
       05   CDM-A-ERROR-MESSAGE        PIC X.
       05   CDM-D-ERROR-MESSAGE        PIC X(77).
*
       05   CDM-L-DUMMY                PIC S9(4)   COMP.
       05   CDM-A-DUMMY                PIC X.
       05   CDM-D-DUMMY                PIC X.
*
```

Figure 9-17 Programmer-generated symbolic map for the customer-maintenance
program (part 2 of 2)

or PA key before he enters a customer number. Another is to implement the add, delete, and change functions as separate programs.
In any event, the customer-maintenance program illustrates the
basic requirements of any file-maintenance program.

Incidentally, a minor problem involving shared files may occur
when two operators attempt to update the same record using this
maintenance program. While it's true that the READ/UPDATE
command holds a record for update until a REWRITE, DELETE,
or UNLOCK command is issued, that only applies during a single
program execution. CICS provides no way to hold a record for
update *between* executions of a program in a pseudo-conversational
session. So, in a pseudo-conversational program, while the data for
update is displayed on the screen, the record in the field isn't held for
update because the task isn't active. As a result, it's possible for a
second operator to modify or delete the record before the first operator's task is restarted.

In some applications, this can be a major problem. If it is,
there are a couple of things you can do. The first is to save the record between program executions in the communication area. Then,
when your program issues a READ/UPDATE command, it com-
pares the newly read record with the one saved in the communication area. If the records differ, it means someone has changed the
record.

The second option is to place an indicator field in the record
itself. When your program reads the record for the first time, it
turns on the indicator and rewrites the record. When it updates the
record in its next execution, it turns the indicator off. Then, each
program must check the indicator when it reads a record. If the
indicator is on, it means the record is being processed by another
user, and the program shouldn't attempt to update it.

```
        IDENTIFICATION DIVISION.
    *
        PROGRAM-ID.   CUSTMNT.
    *AUTHOR.          DOUG LOWE.
    *DATE.            MAY 25, 1984.
    *NOTES.           THIS PROGRAM PROCESSES ADDS, CHANGES, AND DELETES
    *                 FOR THE CUSTOMER MASTER FILE.
    *
        ENVIRONMENT DIVISION.
    *
        DATA DIVISION.
    *
        WORKING-STORAGE SECTION.
    *
        01   SWITCHES.
    *
            05   END-SESSION-SW          PIC X          VALUE 'N'.
                 88   END-SESSION                        VALUE 'Y'.
            05   CANCEL-ENTRY-SW         PIC X          VALUE 'N'.
                 88   CANCEL-ENTRY                       VALUE 'Y'.
            05   VALID-DATA-SW           PIC X          VALUE 'Y'.
                 88   VALID-DATA                         VALUE 'Y'.
            05   PF-KEY-1-SW             PIC X          VALUE 'N'.
                 88   PF-KEY-1                           VALUE 'Y'.
    *
        01   COMMUNICATION-AREA.
    *
            05   CA-PROCESS-FLAG         PIC X.
                 88   PROCESS-KEY-SCREEN                 VALUE '1'.
                 88   PROCESS-CUSTOMER-SCREEN            VALUE '2'.
            05   CA-CUSTOMER-FOUND-SW    PIC X          VALUE 'Y'.
                 88   CA-CUSTOMER-FOUND                  VALUE 'Y'.
    *
        COPY MNTSET1.
    *
        COPY CUSTMAST.
    *
        LINKAGE SECTION.
    *
        01   DFHCOMMAREA                 PIC X(2).
    *
        PROCEDURE DIVISION.
    *
        000-MAINTAIN-CUSTOMER-FILE SECTION.
    *
            MOVE LOW-VALUE TO KEY-MAP
                             CUSTOMER-DATA-MAP.
            IF EIBCALEN = ZERO
                PERFORM 8000-START-TERMINAL-SESSION
            ELSE
                MOVE DFHCOMMAREA TO COMMUNICATION-AREA
                IF PROCESS-KEY-SCREEN
                    PERFORM 1000-PROCESS-KEY-SCREEN
                ELSE
                    PERFORM 2000-PROCESS-CUSTOMER-SCREEN.
```

Figure 9-18   Source listing for the customer-maintenance program (part 1 of 7)

```
        IF END-SESSION
            EXEC CICS
                XCTL PROGRAM('INVMENU')
            END-EXEC
        ELSE
            EXEC CICS
                RETURN TRANSID('MNT1')
                        COMMAREA(COMMUNICATION-AREA)
                        LENGTH(2)
            END-EXEC.
*
 1000-PROCESS-KEY-SCREEN SECTION.
*
        PERFORM 1100-RECEIVE-KEY-SCREEN.
        IF NOT END-SESSION
            IF NOT VALID-DATA
                PERFORM 1400-SEND-KEY-SCREEN
            ELSE
                IF        KM-D-CUSTOMER-NUMBER = SPACE
                    OR KM-L-CUSTOMER-NUMBER = ZERO
                    MOVE 'YOU MUST ENTER A CUSTOMER NUMBER'
                        TO KM-D-ERROR-MESSAGE
                    PERFORM 1400-SEND-KEY-SCREEN
                ELSE
                    PERFORM 1200-READ-CUSTOMER-RECORD
                    MOVE KM-D-CUSTOMER-NUMBER TO CDM-D-CUSTOMER-NUMBER
                    MOVE CM-NAME              TO CDM-D-NAME
                    MOVE CM-ADDRESS           TO CDM-D-ADDRESS
                    MOVE CM-CITY              TO CDM-D-CITY
                    MOVE CM-STATE             TO CDM-D-STATE
                    MOVE CM-ZIP-CODE          TO CDM-D-ZIP-CODE
                    MOVE -1 TO CDM-L-NAME
                    MOVE '2' TO CA-PROCESS-FLAG
                    PERFORM 1300-SEND-CUSTOMER-SCREEN.
*
 1100-RECEIVE-KEY-SCREEN SECTION.
*
        EXEC CICS
            HANDLE AID CLEAR(1100-CLEAR-KEY)
                        ANYKEY(1100-ANYKEY)
        END-EXEC.
        EXEC CICS
            RECEIVE MAP('MNTMAP1')
                    MAPSET('MNTSET1')
                    INTO(KEY-MAP)
        END-EXEC.
        GO TO 1100-EXIT.
*
 1100-CLEAR-KEY.
*
        MOVE 'Y' TO END-SESSION-SW.
        GO TO 1100-EXIT.
*
 1100-ANYKEY.
```

Figure 9-18   Source listing for the customer-maintenance program (part 2 of 7)

```
*
        MOVE 'N' TO VALID-DATA-SW.
        MOVE 'INVALID KEY PRESSED' TO KM-D-ERROR-MESSAGE.
*
   1100-EXIT.
*
        EXIT.
*
   1200-READ-CUSTOMER-RECORD SECTION.
*
        MOVE 'Y' TO CA-CUSTOMER-FOUND-SW.
        EXEC CICS
            HANDLE CONDITION NOTFND(1200-NOTFND)
        END-EXEC.
        EXEC CICS
            READ DATASET('CUSTMAS')
                INTO(CUSTOMER-MASTER-RECORD)
                RIDFLD(KM-D-CUSTOMER-NUMBER)
        END-EXEC.
        MOVE 'ENTER CHANGES OR PRESS PF1 TO DELETE CUSTOMER OR CLEAR
-           'TO START OVER' TO CDM-D-OPERATOR-MESSAGE.
        MOVE SPACE TO CDM-D-ERROR-MESSAGE.
        GO TO 1200-EXIT.
*
   1200-NOTFND.
*
        MOVE SPACE TO CUSTOMER-MASTER-RECORD.
        MOVE 'N' TO CA-CUSTOMER-FOUND-SW.
        MOVE 'ENTER DATA FOR NEW CUSTOMER OR PRESS CLEAR TO START OVE
-           'R' TO CDM-D-OPERATOR-MESSAGE.
        MOVE SPACE TO CDM-D-ERROR-MESSAGE.
*
   1200-EXIT.
*
        EXIT.
*
   1300-SEND-CUSTOMER-SCREEN SECTION.
*
        EXEC CICS
            SEND MAP('MNTMAP2')
                MAPSET('MNTSET1')
                FROM(CUSTOMER-DATA-MAP)
                CURSOR
        END-EXEC.
*
   1400-SEND-KEY-SCREEN SECTION.
*
        MOVE 'PRESS CLEAR TO END SESSION' TO KM-D-OPERATOR-MESSAGE.
        EXEC CICS
            SEND MAP('MNTMAP1')
                MAPSET('MNTSET1')
                FROM(KEY-MAP)
                ERASE
        END-EXEC.
```

Figure 9-18   Source listing for the customer-maintenance program (part 3 of 7)

```
*
   2000-PROCESS-CUSTOMER-SCREEN SECTION.
*
        PERFORM 2100-RECEIVE-CUSTOMER-SCREEN.
        IF VALID-DATA
            IF NOT CANCEL-ENTRY
                IF CA-CUSTOMER-FOUND
                    IF PF-KEY-1
                        PERFORM 2400-DELETE-CUSTOMER-MASTER
                    ELSE
                        PERFORM 2300-CHANGE-CUSTOMER-MASTER
                ELSE
                    PERFORM 2200-ADD-CUSTOMER-MASTER
            ELSE
                MOVE 'NO ACTION TAKEN' TO KM-D-ERROR-MESSAGE.
        IF VALID-DATA
            PERFORM 1400-SEND-KEY-SCREEN
            MOVE '1' TO CA-PROCESS-FLAG
        ELSE
            PERFORM 1300-SEND-CUSTOMER-SCREEN
            MOVE '2' TO CA-PROCESS-FLAG.
*
   2100-RECEIVE-CUSTOMER-SCREEN SECTION.
*
        EXEC CICS
            HANDLE AID CLEAR(2100-CLEAR-KEY)
                       PF1(2100-PF1-KEY)
                       ANYKEY(2100-ANYKEY)
        END-EXEC.
        EXEC CICS
            RECEIVE MAP('MNTMAP2')
                    MAPSET('MNTSET1')
                    INTO(CUSTOMER-DATA-MAP)
        END-EXEC.
        GO TO 2100-EXIT.
*
   2100-CLEAR-KEY.
*
        MOVE 'Y' TO CANCEL-ENTRY-SW.
        GO TO 2100-EXIT.
*
   2100-PF1-KEY.
*
        IF CA-CUSTOMER-FOUND
            MOVE 'Y' TO PF-KEY-1-SW
        ELSE
            MOVE 'N' TO VALID-DATA-SW
            MOVE 'INVALID KEY PRESSED' TO CDM-D-ERROR-MESSAGE.
        GO TO 2100-EXIT.
*
   2100-ANYKEY.
*
        MOVE 'N' TO VALID-DATA-SW.
        MOVE 'INVALID KEY PRESSED' TO CDM-D-ERROR-MESSAGE.
```

Figure 9-18   Source listing for the customer-maintenance program (part 4 of 7)

```
 *
  2100-EXIT.

 *     EXIT.

 *
  2200-ADD-CUSTOMER-MASTER SECTION.
 *
       PERFORM 2210-EDIT-CUSTOMER-DATA.
       IF VALID-DATA
           MOVE CDM-D-CUSTOMER-NUMBER TO CM-CUSTOMER-NUMBER
           MOVE CDM-D-NAME             TO CM-NAME
           MOVE CDM-D-ADDRESS          TO CM-ADDRESS
           MOVE CDM-D-CITY             TO CM-CITY
           MOVE CDM-D-STATE            TO CM-STATE
           MOVE CDM-D-ZIP-CODE         TO CM-ZIP-CODE
           MOVE 'RECORD ADDED' TO KM-D-ERROR-MESSAGE
           PERFORM 2200-WRITE-CUSTOMER-RECORD.
 *
  2210-EDIT-CUSTOMER-DATA SECTION.
 *
       IF      CDM-D-ZIP-CODE = SPACE
           OR CDM-L-ZIP-CODE = ZERO
           MOVE -1 TO CDM-L-ZIP-CODE
           MOVE 'YOU MUST ENTER A ZIP CODE'
               TO CDM-D-ERROR-MESSAGE.
 *
       IF      CDM-D-STATE = SPACE
           OR CDM-L-STATE = ZERO
           MOVE -1 TO CDM-L-STATE
           MOVE 'YOU MUST ENTER A STATE'
               TO CDM-D-ERROR-MESSAGE.
 *
       IF      CDM-D-CITY = SPACE
           OR CDM-L-CITY = ZERO
           MOVE -1 TO CDM-L-CITY
           MOVE 'YOU MUST ENTER A CITY'
               TO CDM-D-ERROR-MESSAGE.
 *
       IF      CDM-D-ADDRESS = SPACE
           OR CDM-L-ADDRESS = ZERO
           MOVE -1 TO CDM-L-ADDRESS
           MOVE 'YOU MUST ENTER AN ADDRESS'
               TO CDM-D-ERROR-MESSAGE.
 *
       IF      CDM-D-NAME = SPACE
           OR CDM-L-NAME = ZERO
           MOVE -1 TO CDM-L-NAME
           MOVE 'YOU MUST ENTER A NAME'
               TO CDM-D-ERROR-MESSAGE.
 *
       IF CDM-D-ERROR-MESSAGE NOT = LOW-VALUE
           MOVE 'N' TO VALID-DATA-SW.
```

Figure 9-18   Source listing for the customer-maintenance program (part 5 of 7)

```
*
 2200-WRITE-CUSTOMER-RECORD SECTION.
*
     EXEC CICS
         HANDLE CONDITION DUPREC(2200-DUPREC)
     END-EXEC.
     EXEC CICS
         WRITE DATASET('CUSTMAS')
                 FROM(CUSTOMER-MASTER-RECORD)
                 RIDFLD(CM-CUSTOMER-NUMBER)
     END-EXEC.
     GO TO 2200-EXIT.
*
 2200-DUPREC.
*
     MOVE 'ERROR--CUSTOMER RECORD ALREADY EXISTS'
         TO KM-D-ERROR-MESSAGE.
*
 2200-EXIT.
*
     EXIT.
*
 2300-CHANGE-CUSTOMER-MASTER SECTION.
*
     PERFORM 2210-EDIT-CUSTOMER-DATA.
     IF VALID-DATA
         PERFORM 2310-READ-CUSTOMER-FOR-UPDATE
         IF CA-CUSTOMER-FOUND
             MOVE CDM-D-NAME          TO CM-NAME
             MOVE CDM-D-ADDRESS       TO CM-ADDRESS
             MOVE CDM-D-CITY          TO CM-CITY
             MOVE CDM-D-STATE         TO CM-STATE
             MOVE CDM-D-ZIP-CODE      TO CM-ZIP-CODE
             PERFORM 2320-REWRITE-CUSTOMER-RECORD
             MOVE 'RECORD UPDATED' TO KM-D-ERROR-MESSAGE.
*
 2310-READ-CUSTOMER-FOR-UPDATE SECTION.
*
     EXEC CICS
         HANDLE CONDITION NOTFND(2310-NOTFND)
     END-EXEC.
     EXEC CICS
         READ DATASET('CUSTMAS')
                 INTO(CUSTOMER-MASTER-RECORD)
                 RIDFLD(CDM-D-CUSTOMER-NUMBER)
                 UPDATE
     END-EXEC.
     MOVE 'Y' TO CA-CUSTOMER-FOUND-SW.
     GO TO 2310-EXIT.
```

Figure 9-18   Source listing for the customer-maintenance program (part 6 of 7)

```
*
 2310-NOTFND.
*
     MOVE 'ERROR--CUSTOMER RECORD DOES NOT EXIST'
         TO KM-D-ERROR-MESSAGE.
     MOVE 'N' TO CA-CUSTOMER-FOUND-SW.
*
 2310-EXIT.
*
     EXIT.
*
 2320-REWRITE-CUSTOMER-RECORD SECTION.
*
     EXEC CICS
         REWRITE DATASET('CUSTMAS')
                 FROM(CUSTOMER-MASTER-RECORD)
     END-EXEC.
*
 2400-DELETE-CUSTOMER-MASTER SECTION.
*
     PERFORM 2310-READ-CUSTOMER-FOR-UPDATE.
     IF CA-CUSTOMER-FOUND
         PERFORM 2410-DELETE-CUSTOMER-RECORD
         MOVE 'RECORD DELETED' TO KM-D-ERROR-MESSAGE.
*
 2410-DELETE-CUSTOMER-RECORD SECTION.
*
     EXEC CICS
         DELETE DATASET('CUSTMAS')
     END-EXEC.
*
 8000-START-TERMINAL-SESSION SECTION.
*
     PERFORM 1400-SEND-KEY-SCREEN.
     MOVE '1' TO CA-PROCESS-FLAG.
```

Figure 9-18   Source listing for the customer-maintenance program (part 7 of 7)

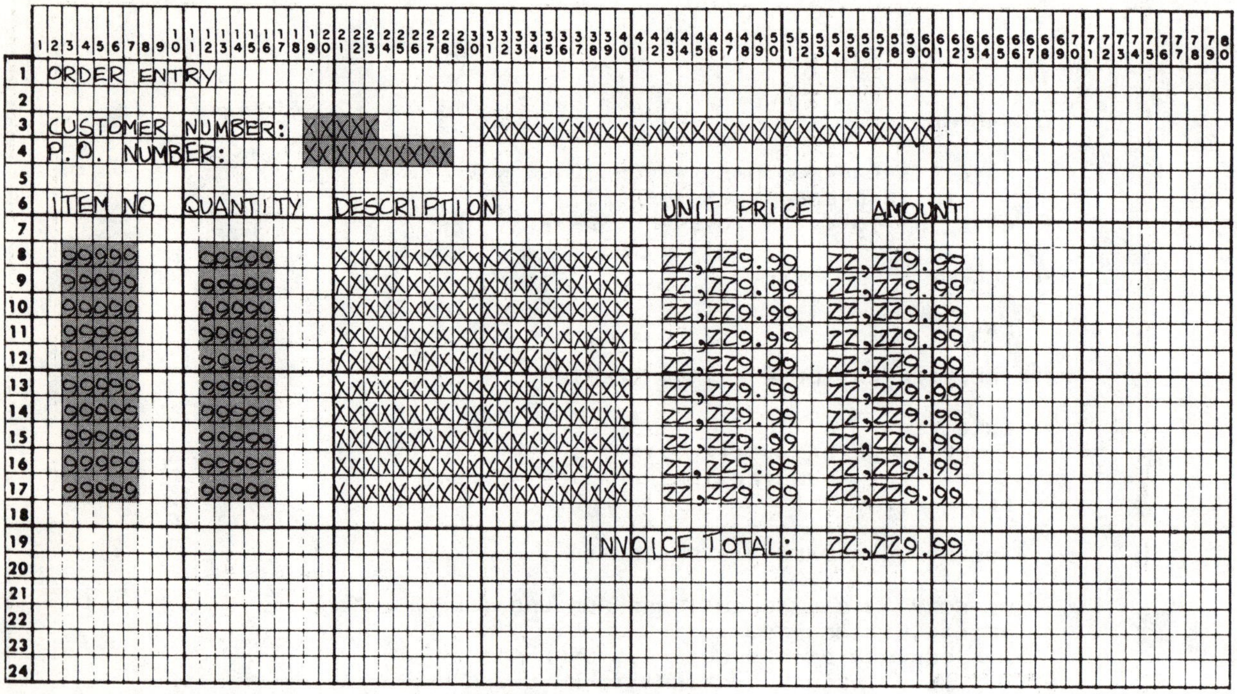

Figure 9-19   Screen layout for the order-entry program

The order-entry program

Figures 9-19 through 9-23 present the order-entry program that was designed in chapter 7. The screen layout is shown in figure 9-19; you can refer back to figure 7-1 to review the complete specifications for the program. In brief, the program accepts data for an order, edits it, requires the operator to sight-verify the data, and creates an invoice record for each verified order.

Figure 9-20 gives the structure chart for this program. Since I explained how I created this chart in chapter 7, I won't discuss it here. However, if you want to refresh your memory on how this program works, review chapter 7 before you go on.

Figure 9-21 gives a portion of the mapset listing for the order-entry program. Since the coding for the line items is repetitive, I include the coding for only the first one.

Figure 9-22 shows the symbolic map I created for this program. Notice how I use an OCCURS clause for the ten groups of line-item fields. In contrast, the symbolic map that BMS generated is full of short, cryptic names and is six and one-half pages long. I think you can imagine how much easier mine is to use.

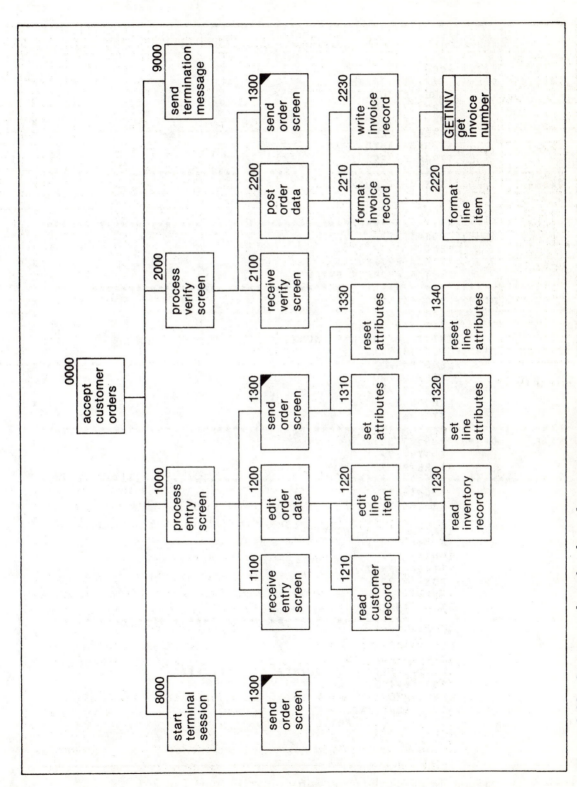

Figure 9-20 Structure chart for the order-entry program

```
          PRINT NOGEN
ORDSET1   DFHMSD TYPE=&SYSPARM,                                            X
                 LANG=COBOL,                                               X
                 TERM=3270-2,                                              X
                 MODE=INOUT,                                               X
                 CTRL=FREEKB,                                              X
                 STORAGE=AUTO,                                             X
                 TIOAPFX=YES
***************************************************************************
ORDMAP1   DFHMDI SIZE=(24,80),                                            X
                 LINE=1,                                                   X
                 COLUMN=1
***************************************************************************
          DFHMDF POS=(1,1),                                              X
                 LENGTH=11,                                               X
                 ATTRB=(BRT,PROT),                                        X
                 INITIAL='ORDER ENTRY'
***************************************************************************
          DFHMDF POS=(3,1),                                              X
                 LENGTH=16,                                               X
                 ATTRB=(BRT,PROT),                                        X
                 INITIAL='CUSTOMER NUMBER:'
CUSTNO    DFHMDF POS=(3,18),                                             X
                 LENGTH=5,                                                X
                 ATTRB=UNPROT
          DFHMDF POS=(3,24),                                             X
                 LENGTH=1,                                                X
                 ATTRB=ASKIP
***************************************************************************
NAME      DFHMDF POS=(3,30),                                             X
                 LENGTH=30,                                               X
                 ATTRB=PROT
***************************************************************************
          DFHMDF POS=(4,1),                                              X
                 LENGTH=12,                                               X
                 ATTRB=(BRT,PROT),                                        X
                 INITIAL='P.O. NUMBER:'
PO        DFHMDF POS=(4,18),                                             X
                 LENGTH=10,                                               X
                 ATTRB=UNPROT
          DFHMDF POS=(4,29),                                             X
                 LENGTH=1,                                                X
                 ATTRB=ASKIP
***************************************************************************
          DFHMDF POS=(6,1),                                              X
                 LENGTH=30,                                               X
                 ATTRB=(BRT,PROT),                                        X
                 INITIAL='ITEM NO  QUANTITY   DESCRIPTION'
          DFHMDF POS=(6,42),                                             X
                 LENGTH=20,                                               X
                 ATTRB=(BRT,PROT),                                        X
                 INITIAL='UNIT PRICE     AMOUNT'
```

Figure 9-21   Mapset listing for the order-entry program (part 1 of 2)

```
*******************************************************************
*          LINE ITEM 1                                           *
*******************************************************************
ITEMNO1    DFHMDF POS=(8,2),                                     X
                  LENGTH=5,                                      X
                  ATTRB=(UNPROT,NUM),                            X
                  PICIN='9(5)'
           DFHMDF POS=(8,8),                                     X
                  LENGTH=1,                                      X
                  ATTRB=ASKIP
QTY1       DFHMDF POS=(8,11),                                    X
                  LENGTH=5,                                      X
                  ATTRB=(UNPROT,NUM),                            X
                  PICIN='9(5)'
           DFHMDF POS=(8,17),                                    X
                  LENGTH=1,                                      X
                  ATTRB=ASKIP
DESCR1     DFHMDF POS=(8,20),                                    X
                  LENGTH=20,                                     X
                  ATTRB=PROT
UPRICE1    DFHMDF POS=(8,42),                                    X
                  LENGTH=9,                                      X
                  ATTRB=PROT,                                    X
                  PICOUT='ZZ,ZZ9.99'
AMOUNT1    DFHMDF POS=(8,53),                                    X
                  LENGTH=9,                                      X
                  ATTRB=PROT,                                    X
                  PICOUT='ZZ,ZZ9.99'
                  .
                  .          The BMS macro instructions that define line items
                  .          2 through 10 are similar to those that define
                  .          line item 1.
                  .
*******************************************************************
           DFHMDF POS=(19,37),                                  X
                  LENGTH=14,                                    X
                  ATTRB=(BRT,PROT),                             X
                  INITIAL='INVOICE TOTAL:'
TOTAL      DFHMDF POS=(19,53),                                  X
                  LENGTH=9,                                     X
                  ATTRB=PROT,                                   X
                  PICOUT='ZZ,ZZ9.99'
*******************************************************************
MESSAGE    DFHMDF POS=(23,1),                                  X
                  LENGTH=79,                                   X
                  ATTRB=(BRT,PROT)
ERROR      DFHMDF POS=(24,1),                                  X
                  LENGTH=77,                                   X
                  ATTRB=(BRT,PROT)
DUMMY      DFHMDF POS=(24,79),                                 X
                  LENGTH=1,                                    X
                  ATTRB=(DRK,PROT,FSET),                       X
                  INITIAL=' '
*******************************************************************
           DFHMSD TYPE=FINAL
           END
```

Figure 9-21   Mapset listing for the order-entry program (part 2 of 2)

```
    01   ORDER-ENTRY-MAP.
*
     05   FILLER                           PIC X(12).
*
     05   OEM-L-CUSTOMER-NUMBER            PIC S9(4)   COMP.
     05   OEM-A-CUSTOMER-NUMBER            PIC X.
     05   OEM-D-CUSTOMER-NUMBER            PIC X(5).
*
     05   OEM-L-NAME                       PIC S9(4)   COMP.
     05   OEM-A-NAME                       PIC X.
     05   OEM-D-NAME                       PIC X(30).
*
     05   OEM-L-PO-NUMBER                  PIC S9(4)   COMP.
     05   OEM-A-PO-NUMBER                  PIC X.
     05   OEM-D-PO-NUMBER                  PIC X(10).
*
     05   OEM-LINE-ITEM                    OCCURS 10.
*
          10   OEM-L-ITEM-NUMBER           PIC S9(4)   COMP.
          10   OEM-A-ITEM-NUMBER           PIC X.
          10   OEM-D-ITEM-NUMBER           PIC 9(5).
*
          10   OEM-L-QUANTITY              PIC S9(4)   COMP.
          10   OEM-A-QUANTITY              PIC X.
          10   OEM-D-QUANTITY              PIC 9(5).
*
          10   OEM-L-ITEM-DESCRIPTION      PIC S9(4)   COMP.
          10   OEM-A-ITEM-DESCRIPTION      PIC X.
          10   OEM-D-ITEM-DESCRIPTION      PIC X(20).
*
          10   OEM-L-UNIT-PRICE            PIC S9(4)   COMP.
          10   OEM-A-UNIT-PRICE            PIC X.
          10   OEM-D-UNIT-PRICE            PIC ZZ,ZZ9.99
                                           BLANK WHEN ZERO.
*
          10   OEM-L-EXTENSION             PIC S9(4)   COMP.
          10   OEM-A-EXTENSION             PIC X.
          10   OEM-D-EXTENSION             PIC ZZ,ZZ9.99
                                           BLANK WHEN ZERO.
*
     05   OEM-L-INVOICE-TOTAL             PIC S9(4)   COMP.
     05   OEM-A-INVOICE-TOTAL             PIC X.
     05   OEM-D-INVOICE-TOTAL             PIC ZZ,ZZ9.99
                                           BLANK WHEN ZERO.
*
     05   OEM-L-OPERATOR-MESSAGE           PIC S9(4)   COMP.
     05   OEM-A-OPERATOR-MESSAGE           PIC X.
     05   OEM-D-OPERATOR-MESSAGE           PIC X(79).
*
     05   OEM-L-ERROR-MESSAGE              PIC S9(4)   COMP.
     05   OEM-A-ERROR-MESSAGE              PIC X.
     05   OEM-D-ERROR-MESSAGE              PIC X(77).
*
     05   OEM-L-DUMMY                      PIC S9(4)   COMP.
     05   OEM-A-DUMMY                      PIC X.
     05   OEM-D-DUMMY                      PIC X.
*
```

Figure 9-22   Programmer-generated symbolic map for the order-entry program

The source listing for the order-entry program is given in figure 9-23. Some of the key points are as follows:

1. As usual, module 0000 handles the pseudo-conversational coding requirements. Like the customer-maintenance program, the order-entry program uses a communication-area flag, CA-PROCESS-FLAG, to determine which screen to process (in this case, either a data-entry screen or a verify screen). The communication area also contains unit-price fields that correspond to the ten line items. They're used in module 2220 to calculate each line-item extension for the invoice record. The unit-price fields aren't taken directly from the screen via the symbolic map because they're displayed in an edited format. Most of the other data the program uses, however, does come from the symbolic map. Finally, the communication-area field CA-TOTAL-ORDERS contains a count of the number of orders posted; this total is displayed when the operator ends the terminal session.

2. The order-entry program accesses the Common Work Area to obtain the current date in the form MMDDYY. As a result, BLL-CELLS and COMMON-WORK-AREA are defined in the Linkage Section, and an ADDRESS command is issued at the start of module 0000. In module 2210, CWA-DATE is moved to the invoice record's date field.

3. The order-entry program returns to the master-menu program by issuing a RETURN command with the TRANSID option. That way, no task is active while the total line is displayed. (You should remember that the customer-maintenance program doesn't display a termination message and, as a result, can pass control directly back to the master-menu program by issuing an XCTL command.)

4. Module 1200 edits the order data the operator enters. First, it performs module 1220 ten times to edit each line item. Notice how the PERFORM statement varies the subscript from 10 to 1 by −1. That way, the line items are edited from the bottom up. Module 1220 edits the item number (by performing module 1230 to read the proper inventory record) and the quantity field for each line item. If the data is valid, module 1220 multiplies the quantity by the unit price (from the inventory record) and adds the resulting extension to the invoice total. ON SIZE ERROR clauses ensure the operator doesn't enter

data that will cause an extension field or the invoice total field to exceed its capacity. Then, module 1200 edits the customer-number field to ensure the customer is in the customer file.

5. Module 2210 (format invoice record) gets the data it uses from three sources: (1) the invoice control file, via the subprogram GETINV, (2) the Common Work Area, and (3) the symbolic map.

A LINK command invokes GETINV to retrieve an invoice number from the invoice control file. GETINV returns the number in the communication area specified on the LINK command.

Most of the data module 2210 uses comes from the symbolic map. Because modules 1310 and 1320 set the attribute characters so the MDTs are on, the invoice fields are sent to the program when a verify screen is received. Remember, I can't use the unit-price field in the symbolic map because it's not numeric. That's why I included the unit-price fields in the communication area.

Incidentally, for efficiency reasons, you may object to the way I modify the attributes in modules 1310 through 1340. If I were fine-tuning this program to make it as efficient as possible, I'd probably eliminate these modules altogether. Instead, I'd modify the attribute bytes in module 1300, coding the subscripts as literals, like this:

```
IF SET-PROTECTED
    MOVE FAC-PROT-MDT TO OEM-A-CUSTOMER-NUMBER
                         OEM-A-PO-NUMBER
                         OEM-A-ITEM-NUMBER(1)
                         OEM-A-QUANTITY(1)
                         OEM-A-ITEM-NUMBER(2)
                         OEM-A-QUANTITY(2)

            .
            .
            .
```

and so on. Here, straight-line coding makes the program more efficient. However, the efficiency savings are marginal. So I kept my original design, which more clearly reflects the functional requirements of the program.

```
 IDENTIFICATION DIVISION.
*
 PROGRAM-ID.   ORDRENT.
*AUTHOR.        DOUG LOWE.
*DATE.          OCTOBER 14, 1983.
*NOTES.         THIS PROGRAM ACCEPTS AN ORDER FROM THE OPERATOR
*               AND WRITES IT TO THE INVOICE FILE.
*
 ENVIRONMENT DIVISION.
*
 DATA DIVISION.
*
 WORKING-STORAGE SECTION.
*
 01  SWITCHES.
*
     05   END-SESSION-SW               PIC X   VALUE 'N'.
          88   END-SESSION                     VALUE 'Y'.
     05   VALID-DATA-SW                PIC X   VALUE 'Y'.
          88   VALID-DATA                      VALUE 'Y'.
     05   CUSTOMER-FOUND-SW            PIC X   VALUE 'Y'.
          88   CUSTOMER-FOUND                  VALUE 'Y'.
     05   ITEM-FOUND-SW                PIC X   VALUE 'Y'.
          88   ITEM-FOUND                      VALUE 'Y'.
     05   VALID-QUANTITY-SW            PIC X   VALUE 'Y'.
          88   VALID-QUANTITY                  VALUE 'Y'.
*
 01  FLAGS.
*
     05   ORDER-VERIFICATION-FLAG      PIC X   VALUE '0'.
          88   POST-ORDER                      VALUE '1'.
          88   MODIFY-ORDER                    VALUE '2'.
          88   CANCEL-ORDER                    VALUE '3'.
     05   ATTRIBUTE-CONTROL-FLAG       PIC X   VALUE '0'.
          88   SET-PROTECTED                   VALUE '1'.
          88   SET-UNPROTECTED                 VALUE '2'.
     05   SEND-CONTROL-FLAG            PIC X   VALUE '0'.
          88   SEND-ALL                        VALUE '1'.
          88   SEND-DATAONLY                   VALUE '2'.
*
 01  WORK-FIELDS.
*
     05   LINE-ITEM-SUB                PIC S9(4)      COMP.
     05   LINE-ITEM-COUNT              PIC S9(4)      COMP.
*
 01  TOTAL-LINE.
*
     05   TL-TOTAL-ORDERS     PIC ZZ9.
     05   FILLER              PIC X(15)   VALUE ' ORDERS ENTERED'.
     05   FILLER              PIC X(15)   VALUE '.  PRESS ENTER '.
     05   FILLER              PIC X(15)   VALUE 'TO RETURN TO ME'.
     05   FILLER              PIC X(3)    VALUE 'NU.'.
```

Figure 9-23   Source listing for the order-entry program (part 1 of 10)

```
01   COMMUNICATION-AREA.
*
     05   CA-PROCESS-FLAG            PIC X.
          88   PROCESS-ENTRY-SCREEN    VALUE '1'.
          88   PROCESS-VERIFY-SCREEN   VALUE '2'.
     05   CA-UNIT-PRICE             OCCURS 10
                                    PIC S9(5)V99  COMP-3.
     05   CA-TOTAL-ORDERS           PIC S9(3)     COMP-3
                                    VALUE ZERO.
*
 COPY INVOICE.
*
 COPY CUSTMAST.
*
 COPY INVMAST.
*
 COPY ORDSET1.
*
 COPY FACDEFN.
*
 LINKAGE SECTION.
*
 01   DFHCOMMAREA                   PIC X(43).
*
 01   BLL-CELLS.
*
     05   FILLER                    PIC S9(8)   COMP.
     05   BLL-CWA                   PIC S9(8)   COMP.
*
 01   COMMON-WORK-AREA.
*
     05   CWA-DATE                  PIC 9(6).
*
 PROCEDURE DIVISION.
*
 0000-ACCEPT-CUSTOMER-ORDERS SECTION.
*
     EXEC CICS
         ADDRESS CWA(BLL-CWA)
     END-EXEC.
     IF EIBCALEN = ZERO
         PERFORM 8000-START-TERMINAL-SESSION
     ELSE
         MOVE DFHCOMMAREA TO COMMUNICATION-AREA
         IF PROCESS-ENTRY-SCREEN
             PERFORM 1000-PROCESS-ENTRY-SCREEN
         ELSE IF PROCESS-VERIFY-SCREEN
             PERFORM 2000-PROCESS-VERIFY-SCREEN.
```

Figure 9-23   Source listing for the order-entry program (part 2 of 10)

```
/
        IF END-SESSION
            PERFORM 9000-SEND-TERMINATION-MESSAGE
            EXEC CICS
                RETURN TRANSID('MENU')
            END-EXEC
        ELSE
            EXEC CICS
                RETURN TRANSID('ORD1')
                       COMMAREA(COMMUNICATION-AREA)
                       LENGTH(43)
            END-EXEC.
*
 1000-PROCESS-ENTRY-SCREEN SECTION.
*
        PERFORM 1100-RECEIVE-ENTRY-SCREEN.
        IF NOT END-SESSION
            IF VALID-DATA
                PERFORM 1200-EDIT-ORDER-DATA.
        IF NOT END-SESSION
            IF VALID-DATA
                MOVE 'PRESS ENTER TO POST ORDER, PA1 TO MODIFY ORDER,
                    ' OR CLEAR TO CANCEL ORDER'
                    TO OEM-D-OPERATOR-MESSAGE
                MOVE SPACE TO OEM-D-ERROR-MESSAGE
                MOVE '1' TO ATTRIBUTE-CONTROL-FLAG
                MOVE '2' TO SEND-CONTROL-FLAG
                PERFORM 1300-SEND-ORDER-SCREEN
                MOVE '2' TO CA-PROCESS-FLAG
            ELSE
                MOVE 'ERRORS DETECTED--MAKE CORRECTIONS OR PRESS CLEA
                    'R TO END SESSION' TO OEM-D-OPERATOR-MESSAGE
                MOVE '0' TO ATTRIBUTE-CONTROL-FLAG
                MOVE '2' TO SEND-CONTROL-FLAG
                PERFORM 1300-SEND-ORDER-SCREEN
                MOVE '1' TO CA-PROCESS-FLAG.
*
 1100-RECEIVE-ENTRY-SCREEN SECTION.
*
        EXEC CICS
            HANDLE AID CLEAR(1100-CLEAR-KEY)
                       ANYKEY(1100-ANYKEY)
        END-EXEC.
        EXEC CICS
            RECEIVE MAP('ORDMAP1')
                    MAPSET('ORDSET1')
                    INTO(ORDER-ENTRY-MAP)
        END-EXEC.
        GO TO 1100-EXIT.
*
 1100-CLEAR-KEY.
*
        MOVE 'Y' TO END-SESSION-SW.
        GO TO 1100-EXIT.
```

Figure 9-23   Source listing for the order-entry program (part 3 of 10)

```
/
 1100-ANYKEY.
*
     MOVE LOW-VALUE TO ORDER-ENTRY-MAP.
     MOVE -1 TO OEM-L-CUSTOMER-NUMBER.
     MOVE 'N' TO VALID-DATA-SW.
     MOVE 'INVALID KEY PRESSED' TO OEM-D-ERROR-MESSAGE.
*
 1100-EXIT.
*
     EXIT.
*
 1200-EDIT-ORDER-DATA SECTION.
*
     MOVE FAC-UNPROT-NUM-MDT TO OEM-A-CUSTOMER-NUMBER.
*
     MOVE ZERO TO LINE-ITEM-COUNT
                  INV-INVOICE-TOTAL.
     PERFORM 1220-EDIT-LINE-ITEM
         VARYING LINE-ITEM-SUB FROM 10 BY -1
         UNTIL LINE-ITEM-SUB < 1.
     MOVE INV-INVOICE-TOTAL TO OEM-D-INVOICE-TOTAL.
     IF LINE-ITEM-COUNT = ZERO
         MOVE FAC-UNPROT-NUM-BRT-MDT TO OEM-A-ITEM-NUMBER(1)
         MOVE -1 TO OEM-L-ITEM-NUMBER(1)
         MOVE 'YOU MUST ENTER AT LEAST ONE LINE ITEM'
             TO OEM-D-ERROR-MESSAGE.
*
     IF OEM-L-CUSTOMER-NUMBER = ZERO
         MOVE FAC-UNPROT-NUM-MDT TO OEM-A-CUSTOMER-NUMBER
         MOVE -1 TO OEM-L-CUSTOMER-NUMBER
         MOVE 'YOU MUST ENTER A CUSTOMER NUMBER'
             TO OEM-D-ERROR-MESSAGE
         MOVE SPACE TO OEM-D-NAME
     ELSE
         PERFORM 1210-READ-CUSTOMER-RECORD
         IF CUSTOMER-FOUND
             MOVE CM-NAME TO OEM-D-NAME
         ELSE
             MOVE FAC-UNPROT-NUM-MDT TO OEM-A-CUSTOMER-NUMBER
             MOVE -1 TO OEM-L-CUSTOMER-NUMBER
             MOVE 'CUSTOMER NOT IN FILE' TO OEM-D-ERROR-MESSAGE
             MOVE SPACE TO OEM-D-NAME.
*
     IF OEM-D-ERROR-MESSAGE NOT = LOW-VALUE
         MOVE 'N' TO VALID-DATA-SW.
*
 1210-READ-CUSTOMER-RECORD SECTION.
*
     EXEC CICS
         HANDLE CONDITION NOTFND(1210-NOTFND)
     END-EXEC.
```

Figure 9-23   Source listing for the order-entry program (part 4 of 10)

```
    /
        EXEC CICS
            READ DATASET('CUSTMAST')
                INTO(CUSTOMER-MASTER-RECORD)
                RIDFLD(OEM-D-CUSTOMER-NUMBER)
        END-EXEC.
        GO TO 1210-EXIT.
*
  1210-NOTFND.
*
        MOVE SPACE TO CM-NAME.
        MOVE 'N' TO CUSTOMER-FOUND-SW.
*
  1210-EXIT.
*
        EXIT.
*
  1220-EDIT-LINE-ITEM SECTION.
*
        MOVE 'N' TO ITEM-FOUND-SW.
        MOVE 'Y' TO VALID-QUANTITY-SW.
        MOVE FAC-UNPROT-NUM-MDT TO OEM-A-ITEM-NUMBER(LINE-ITEM-SUB)
                                   OEM-A-QUANTITY(LINE-ITEM-SUB).
*
        IF OEM-L-ITEM-NUMBER(LINE-ITEM-SUB) = ZERO
            IF OEM-L-QUANTITY(LINE-ITEM-SUB) NOT = ZERO
                MOVE FAC-UNPROT-NUM-BRT-MDT
                    TO OEM-A-QUANTITY(LINE-ITEM-SUB)
                MOVE -1 TO OEM-L-QUANTITY(LINE-ITEM-SUB)
                MOVE 'QUANTITY INVALID WITHOUT ITEM NUMBER'
                    TO OEM-D-ERROR-MESSAGE.
*
        IF OEM-L-ITEM-NUMBER(LINE-ITEM-SUB) NOT = ZERO
            IF OEM-L-QUANTITY(LINE-ITEM-SUB) = ZERO
                MOVE 'N' TO VALID-QUANTITY-SW
                MOVE FAC-UNPROT-NUM-BRT-MDT
                    TO OEM-A-QUANTITY(LINE-ITEM-SUB)
                MOVE -1 TO OEM-L-QUANTITY(LINE-ITEM-SUB)
                MOVE 'YOU MUST ENTER A QUANTITY'
                    TO OEM-D-ERROR-MESSAGE
            ELSE IF OEM-D-QUANTITY(LINE-ITEM-SUB) NOT NUMERIC
                MOVE 'N' TO VALID-QUANTITY-SW
                MOVE FAC-UNPROT-NUM-BRT-MDT
                    TO OEM-A-QUANTITY(LINE-ITEM-SUB)
                MOVE -1 TO OEM-L-QUANTITY(LINE-ITEM-SUB)
                MOVE 'QUANTITY MUST BE NUMERIC'
                    TO OEM-D-ERROR-MESSAGE
            ELSE IF OEM-D-QUANTITY(LINE-ITEM-SUB) NOT > ZERO
                MOVE 'N' TO VALID-QUANTITY-SW
                MOVE FAC-UNPROT-NUM-BRT-MDT
                    TO OEM-A-QUANTITY(LINE-ITEM-SUB)
                MOVE -1 TO OEM-L-QUANTITY(LINE-ITEM-SUB)
                MOVE 'QUANTITY MUST BE GREATER THAN ZERO'
                    TO OEM-D-ERROR-MESSAGE.
```

Figure 9-23   Source listing for the order-entry program (part 5 of 10)

```
/
       IF OEM-L-ITEM-NUMBER(LINE-ITEM-SUB) = ZERO
           MOVE SPACE TO OEM-D-ITEM-DESCRIPTION(LINE-ITEM-SUB)
           MOVE ZERO  TO OEM-D-UNIT-PRICE(LINE-ITEM-SUB)
                         OEM-D-EXTENSION(LINE-ITEM-SUB)
       ELSE
           ADD 1 TO LINE-ITEM-COUNT
           PERFORM 1230-READ-INVENTORY-RECORD
           IF ITEM-FOUND
               MOVE IM-ITEM-DESCRIPTION
                   TO OEM-D-ITEM-DESCRIPTION(LINE-ITEM-SUB)
               MOVE IM-UNIT-PRICE
                   TO OEM-D-UNIT-PRICE(LINE-ITEM-SUB)
                      CA-UNIT-PRICE(LINE-ITEM-SUB)
           ELSE
               MOVE SPACE TO OEM-D-ITEM-DESCRIPTION(LINE-ITEM-SUB)
               MOVE ZERO  TO OEM-D-UNIT-PRICE(LINE-ITEM-SUB)
                             OEM-D-EXTENSION(LINE-ITEM-SUB)
               MOVE FAC-UNPROT-NUM-BRT-MDT
                   TO OEM-A-ITEM-NUMBER(LINE-ITEM-SUB)
               MOVE -1 TO OEM-L-ITEM-NUMBER(LINE-ITEM-SUB)
               MOVE 'ITEM NOT IN INVENTORY FILE'
                   TO OEM-D-ERROR-MESSAGE.
*
       IF       ITEM-FOUND
          AND VALID-QUANTITY
           MULTIPLY OEM-D-QUANTITY(LINE-ITEM-SUB)
               BY IM-UNIT-PRICE
               GIVING OEM-D-EXTENSION(LINE-ITEM-SUB)
                      INV-EXTENSION(LINE-ITEM-SUB)
               ON SIZE ERROR
                   MOVE 'N' TO VALID-QUANTITY-SW
                   MOVE ZERO TO OEM-D-EXTENSION(LINE-ITEM-SUB)
                   MOVE FAC-UNPROT-NUM-BRT-MDT
                       TO OEM-A-QUANTITY(LINE-ITEM-SUB)
                   MOVE -1 TO OEM-L-QUANTITY(LINE-ITEM-SUB)
                   MOVE 'QUANTITY TOO LARGE'
                       TO OEM-D-ERROR-MESSAGE.
*
       IF       ITEM-FOUND
          AND VALID-QUANTITY
           ADD INV-EXTENSION(LINE-ITEM-SUB)
               TO INV-INVOICE-TOTAL
               ON SIZE ERROR
                   MOVE 99999.99 TO INV-INVOICE-TOTAL
                   MOVE -1 TO OEM-L-ITEM-NUMBER(1)
                   MOVE 'INVOICE TOTAL TOO LARGE'
                       TO OEM-D-ERROR-MESSAGE.
*
  1230-READ-INVENTORY-RECORD SECTION.
*
       EXEC CICS
           HANDLE CONDITION NOTFND(1230-NOTFND)
       END-EXEC.
```

Figure 9-23   Source listing for the order-entry program (part 6 of 10)

```
/        MOVE 'Y' TO ITEM-FOUND-SW.
         MOVE OEM-D-ITEM-NUMBER(LINE-ITEM-SUB) TO IM-ITEM-NUMBER.
         EXEC CICS
             READ DATASET('INVMAST')
                 INTO(INVENTORY-MASTER-RECORD)
                 RIDFLD(IM-ITEM-NUMBER)
         END-EXEC.
         GO TO 1230-EXIT.
*
     1230-NOTFND.
*
         MOVE SPACE TO IM-ITEM-DESCRIPTION.
         MOVE ZERO  TO IM-UNIT-PRICE.
         MOVE 'N' TO ITEM-FOUND-SW.
*
     1230-EXIT.
*
         EXIT.
*
     1300-SEND-ORDER-SCREEN SECTION.
*
         IF SET-PROTECTED
             PERFORM 1310-SET-ATTRIBUTES
         ELSE IF SET-UNPROTECTED
             PERFORM 1330-RESET-ATTRIBUTES.
         IF SEND-ALL
             EXEC CICS
                 SEND MAP('ORDMAP1')
                     MAPSET('ORDSET1')
                     FROM(ORDER-ENTRY-MAP)
                     ERASE
                     CURSOR
             END-EXEC
         ELSE IF SEND-DATAONLY
             EXEC CICS
                 SEND MAP('ORDMAP1')
                     MAPSET('ORDSET1')
                     FROM(ORDER-ENTRY-MAP)
                     DATAONLY
                     CURSOR
             END-EXEC.
*
     1310-SET-ATTRIBUTES SECTION.
*
         MOVE FAC-PROT-MDT TO OEM-A-CUSTOMER-NUMBER
                             OEM-A-PO-NUMBER.
         PERFORM 1320-SET-LINE-ATTRIBUTES
             VARYING LINE-ITEM-SUB FROM 1 BY 1
             UNTIL LINE-ITEM-SUB > 10.
*
     1320-SET-LINE-ATTRIBUTES SECTION.
*
         MOVE FAC-PROT-MDT TO OEM-A-ITEM-NUMBER(LINE-ITEM-SUB)
                             OEM-A-QUANTITY(LINE-ITEM-SUB).
```

Figure 9-23 Source listing for the order-entry program (part 7 of 10)

```
/
 1330-RESET-ATTRIBUTES SECTION.
*
     MOVE FAC-UNPROT-MDT TO OEM-A-CUSTOMER-NUMBER
                            OEM-A-PO-NUMBER.
     PERFORM 1340-RESET-LINE-ATTRIBUTES
         VARYING LINE-ITEM-SUB FROM 1 BY 1
         UNTIL LINE-ITEM-SUB > 10.
*
 1340-RESET-LINE-ATTRIBUTES SECTION.
*
     MOVE FAC-UNPROT-NUM-MDT TO OEM-A-ITEM-NUMBER(LINE-ITEM-SUB)
                               OEM-A-QUANTITY(LINE-ITEM-SUB).
*
 2000-PROCESS-VERIFY-SCREEN SECTION.
*
     PERFORM 2100-RECEIVE-VERIFY-SCREEN.
     IF POST-ORDER
         PERFORM 2200-POST-ORDER-DATA
         MOVE LOW-VALUE TO ORDER-ENTRY-MAP
         MOVE -1 TO OEM-L-CUSTOMER-NUMBER
         MOVE 'ORDER POSTED--ENTER NEXT ORDER OR PRESS CLEAR TO EN
               'D SESSION' TO OEM-D-OPERATOR-MESSAGE
         MOVE '0' TO ATTRIBUTE-CONTROL-FLAG
         MOVE '1' TO SEND-CONTROL-FLAG
         PERFORM 1300-SEND-ORDER-SCREEN
         MOVE '1' TO CA-PROCESS-FLAG
     ELSE IF MODIFY-ORDER
         MOVE LOW-VALUE TO ORDER-ENTRY-MAP
         MOVE -1 TO OEM-L-CUSTOMER-NUMBER
         MOVE 'ENTER MODIFICATIONS OR PRESS CLEAR TO END SESSION'
              TO OEM-D-OPERATOR-MESSAGE
         MOVE '2' TO ATTRIBUTE-CONTROL-FLAG
         MOVE '2' TO SEND-CONTROL-FLAG
         PERFORM 1300-SEND-ORDER-SCREEN
         MOVE '1' TO CA-PROCESS-FLAG
     ELSE IF CANCEL-ORDER
         MOVE LOW-VALUE TO ORDER-ENTRY-MAP
         MOVE -1 TO OEM-L-CUSTOMER-NUMBER
         MOVE 'ORDER CANCELLED--ENTER NEXT ORDER OR PRESS CLEAR TO
              ' END SESSION' TO OEM-D-OPERATOR-MESSAGE
         MOVE '0' TO ATTRIBUTE-CONTROL-FLAG
         MOVE '1' TO SEND-CONTROL-FLAG
         PERFORM 1300-SEND-ORDER-SCREEN
         MOVE '1' TO CA-PROCESS-FLAG
     ELSE
         MOVE LOW-VALUE TO ORDER-ENTRY-MAP
         MOVE 'PRESS ENTER TO POST ORDER, PA1 TO MODIFY ORDER, OR
              'CLEAR TO CANCEL ORDER' TO OEM-D-OPERATOR-MESSAGE
         MOVE 'INVALID KEY PRESSED' TO OEM-D-ERROR-MESSAGE
         MOVE '0' TO ATTRIBUTE-CONTROL-FLAG
         MOVE '2' TO SEND-CONTROL-FLAG
         PERFORM 1300-SEND-ORDER-SCREEN
         MOVE '2' TO CA-PROCESS-FLAG.
```

Figure 9-23   Source listing for the order-entry program (part 8 of 10)

```
/
 2100-RECEIVE-VERIFY-SCREEN SECTION.
*
     EXEC CICS
         HANDLE AID PA1(2100-PA1-KEY)
                    CLEAR(2100-CLEAR-KEY)
                    ANYKEY(2100-ANYKEY)
     END-EXEC.
     MOVE '1' TO ORDER-VERIFICATION-FLAG.
     EXEC CICS
         RECEIVE MAP('ORDMAP1')
                 MAPSET('ORDSET1')
                 INTO(ORDER-ENTRY-MAP)
     END-EXEC.
     GO TO 2100-EXIT.
*
 2100-PA1-KEY.
*
     MOVE '2' TO ORDER-VERIFICATION-FLAG.
     GO TO 2100-EXIT.
*
 2100-CLEAR-KEY.
*
     MOVE '3' TO ORDER-VERIFICATION-FLAG.
     GO TO 2100-EXIT.
*
 2100-ANYKEY.
*
     MOVE '0' TO ORDER-VERIFICATION-FLAG.
*
 2100-EXIT.
*
     EXIT.
*
 2200-POST-ORDER-DATA SECTION.
*
     PERFORM 2210-FORMAT-INVOICE-RECORD.
     PERFORM 2230-WRITE-INVOICE-RECORD.
     ADD 1 TO CA-TOTAL-ORDERS.
*
 2210-FORMAT-INVOICE-RECORD SECTION.
*
     EXEC CICS
         LINK PROGRAM('GETINV')
              COMMAREA(INV-INVOICE-NUMBER)
              LENGTH(5)
     END-EXEC.
     MOVE OEM-D-CUSTOMER-NUMBER TO INV-CUSTOMER-NUMBER.
     MOVE OEM-D-PO-NUMBER       TO INV-PO-NUMBER.
     MOVE CWA-DATE              TO INV-INVOICE-DATE.
     MOVE ZERO TO INV-INVOICE-TOTAL.
```

Figure 9-23   Source listing for the order-entry program (part 9 of 10)

```
/
      PERFORM 2220-FORMAT-LINE-ITEM
          VARYING LINE-ITEM-SUB FROM 1 BY 1
          UNTIL LINE-ITEM-SUB > 10.
*
 2220-FORMAT-LINE-ITEM SECTION.
*
      IF OEM-L-ITEM-NUMBER(LINE-ITEM-SUB) = ZERO
          MOVE ZERO TO INV-ITEM-NUMBER(LINE-ITEM-SUB)
                       INV-QUANTITY(LINE-ITEM-SUB)
                       INV-UNIT-PRICE(LINE-ITEM-SUB)
                       INV-EXTENSION(LINE-ITEM-SUB)
      ELSE
          MOVE OEM-D-ITEM-NUMBER(LINE-ITEM-SUB)
              TO INV-ITEM-NUMBER(LINE-ITEM-SUB)
          MOVE OEM-D-QUANTITY(LINE-ITEM-SUB)
              TO INV-QUANTITY(LINE-ITEM-SUB)
          MOVE CA-UNIT-PRICE(LINE-ITEM-SUB)
              TO INV-UNIT-PRICE(LINE-ITEM-SUB)
          COMPUTE INV-EXTENSION(LINE-ITEM-SUB)=
                  INV-QUANTITY(LINE-ITEM-SUB) *
                  INV-UNIT-PRICE(LINE-ITEM-SUB)
          ADD INV-EXTENSION(LINE-ITEM-SUB) TO INV-INVOICE-TOTAL.
*
 2230-WRITE-INVOICE-RECORD SECTION.
*
      EXEC CICS
          WRITE DATASET('INVOICE')
                FROM(INVOICE-RECORD)
                RIDFLD(INV-INVOICE-NUMBER)
      END-EXEC.
*
 8000-START-TERMINAL-SESSION SECTION.
*
      MOVE LOW-VALUE TO ORDER-ENTRY-MAP.
      MOVE -1 TO OEM-L-CUSTOMER-NUMBER.
      MOVE 'PRESS CLEAR TO END SESSION' TO OEM-D-OPERATOR-MESSAGE.
      MOVE '0' TO ATTRIBUTE-CONTROL-FLAG.
      MOVE '1' TO SEND-CONTROL-FLAG.
      PERFORM 1300-SEND-ORDER-SCREEN.
      MOVE '1' TO CA-PROCESS-FLAG.
*
 9000-SEND-TERMINATION-MESSAGE SECTION.
*
      MOVE CA-TOTAL-ORDERS TO TL-TOTAL-ORDERS.
      EXEC CICS
          SEND TEXT FROM(TOTAL-LINE)
                    LENGTH(51)
                    ERASE
                    FREEKB
      END-EXEC.
```

Figure 9-23   Source listing for the order-entry program (part 10 of 10)

```
    IDENTIFICATION DIVISION.
*
   PROGRAM-ID.   GETINV.
*AUTHOR.         DOUG LOWE.
*DATE.           OCTOBER 14, 1983.
*NOTES.          THIS PROGRAM RETURNS AN INVOICE NUMBER VIA DFHCOMMAREA.
*                THE VALUE IN INVCTL IS INCREMENTED BY 1.
*
   ENVIRONMENT DIVISION.
*
   DATA DIVISION.
*
   WORKING-STORAGE SECTION.
*
   01   INVCTL-RECORD.
*
        05   IR-RECORD-KEY            PIC X      VALUE '0'.
        05   IR-NEXT-INVOICE-NUMBER   PIC 9(5).
*
   LINKAGE SECTION.
*
   01   DFHCOMMAREA                   PIC 9(5).
*
   PROCEDURE DIVISION.
*
   000-GET-INVOICE-NUMBER SECTION.
*
        EXEC CICS
            READ DATASET('INVCTL')
                 INTO(INVCTL-RECORD)
                 RIDFLD(IR-RECORD-KEY)
                 UPDATE
        END-EXEC.
        MOVE IR-NEXT-INVOICE-NUMBER TO DFHCOMMAREA.
        ADD 1 TO IR-NEXT-INVOICE-NUMBER.
        EXEC CICS
            REWRITE DATASET('INVCTL')
                    FROM(INVCTL-RECORD)
        END-EXEC.
        EXEC CICS
            RETURN
        END-EXEC.
```

Figure 9-24   Source listing for the GETINV subprogram

The GETINV subprogram

Figure 9-24 shows the source listing for the GETINV subprogram.
As you can see, this program simply reads a record from the invoice
control file, moves the invoice number to the communication area,
adds 1 to the invoice number in the invoice control record, and

rewrites the record. By using this subprogram, the order-entry program produces invoices with ascending invoice numbers, even if several users are entering orders at once.

Discussion

As I said at the beginning of this topic, you shouldn't feel overwhelmed if you don't understand all of these programs the first few times you read them. CICS is complicated, and you need to understand many concepts before you can use any of them. Even so, as you apply the CICS commands and the programming and design techniques these programs illustrate, you'll come to feel more and more comfortable with CICS.

Objective

Given specifications for a CICS program using the features this book presents, code it using the model programs in this chapter as guides.

Chapter 10

Testing and debugging

In this chapter, I present some useful techniques for testing and
debugging CICS programs. This chapter has two topics. The first
explains the process of testing a CICS program, and the second
covers debugging techniques.

Topic 1   Testing a CICS program

One of the major pitfalls of program development is inadequate testing. All too often, programs aren't tried on enough combinations of input data to be sure all of their routines work, but they're put into production anyway. Then, when a program produces inaccurate results or simply fails, a crisis can occur. It's your responsibility as a programmer to develop programs that work properly. As a result, you've got to take testing seriously.

The test plan

To prepare to test your program, you should develop a *test plan*. The test plan is a strategy you'll follow when you test your program. Since the burden of proof is on the programmer, you should prepare the test plan carefully.

To begin the test plan, analyze your program's structure chart and code. Consider each module, one at a time, and decide what conditions must be tested for each. If your test data accounts for all of the conditions you identify, you can feel sure your program will be tested adequately. Figure 10-1 is a list of conditions that I developed for the order-entry program in chapter 9. It gives all of the conditions that should be tested for the critical modules of the program. Making a list like this can be a laborious job if a program is large and has many modules. However, it's the most systematic way to insure your testing will be adequate.

After you've listed the conditions to test, you need to decide in what sequence you'll test them. Your intent here is to discover major problems first. For example, you shouldn't start by testing to see if the customer-number field is edited properly. Instead, start by testing to see if the major modules are executed in the proper sequence.

In general, your test plan should have three steps. First, you should test the major modules of the program using only valid data; that is, don't test for error conditions. Second, you should test independent error conditions one at a time. And third, you should test combinations of error conditions to see if one error has an effect on another. In general, the first two steps are fairly easy to manage. It's the third one that becomes complicated and is often done inadequately.

Module	Error condition
0000	Does the pseudo-conversational logic work properly? Are modules 8000 and 9000 executed at the right time? Are modules 1000 and 2000 executed at the right time? Is the CWA addressed properly?
1000	Does the end-session test work? Are the switches for the SEND module set properly?
1100	Are all AID keys handled correctly? What if no data is entered? What if the map doesn't exist?
1200	Are all invalid fields tested and marked accordingly? What if there are no line items? Does the customer lookup routine work properly?
1210	What if the file isn't open or doesn't exist? Does the NOTFND condition work properly?
1220	Same ideas as 1200 plus: If data is invalid, are all computations bypassed? What if computations exceed field sizes?
1230	Same ideas as 1210.
1300	Is the correct screen sent? Are the SEND statements executed with the best selection of options? Are the attributes properly set for all fields?
2000	Are the switches for the SEND module set properly? Is the communication area process flag set properly?

Figure 10-1   Possible error conditions for the order-entry program (part 1 of 2)

Module	Error condition
2100	
	Same ideas as 1100.
2200	
	Is the control total accumulated properly?
2210	
	Are all fields formatted properly?
	Does the LINK to GETINV work?
	Are line items that weren't entered set to hexadecimal zeros?
2220	
	Same ideas as 2210.
2230	
	What if the file isn't open?
	What if there's a duplicate key?
	What if the file doesn't have a null record?

Figure 10-1   Possible error conditions for the order-entry program (part 2 of 2)

Figure 10-2 gives a test plan for the order-entry program. Although it's limited, it gives you an idea of what a test plan looks like. This plan proceeds in the three steps I just described.

The test data

Too often, test data is created without a test plan. Is it any wonder, then, that programs are often put into production with dozens, even hundreds, of bugs and that bugs often appear years later? In contrast, you should create test data based on your test plan and determine exactly what output to expect. After your program proves itself on the data you created, you can feel confident it's bug-free.

I suggest you limit the test data for the early phases of testing to just a few transactions. That way, it won't be difficult to determine the expected output. For example, in the plan for the order-entry program in figure 10-2, three orders are enough for the first step.

Test phase	Data
1. Valid transactions	Three orders, each with valid data; one with a single line item, another with two or three line items, and the third with ten line items.
2. Single errors	Invalid orders with data that will test all edits for each field.
3. Combined errors	Invalid orders with data that test edits in combination.

Figure 10-2 Test plan for the order-entry program

What to look for when you test your program

Figure 10-3 summarizes some of the common programming errors you should look for as you test a program. Naturally, the first thing you should do when you run a program is examine the screens carefully. Are the screens defined properly? Are all attribute bytes properly set? Does the cursor move from field to field as it should?

Next, begin your test using the test plan you've created. As you enter valid data, single errors, and errors in combination, make sure your program performs properly. Keep a list of errors you find so you'll remember to correct them.

The general idea when testing an interactive program is to do your best to make the program fail. If you try everything you can think of and the program still functions properly, it's probably correct.

Top-down testing

One of the problems with testing a program is that it may contain dozens of bugs the first time it's run. As a result, it's often impossible to isolate each problem the first time around, so several test runs may be necessary. The purpose of *top-down testing* is to simplify each run by reducing the amount of code tested during each.

When you use top-down testing, you don't code the entire program and then test it. Instead, you code and test in phases. You normally start by coding and testing the level-0 and level-1 modules. Then, after correcting any bugs, you add one or more mod-

---

What to check for as you examine the appearance of the screen:

> Are all headings and captions placed correctly?
> Is there any garbage on the screen?
> Are there any misspellings?
> Do all the fields have the correct attributes?
> Is the cursor in the correct initial location?
> Does the cursor move correctly from field to field?

What to check for as you enter valid data:

> Are all program screens displayed in the correct sequence?
> Do all AID keys work correctly?
> Are the operator messages always correct?
> Are the functions of all AID keys shown?
> Does the program properly acknowledge receipt of valid data?
> Are work fields properly cleared after each valid transaction?
> Are control totals accumulated properly?
> Are files updated properly?

What to check for as you enter single errors:

> Does each case of invalid data for each field yield a correct error message?
> Do lookup routines work properly?
> Is the field in error highlighted?
> Is the cursor positioned at the field in error?
> When you correct the error, does the error message go away?
> Does the program post transactions even though errors are detected?

What to check for as you enter compound errors:

> Are all errors detected, or does the program stop after the first?
> Is the cursor positioned under the first field in error, and is the corresponding error message displayed?
> Are all errors highlighted?

Figure 10-3   What to check for when you test a program

ules and test again. You continue until all of the modules have been coded and you've tested the entire program. Because top-down coding and testing always go together, the term top-down testing implies top-down coding as well.

To illustrate, consider the first phase of coding for the order-entry program shown in figure 10-4. Rather than test all the modules at once, I decided to code and test only the level-0, level-1,

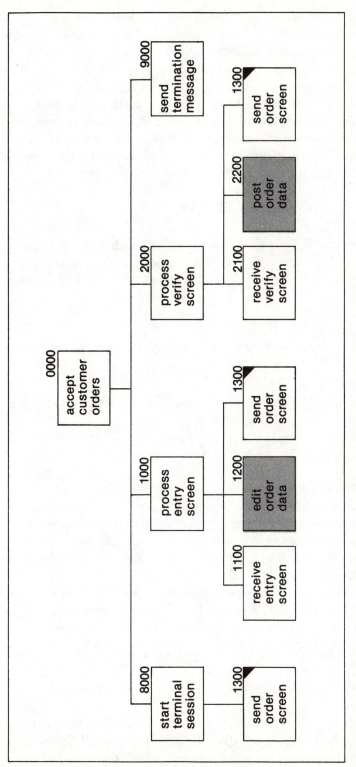

Figure 10-4 First phase of coding and testing for the order-entry program

and simple level-2 modules (the RECEIVE and SEND modules). Once I've tested and debugged these modules, I'll add the edit and post modules, probably one at a time.

To use top-down testing, you must code *program stubs* for all modules called by the modules being tested. In figure 10-4, for example, modules 1200 and 2200 are program stubs for the first phase of testing. The coding for a program stub is brief. It does the minimum amount of work necessary for the calling module to continue. For example, the program stub for module 1200 might contain a single MOVE statement, like this:

```
MOVE 'Y' TO VALID-DATA-SW.
```

In other words, the edit module always indicates that the data is valid, whether it is or not. If you need to know when a stub is executed as you test your program, you can insert a SEND TEXT command, like this:

```
EXEC CICS
    SEND TEXT FROM(STUB-2200-MESSAGE)
END-EXEC.
```

where STUB-2200-MESSAGE is the name of a working storage field containing an appropriate message.

Discussion

The benefits of structured programming are perhaps most obvious during testing. Because a structured program consists of independent modules, it's almost sure to have fewer bugs than an unstructured program. In addition, the bugs that do exist will probably be easier to isolate and correct.

Furthermore, if you use top-down testing, you'll gain the advantage of isolating major bugs early. In general, bugs at a higher level in the structure chart are more serious than those at lower levels. By coding and testing the higher-level modules first, you'll find and correct the serious errors first.

Terminology

test plan
top-down testing
program stub

Objective

Given the specifications and design for a CICS program, create an
appropriate top-down test plan and complete test data.

Topic 2   Debugging a CICS abend

When a CICS program encounters an invalid condition during its execution, it ends in an *abnormal termination*, or *abend*. This topic presents two common techniques for finding the cause of an abend: (1) using an IBM-supplied debugging aid called the Execution Diagnostics Facility, or EDF, and (2) interpreting the storage dump that results from the abend. Before I can show you these techniques, you need to know two things: the two most commonly encountered conditions that lead to an abend, and the compiler output used for debugging.

Abend codes

When a CICS program terminates abnormally, an *abnormal termination message* (or just *abend message*) is sent to the terminal. Figure 10-5 shows a typical abend message. Here, the transaction MOR1 was running the program MORCAL1 when the abend occurred. Each type of CICS abend has its own *abend code*; in this case, the abend code is ASRA. The "AT H400" indicates that the task was running at the terminal named H400. Almost always, it's the abend code that gives you the information you need to begin debugging your program.

IBM's *CICS Messages and Codes* manual documents the more than 300 possible abend codes. Fortunately, you only need to know a few, and they fall into just two categories: exceptional condition abends and program check abends.

Exceptional condition abends   As you know, when a CICS exceptional condition (such as NOTFND) occurs and the program doesn't include a HANDLE CONDITION command for the condition, the task is terminated. Then, CICS displays an abend code that identifies the exceptional condition that caused the abend.

Figure 10-6 lists these codes. As you can see, all of the abend codes for exceptional conditions begin with the letters AEI or AEY. So when you encounter one of these codes, you can refer to this list to see which condition was raised. The shaded codes in figure 10-6 represent exceptional conditions that the CICS commands in this book can raise.

```
DFH006I TRANSACTION MOR1 PROGRAM MORCAL1   ABEND ASRA AT H400
```

Figure 10-5   CICS transaction abend message

Usually, an exceptional condition abend is caused by a programming error. For example, if you forget to code a HANDLE CONDITION command for the NOTFND condition, your program will abend with code AEIM if it tries to read a record that doesn't exist. Similarly, if you execute a REWRITE command without first executing a READ/UPDATE command, your program will abend with code AEIP.

In some cases, an exceptional condition is caused by a problem outside of your program. For example, if you try to write a record to a file that's specified in the FCT as read-only, your program abends with code AEIP. Here, the problem is probably in the FCT entry, not your program.

Program check abends   When a program tries to perform an invalid machine operation, a *program check* occurs. For example, trying to perform an arithmetic operation on non-numeric data results in a *data exception* program check. A program check always causes your program to abend with the code ASRA. As a result, ASRA is the abend code you'll probably see most often. Fifteen different types of program checks can occur on a System/370. The technique you use to find out which program check occurred depends on whether you're using EDF or a storage dump, as I'll explain later.

Compiler output used for debugging

Whether you use the Execution Diagnostics Facility or a CICS storage dump to debug an abend, you need two pieces of compiler output in addition to the source listing: the Data Division Map (DMAP) and the Condensed Procedure Listing (CLIST). To get this output, you must specify the DMAP and CLIST options for the compiler (*not* the translator). You can use the Procedure Map (PMAP) rather than the CLIST, but it's more cumbersome. So I recommend you use the CLIST instead.

Code	Condition	Code	Condition
AEIA	ERROR	AEI9	MAPFAIL
AEID	EOF	AEYA	INVERRTERM
AEIE	EODS	AEYB	INVMPSZ
AEIG	INBFMH	AEYC	IGREQID
AEIH	ENDINPT	AEYE	INVLDC
AEII	NONVAL	AEYG	JIDERR
AEIJ	NOSTART	AEYH	QIDERR
AEIK	TERMIDERR	AEYJ	DSSTAT
AEIL	DSIDERR	AEYK	SELNERR
AEIM	NOTFND	AEYL	FUNCERR
AEIN	DUPREC	AEYM	UNEXPIN
AEIO	DUPKEY	AEYN	NOPASSBKRD
AEIP	INVREQ	AEYO	NOPASSBKWR
AEIQ	IOERR	AEYP	SEGIDERR
AEIR	NOSPACE	AEYQ	SYSIDERR
AEIS	NOTOPEN	AEYR	ISINVREQ
AEIT	ENDFILE	AEYT	ENVDEFERR
AEIU	ILLOGIC	AEYU	IGREQCD
AEIV	LENGERR	AEYV	SESSERR
AEIW	QZERO	AEYY	NOTALLOC
AEIZ	ITEMERR	AEYZ	CBIDERR
AEIO	PGMIDERR	AEYO	INVEXITREQ
AEI1	TRANSIDERR	AEY1	INVPARTNSET
AEI2	ENDDATA	AEY2	INVPARTN
AEI3	INVTSREQ	AEY3	PARTNFAIL
AEI8	TSIOERR		

Figure 10-6 Transaction abend codes for exceptional conditions

Figure 10-7 presents the compiler output for a version of the mortgage-calculation program presented in chapter 6 that contains a bug. The compiler's source listing is contained in the first six parts of figure 10-7. I included it here because other debugging documents refer to the statement numbers in the compiler's source listing.

After the source listing, part 7 of figure 10-7 presents the first page of the DMAP for the mortgage-calculation program. The DMAP lists the characteristics of each data field defined in your program. Here, the entry for MCM-D-INTEREST-RATE is shaded. The only items in the DMAP you need to be concerned with are the base locator, found in the BASE column, and the displacement, found in the DISPL column. You use these items to determine the address of a field in working storage.

BASE specifies a *base locator* you use to calculate the address of a field. A base locator is one of the system's general registers. To determine which register is assigned to a base locator, you use the REGISTER ASSIGNMENT output, which follows the DMAP and is shown in part 8 of figure 10-7. Here, you can see that base locator 1 is assigned to general register 6.

To determine the address of a field in working storage, you add the field's displacement (shown in the DISPL column of the DMAP) to the value contained in the field's base locator register. You'll see how this works later in this topic.

Part 9 of figure 10-7 shows the CLIST for the mortgage-calculation program. For each executable statement in the Procedure Division, the CLIST shows three things: the statement number, the verb name, and the statement's offset from the beginning of the Procedure Division. The offset indicates the position of the first machine-language instruction generated for the statement. For example, the shaded portion in part 9 of figure 10-7 indicates that the first instruction generated for statement 303, a COMPUTE statement, begins at location DFA (the offset is in hexadecimal). You use the CLIST primarily to find out which statement is executing when an abend occurs.

The Execution Diagnostics Facility

The *Execution Diagnostics Facility*, or *EDF*, is an interactive debugging tool that lets you trace the progress of a program as it executes. To illustrate how EDF is used, I'll present several screens from a debugging session for the mortgage-calculation program.

You can use EDF in two ways. To use EDF for *same-terminal checkout*, you enter the transaction identifier CEDF at your terminal. When CICS responds with this message:

```
THIS TERMINAL: EDF MODE ON
```

you enter the trans-id for the program you want to debug. Then, your terminal alternates between screens displayed by your program and screens displayed by EDF.

```
PP 5740-CB¹ RELEASE 2.3 + PTF 8 - UP13477           IBM OS/VS COBOL  JULY 24, 1978


   1                        14.45.40      OCT 18,1983


00001    010000 IDENTIFICATION DIVISION.
00002    010100*
00003    010200 PROGRAM-ID.  MORCAL1.
00004    010300*AUTHOR.      DOUG LOWE.
00005    010400*DATE.        MAY 10, 1983.
00006    010500*NOTES.       THIS PROGRAM CALCULATES MONTHLY MORTGAGE PAYMENTS
00007    010600*             BASED ON PRINCIPAL AMOUNT, NO. OF YEARS, AND
00008    010700*             INTEREST RATE ENTERED BY THE OPERATOR.
00009    010800*
00010    010900 ENVIRONMENT DIVISION.
00011    011000*
00012    011100 DATA DIVISION.
00013    011200*
00014    011300 WORKING-STORAGE SECTION.
00015    011400*
00016    011500 01  SWITCHES.
00017    011600*
00018    011700     05  END-SESSION-SW            PIC X         VALUE 'N'.
00019    011800         88  END-SESSION                         VALUE 'Y'.
00020    011900     05  VALID-DATA-SW             PIC X         VALUE 'Y'.
00021    012000         88  VALID-DATA                          VALUE 'Y'.
00022    012500*
00023    012600 01  END-OF-SESSION-MESSAGE        PIC X(13)
00024    012700                                   VALUE 'SESSION ENDED'.
00025    012710*
00026    012800 01  COMMUNICATION-AREA            PIC X.
00027    013200*
00028    013300 COPY MORSET1.
00029  C*000010 01  MORTGAGE-CALCULATION-MAP.
00030  C 000020*
00031  C 000023     05  FILLER                    PIC X(12).
00032  C 000026*
00033  C 000030     05  MCM-L-PRINCIPAL-AMOUNT    PIC S9(4)    COMP.
00034  C 000040     05  MCM-A-PRINCIPAL-AMOUNT    PIC X.
00035  C 000050     05  MCM-D-PRINCIPAL-AMOUNT    PIC 9(6)V99.
00036  C 000060*
00037  C 000070     05  MCM-L-NO-OF-YEARS         PIC S9(4)    COMP.
00038  C 000071     05  MCM-A-NO-OF-YEARS         PIC X.
00039  C 000072     05  MCM-D-NO-OF-YEARS         PIC 99.
00040  C 000073*
00041  C 000074     05  MCM-L-INTEREST-RATE       PIC S9(4)    COMP.
00042  C 000075     05  MCM-A-INTEREST-RATE       PIC X.
00043  C 000076     05  MCM-D-INTEREST-RATE       PIC V9(4).
00044  C 000077*
00045  C 000078     05  MCM-L-MONTHLY-PAYMENT     PIC S9(4)    COMP.
00046  C 000079     05  MCM-A-MONTHLY-PAYMENT     PIC X.
00047  C 000080     05  MCM-D-MONTHLY-PAYMENT     PIC ZZ,ZZ9.99.
00048  C 000081*
00049  C 000082     05  MCM-L-OPERATOR-MESSAGE    PIC S9(4)    COMP.
00050  C 000083     05  MCM-A-OPERATOR-MESSAGE    PIC X.
00051  C 000084     05  MCM-D-OPERATOR-MESSAGE    PIC X(79).
00052  C 000085*
00053  C 000086     05  MCM-L-ERROR-MESSAGE       PIC S9(4)    COMP.
00054  C 000087     05  MCM-A-ERROR-MESSAGE       PIC X.
00055  C 000088     05  MCM-D-ERROR-MESSAGE       PIC X(77).
00056  C 000089*
```

Figure 10-7   Compiler output for the mortgage-calculation program (part 1 of 9)

```
 2                        14.45.40        OCT 18,1983

00057 C 000090      05   MCM-L-DUMMY                PIC S9(4)    COMP.
00058 C 000091      05   MCM-A-DUMMY                PIC X.
00059 C 000092      05   MCM-D-DUMMY                PIC X.
00060 C 000093*
00061   013400*
00062   013410 COPY FACDEFN.
00063 C*000010 01  FIELD-ATTRIBUTE-DEFINITIONS.
00064 C 000020*
00065 C 000030      05   FAC-UNPROT                 PIC X     VALUE ' '.
00066 C 000040      05   FAC-UNPROT-MDT             PIC X     VALUE 'A'.
00067 C 000070      05   FAC-UNPROT-BRT             PIC X     VALUE 'H'.
00068 C 000080      05   FAC-UNPROT-BRT-MDT         PIC X     VALUE 'I'.
00069 C 000090      05   FAC-UNPROT-DARK            PIC X     VALUE '<'.
00070 C 000100      05   FAC-UNPROT-DARK-MDT        PIC X     VALUE '('.
00071 C 000110      05   FAC-UNPROT-NUM             PIC X     VALUE '8'.
00072 C 000120      05   FAC-UNPROT-NUM-MDT         PIC X     VALUE 'J'.
00073 C 000150      05   FAC-UNPROT-NUM-BRT         PIC X     VALUE 'Q'.
00074 C 000160      05   FAC-UNPROT-NUM-BRT-MDT     PIC X     VALUE 'R'.
00075 C 000170      05   FAC-UNPROT-NUM-DARK        PIC X     VALUE '*'.
00076 C 000180      05   FAC-UNPROT-NUM-DARK-MDT    PIC X     VALUE ')'.
00077 C 000190      05   FAC-PROT                   PIC X     VALUE '-'.
00078 C 000191      05   FAC-PROT-MDT               PIC X     VALUE '/'.
00079 C 000194      05   FAC-PROT-BRT               PIC X     VALUE 'Y'.
00080 C 000195      05   FAC-PROT-BRT-MDT           PIC X     VALUE 'Z'.
00081 C 000196      05   FAC-PROT-DARK              PIC X     VALUE '%'.
00082 C 000197      05   FAC-PROT-DARK-MDT          PIC X     VALUE ']'.
00083 C 000198      05   FAC-PROT-SKIP              PIC X     VALUE '0'.
00084 C 000199      05   FAC-PROT-SKIP-MDT          PIC X     VALUE '1'.
00085 C 000202      05   FAC-PROT-SKIP-BRT          PIC X     VALUE '8'.
00086 C 000203      05   FAC-PROT-SKIP-BRT-MDT      PIC X     VALUE '9'.
00087 C 000204      05   FAC-PROT-SKIP-DARK         PIC X     VALUE 'a'.
00088 C 000205      05   FAC-PROT-SKIP-DARK-MDT     PIC X     VALUE QUOTE.
00089   013420*
00090           01   DFHLDVER PIC X(22) VALUE 'LD TABLE DFHEITAB 1.6 '.
00091           01   DFHEIDO PICTURE S9(7) COMPUTATIONAL-3 VALUE ZERO.
00092           01   DFHEIBO PICTURE S9(4) COMPUTATIONAL VALUE ZERO.
00093           01   DFHEICB  PICTURE X(8) VALUE IS '        '.
00094
00095           01   DFHEIV16   COMP PIC S9(8).
00096           01   DFHEIV11   COMP PIC S9(4).
00097           01   DFHEIV12   COMP PIC S9(4).
00098           01   DFHEIV13   COMP PIC S9(4).
00099           01   DFHEIV14   COMP PIC S9(4).
00100           01   DFHEIV15   COMP PIC S9(4).
00101           01   DFHB0025   COMP PIC S9(4).
00102           01   DFHEIV5    PIC X(4).
00103           01   DFHEIV6    PIC X(4).
00104           01   DFHEIV17   PIC X(4).
00105           01   DFHEIV18   PIC X(4).
00106           01   DFHEIV19   PIC X(4).
00107           01   DFHEIV1    PIC X(8).
00108           01   DFHEIV2    PIC X(8).
00109           01   DFHEIV3    PIC X(8).
00110           01   DFHEIV20   PIC X(8).
00111           01   DFHC0084   PIC X(8).
00112           01   DFHC0085   PIC X(8).
00113           01   DFHC0320   PIC X(32).
00114           01   DFHEIV9    PIC X(1).
00115           01   DFHEIV10   PIC S9(7) COMP-3.
```

Figure 10-7   Compiler output for the mortgage-calculation program (part 2 of 9)

```
   3                        14.45.40        OCT 18,1983

00116          01    DFHEIV4   PIC X(6).
00117          01    DFHEIV7   PIC X(2).
00118          01    DFHEIV8   PIC X(2).
00119          01    DFHC0022  PIC X(2).
00120          01    DFHC0023  PIC X(2).
00121          01    DFHC0070  PIC X(7).
00122          01    DFHC0071  PIC X(7).
00123          01    DFHDUMMY COMP PIC S9(4).
00124          01    DFHEIV0  PICTURE X(29).
00125    013500 LINKAGE SECTION.
00126    013600*
00127          01    DFHEIBLK.
00128          02     EIBTIME  PIC S9(7) COMP-3.
00129          02     EIBDATE  PIC S9(7) COMP-3.
00130          02     EIBTRNID PIC X(4).
00131          02     EIBTASKN PIC S9(7) COMP-3.
00132          02     EIBTRMID PIC X(4).
00133          02     DFHEIGDI COMP PIC S9(4).
00134          02     EIBCPOSN COMP PIC S9(4).
00135          02     EIBCALEN COMP PIC S9(4).
00136          02     EIBAID   PIC X(1).
00137          02     EIBFN    PIC X(2).
00138          02     EIBRCODE PIC X(6).
00139          02     EIBDS    PIC X(8).
00140          02     EIBREQID PIC X(8).
00141          02     EIBRSRCE PIC X(8).
00142          02     EIBSYNC  PIC X(1).
00143          02     EIBFREE  PIC X(1).
00144          02     EIBRECV  PIC X(1).
00145          02     EIBFIL02 PIC X(1).
00146          02     EIBATT   PIC X(1).
00147          02     EIBEOC   PIC X(1).
00148          02     EIBFMH   PIC X(1).
00149          02     EIBCOMPL PIC X(1).
00150          02     EIBSIG   PIC X(1).
00151          02     EIBCONF  PIC X(1).
00152          02     EIBERR   PIC X(1).
00153          02     EIBERRCD PIC X(4).
00154          02     EIBSYNRB PIC X(1).
00155          02     EIBNODAT PIC X(1).
00156    013700 01  DFHCOMMAREA                    PIC X.
00157    013800*
00158          01    DFHBLLSLOT1 PICTURE X(1).
00159          01    DFHBLLSLOT2 PICTURE X(1).
00160    013900 PROCEDURE DIVISION USING DFHEIBLK DFHCOMMAREA.
00161              SERVICE RELOAD DFHEIBLK.
00162              SERVICE RELOAD DFHCOMMAREA.
00163    014000*
00164    014100 000-DETERMINE-MONTHLY-PAYMENTS SECTION.
00165    014200*
00166    014300     IF EIBCALEN = ZERO
00167    014310         PERFORM 800-START-TERMINAL-SESSION
00168    014500     ELSE
00169    014600         PERFORM 100-PROCESS-MORTGAGE-SCREEN.
00170    014700     IF END-SESSION
00171    014800         PERFORM 900-SEND-TERMINATION-MESSAGE
00172        *EXEC CICS
00173        *    RETURN
00174        *END-EXEC
```

Figure 10-7   Compiler output for the mortgage-calculation program (part 3 of 9)

```
   4                          14.45.40        OCT 18,1983

00175    014900              MOVE '            00046    ' TO DFHEIVO
00176                        CALL 'DFHEI1' USING DFHEIVO
00177
00178    015200      ELSE
00179          *EXEC CICS
00180          *     RETURN TRANSID('MOR1')                    '
00181          *            COMMAREA(COMMUNICATION-AREA)
00182          *            LENGTH(1)
00183          *END-EXEC.
00184    015300            MOVE '            00050    ' TO DFHEIVO
00185                      MOVE 'MOR1' TO DFHEIV5
00186                      MOVE 1 TO DFHEIV11
00187                      CALL 'DFHEI1' USING DFHEIVO  DFHEIV5  COMMUNICATION-AREA
00188              DFHEIV11.
00189    015800*
00190    015900 100-PROCESS-MORTGAGE-SCREEN SECTION.
00191    016000*
00192    016100      PERFORM 110-RECEIVE-MORTGAGE-SCREEN.
00193    016200      IF NOT END-SESSION
00194    016300          PERFORM 120-EDIT-MORTGAGE-DATA
00195    016400          IF VALID-DATA
00196    016500              PERFORM 130-CALCULATE-MONTHLY-PAYMENT
00197    016600              MOVE 'ENTER NEXT SET OF DATA OR PRESS CLEAR TO END SE
00198         -     'SSION' TO MCM-D-OPERATOR-MESSAGE
00199    016624              MOVE SPACE TO MCM-D-ERROR-MESSAGE
00200    016632              MOVE -1 TO MCM-L-PRINCIPAL-AMOUNT
00201    016648              PERFORM 140-SEND-MORTGAGE-SCREEN
00202    016664          ELSE
00203    016680              MOVE 'ERRORS DETECTED--MAKE CORRECTIONS OR PRESS CLEA
00204         -     'R TO END SESSION' TO MCM-D-OPERATOR-MESSAGE
00205    016800              PERFORM 140-SEND-MORTGAGE-SCREEN.
00206    016850*
00207    016900 110-RECEIVE-MORTGAGE-SCREEN SECTION.
00208    017000*
00209          *EXEC CICS
00210          *     HANDLE AID CLEAR(110-CLEAR-KEY)
00211          *                ANYKEY(110-ANYKEY)
00212          *END-EXEC.
00213    017100      MOVE '                    00075    ' TO DFHEIVO
00214                CALL 'DFHEI1' USING DFHEIVO
00215                GO TO  110-CLEAR-KEY 110-ANYKEY DEPENDING ON DFHEIGDI.
00216
00217          *EXEC CICS
00218          *     RECEIVE MAP('MORMAP1')
00219          *             MAPSET('MORSET1')
00220          *             INTO(MORTGAGE-CALCULATION-MAP)
00221          *END-EXEC.
00222    017500      MOVE '            00079    ' TO DFHEIVO
00223                MOVE 'MORMAP1' TO DFHC0070
00224                MOVE 'MORSET1' TO DFHC0071
00225                CALL 'DFHEI1' USING DFHEIVO  DFHC0070
00226                MORTGAGE-CALCULATION-MAP DFHDUMMY DFHC0071.
00227    018000      GO TO 110-EXIT.
00228    018100*
00229    018200 110-CLEAR-KEY.
00230    018300*
00231    018400      MOVE 'Y' TO END-SESSION-SW.
00232    018500      GO TO 110-EXIT.
00233    018600*
00234    018700 110-ANYKEY.
```

Figure 10-7   Compiler output for the mortgage-calculation program (part 4 of 9)

```
  5                    14.45.40      OCT 18,1983

00235    018800*
00236    019000        MOVE 'N' TO VALID-DATA-SW.
00237    019010        MOVE -1 TO MCM-L-PRINCIPAL-AMOUNT.
00238    019100        MOVE 'INVALID KEY PRESSED' TO MCM-D-ERROR-MESSAGE.
00239    019200*
00240    019300 110-EXIT.
00241    019400*
00242    019500        EXIT.
00243    019600*
00244    019700 120-EDIT-MORTGAGE-DATA SECTION.
00245    019800*
00246    019802        MOVE FAC-UNPROT-NUM-MDT TO MCM-A-PRINCIPAL-AMOUNT
00247    019804                               MCM-A-NO-OF-YEARS
00248    019806                               MCM-A-INTEREST-RATE.
00249    019808*
00250    019810        IF MCM-L-INTEREST-RATE = ZERO
00251    019820            MOVE FAC-UNPROT-NUM-BRT TO MCM-A-INTEREST-RATE
00252    019900            MOVE -1 TO MCM-L-INTEREST-RATE
00253    020000            MOVE 'YOU MUST ENTER AN INTEREST RATE'
00254    020200                TO MCM-D-ERROR-MESSAGE
00255    020300        ELSE IF MCM-D-INTEREST-RATE NOT NUMERIC
00256    020310            MOVE FAC-UNPROT-NUM-BRT TO MCM-A-INTEREST-RATE
00257    020400            MOVE -1 TO MCM-L-INTEREST-RATE
00258    020500            MOVE 'INTEREST RATE MUST BE NUMERIC'
00259    020600                TO MCM-D-ERROR-MESSAGE
00260    020800        ELSE IF MCM-L-INTEREST-RATE NOT > ZERO
00261    020810            MOVE FAC-UNPROT-NUM-BRT TO MCM-A-INTEREST-RATE
00262    020900            MOVE -1 TO MCM-L-INTEREST-RATE
00263    021000            MOVE 'INTEREST RATE MUST BE GREATER THAN ZERO'
00264    021100                TO MCM-D-ERROR-MESSAGE.
00265    021200*
00266    021400        IF MCM-L-NO-OF-YEARS = ZERO
00267    021410            MOVE FAC-UNPROT-NUM-BRT TO MCM-A-NO-OF-YEARS
00268    021500            MOVE -1 TO MCM-L-NO-OF-YEARS
00269    021600            MOVE 'YOU MUST ENTER NO OF YEARS'
00270    021700                TO MCM-D-ERROR-MESSAGE
00271    021800        ELSE IF MCM-D-NO-OF-YEARS NOT NUMERIC
00272    021810            MOVE FAC-UNPROT-NUM-BRT TO MCM-A-NO-OF-YEARS
00273    021900            MOVE -1 TO MCM-L-NO-OF-YEARS
00274    022000            MOVE 'NO OF YEARS MUST BE NUMERIC'
00275    022200                TO MCM-D-ERROR-MESSAGE
00276    022300        ELSE IF MCM-D-NO-OF-YEARS NOT > ZERO
00277    022310            MOVE FAC-UNPROT-NUM-BRT TO MCM-A-NO-OF-YEARS
00278    022400            MOVE -1 TO MCM-L-NO-OF-YEARS
00279    022500            MOVE 'NO OF YEARS MUST BE GREATER THAN ZERO'
00280    022600                TO MCM-D-ERROR-MESSAGE.
00281    022800*
00282    022810        IF MCM-L-PRINCIPAL-AMOUNT = ZERO
00283    022815            MOVE FAC-UNPROT-NUM-BRT TO MCM-A-PRINCIPAL-AMOUNT
00284    022820            MOVE -1 TO MCM-L-PRINCIPAL-AMOUNT
00285    022830            MOVE 'YOU MUST ENTER PRINCIPAL AMOUNT'
00286    022840                TO MCM-D-ERROR-MESSAGE
00287    022850        ELSE IF MCM-D-PRINCIPAL-AMOUNT NOT NUMERIC
00288    022855            MOVE FAC-UNPROT-NUM-BRT TO MCM-A-PRINCIPAL-AMOUNT
00289    022860            MOVE -1 TO MCM-L-PRINCIPAL-AMOUNT
00290    022870            MOVE 'PRINCIPAL AMOUNT MUST BE NUMERIC'
00291    022880                TO MCM-D-ERROR-MESSAGE
00292    022890        ELSE IF MCM-D-PRINCIPAL-AMOUNT NOT > ZERO
00293    022895            MOVE FAC-UNPROT-NUM-BRT TO MCM-A-PRINCIPAL-AMOUNT
00294    022900            MOVE -1 TO MCM-L-PRINCIPAL-AMOUNT
00295    022910            MOVE 'PRINCIPAL AMOUNT MUST BE GREATER THAN ZERO'
00296    022920                TO MCM-D-ERROR-MESSAGE.
```

Figure 10-7 Compiler output for the mortgage-calculation program (part 5 of 9)

```
   6                    14.45.40      OCT 18,1983

00297   022930*
00298   022940       IF MCM-D-ERROR-MESSAGE NOT = LOW-VALUE
00299   022950           MOVE 'N' TO VALID-DATA-SW.
00300   022960*
00301   025800 130-CALCULATE-MONTHLY-PAYMENT SECTION.
00302   025900*
00303   026000       COMPUTE MCM-D-MONTHLY-PAYMENT =
00304   026100           MCM-D-PRINCIPAL-AMOUNT  /
00305   026200             ((1 - (1 / (1 + MCM-D-INTEREST-RATE / 12)
00306   026300               ** (MCM-D-NO-OF-YEARS * 12)))
00307   026400               / (MCM-D-INTEREST-RATE / 12)).
00308   026600*
00309   026700 140-SEND-MORTGAGE-SCREEN SECTION.
00310   026800*
00311          *EXEC CICS
00312          *    SEND MAP('MORMAP1')
00313          *         MAPSET('MORSET1')
00314          *         FROM(MORTGAGE-CALCULATION-MAP)
00315          *         DATAONLY
00316          *         CURSOR
00317          *END-EXEC.
00318   026900       MOVE ' J          00168   ' TO DFHEIVO
00319                 MOVE 'MORMAP1' TO DFHC0070
00320                 MOVE 'MORSET1' TO DFHC0071
00321                 MOVE -1 TO DFHEIV11
00322                 CALL 'DFHEI1' USING DFHEIVO  DFHC0070
00323                 MORTGAGE-CALCULATION-MAP DFHDUMMY DFHC0071 DFHDUMMY DFHDUMMY
00324                 DFHDUMMY DFHEIV11.
00325   027600*
00326   027700 800-START-TERMINAL-SESSION SECTION.
00327   027800*
00328   028000       MOVE LOW-VALUE TO MORTGAGE-CALCULATION-MAP.
00329   028100       MOVE 'PRESS CLEAR TO END SESSION' TO MCM-D-OPERATOR-MESSAGE.
00330   028210       MOVE -1 TO MCM-L-PRINCIPAL-AMOUNT.
00331          *EXEC CICS
00332          *    SEND MAP('MORMAP1')
00333          *         MAPSET('MORSET1')
00334          *         FROM(MORTGAGE-CALCULATION-MAP)
00335          *         ERASE
00336          *         CURSOR
00337          *END-EXEC.
00338   028300       MOVE ' J      S    00181   ' TO DFHEIVO
00339                 MOVE 'MORMAP1' TO DFHC0070
00340                 MOVE 'MORSET1' TO DFHC0071
00341                 MOVE -1 TO DFHEIV11
00342                 CALL 'DFHEI1' USING DFHEIVO  DFHC0070
00343                 MORTGAGE-CALCULATION-MAP DFHDUMMY DFHC0071 DFHDUMMY DFHDUMMY
00344                 DFHDUMMY DFHEIV11.
00345   029600*
00346   029700 900-SEND-TERMINATION-MESSAGE SECTION.
00347   029800*
00348          *EXEC CICS
00349          *    SEND TEXT FROM(END-OF-SESSION-MESSAGE)
00350          *              LENGTH(13)
00351          *              ERASE
00352          *              FREEKB
00353          *END-EXEC.
00354   029900       MOVE ' -    B       00191   ' TO DFHEIVO
00355                 MOVE 13 TO DFHEIV11
00356                 CALL 'DFHEI1' USING DFHEIVO  DFHDUMMY END-OF-SESSION-MESSAGE
00357                 DFHEIV11.
00358
00359
```

Figure 10-7   Compiler output for the mortgage-calculation program (part 6 of 9)

8   MORCAL1   14.45.40   OCT 18,1983

INTRNL NAME	LVL	SOURCE NAME	BASE	DISPL	INTRNL NAME	DEFINITION	USAGE	R	O	Q	M
DNM=1-401	01	SWITCHES	BL=1	000	DNM=1-401	DS 0CL2	GROUP				
DNM=1-22	02	END-SESSION-SW	BL=1	000	DNM=1-422	DS 1C	DISP				
DNM=1-449	88	END-SESSION			DNM=1-449						
DNM=1-474	02	VALID-DATA-SW	BL=1	001	DNM=1-474	DS 1C	DISP				
DNM=2-000	88	VALID-DATA			DNM=2-000	DS 0000					
DNM=2-021	01	END-OF-SESSION-MESSAGE	BL=1	008	DNM=2-021	DS 13C	DISP				
DNM=2-053	01	COMMUNICATION-AREA	BL=1	018	DNM=2-053	DS 1C	DISP				
DNM=2-081	01	MORTGAGE-CALCULATION-MAP	BL=1	020	DNM=2-081	DS 0CL213	GROUP				
DNM=2-118	02	FILLER	BL=1	020	DNM=2-118	DS 12C	DISP				
DNM=2-129	02	MCM-L-PRINCIPAL-AMOUNT	BL=1	02C	DNM=2-129	DS 2C	COMP				
DNM=2-161	02	MCM-A-PRINCIPAL-AMOUNT	BL=1	02E	DNM=2-161	DS 1C	DISP				
DNM=2-193	02	MCM-D-PRINCIPAL-AMOUNT	BL=1	02F	DNM=2-193	DS 8C	DISP-NM				
DNM=2-225	02	MCM-L-NO-OF-YEARS	BL=1	037	DNM=2-225	DS 2C	COMP				
DNM=2-252	02	MCM-A-NO-OF-YEARS	BL=1	039	DNM=2-252	DS 1C	DISP				
DNM=2-279	02	MCM-D-NO-OF-YEARS	BL=1	03A	DNM=2-279	DS 2C	DISP-NM				
DNM=2-306	02	MCM-L-INTEREST-RATE	BL=1	03C	DNM=2-306	DS 2C	COMP				
DNM=2-335	02	MCM-A-INTEREST-RATE	BL=1	03E	DNM=2-335	DS 1C	DISP				
DNM=2-364	02	MCM-D-INTEREST-RATE	BL=1	03F	DNM=2-364	DS 4C	DISP-NM				
DNM=2-393	02	MCM-L-MONTHLY-PAYMENT	BL=1	043	DNM=2-393	DS 2C	COMP				
DNM=2-424	02	MCM-A-MONTHLY-PAYMENT	BL=1	045	DNM=2-424	DS 1C	DISP				
DNM=2-455	02	MCM-D-MONTHLY-PAYMENT	BL=1	046	DNM=2-455	DS 9C	NM-EDIT				
DNM=3-000	02	MCM-L-OPERATOR-MESSAGE	BL=1	04F	DNM=3-000	DS 2C	COMP				
DNM=3-032	02	MCM-A-OPERATOR-MESSAGE	BL=1	051	DNM=3-032	DS 1C	DISP				
DNM=3-064	02	MCM-D-OPERATOR-MESSAGE	BL=1	052	DNM=3-064	DS 79C	DISP				
DNM=3-099	02	MCM-L-ERROR-MESSAGE	BL=1	0A1	DNM=3-099	DS 2C	COMP				
DNM=3-128	02	MCM-A-ERROR-MESSAGE	BL=1	0A3	DNM=3-128	DS 1C	DISP				
DNM=3-157	02	MCM-D-ERROR-MESSAGE	BL=1	0A4	DNM=3-157	DS 77C	DISP				
DNM=3-186	02	MCM-L-DUMMY	BL=1	0F1	DNM=3-186	DS 2C	COMP				
DNM=3-207	02	MCM-A-DUMMY	BL=1	0F3	DNM=3-207	DS 1C	DISP				
DNM=3-228	02	MCM-D-DUMMY	BL=1	0F4	DNM=3-228	DS 1C	DISP				
DNM=3-249	01	FIELD-ATTRIBUTE-DEFINITIONS	BL=1	0F8	DNM=3-249	DS 0CL24	GROUP				
DNM=3-289	02	FAC-UNPROT	BL=1	0F8	DNM=3-289	DS 1C	DISP				
DNM=3-309	02	FAC-UNPROT-MDT	BL=1	0F9	DNM=3-309	DS 1C	DISP				
DNM=3-333	02	FAC-UNPROT-BRT	BL=1	0FA	DNM=3-333	DS 1C	DISP				
DNM=3-357	02	FAC-UNPROT-BRT-MDT	BL=1	0FB	DNM=3-357	DS 1C	DISP				
DNM=3-385	02	FAC-UNPROT-DARK	BL=1	0FC	DNM=3-385	DS 1C	DISP				
DNM=3-410	02	FAC-UNPROT-DARK-MDT	BL=1	0FD	DNM=3-410	DS 1C	DISP				
DNM=3-439	02	FAC-UNPROT-NUM	BL=1	0FE	DNM=3-439	DS 1C	DISP				
DNM=3-463	02	FAC-UNPROT-NUM-MDT	BL=1	0FF	DNM=3-463	DS 1C	DISP				
DNM=4-000	02	FAC-UNPROT-NUM-BRT	BL=1	100	DNM=4-000	DS 1C	DISP				
DNM=4-031	02	FAC-UNPROT-NUM-BRT-MDT	BL=1	101	DNM=4-031	DS 1C	DISP				
DNM=4-063	02	FAC-UNPROT-NUM-DARK	BL=1	102	DNM=4-063	DS 1C	DISP				
DNM=4-092	02	FAC-UNPROT-NUM-DARK-MDT	BL=1	103	DNM=4-092	DS 1C	DISP				
DNM=4-125	02	FAC-PROT	BL=1	104	DNM=4-125	DS 1C	DISP				
DNM=4-143	02	FAC-PROT-MDT	BL=1	105	DNM=4-143	DS 1C	DISP				
DNM=4-165	02	FAC-PROT-BRT	BL=1	106	DNM=4-165	DS 1C	DISP				
DNM=4-187	02	FAC-PROT-BRT-MDT	BL=1	107	DNM=4-187	DS 1C	DISP				
DNM=4-216	02	FAC-PROT-DARK	BL=1	108	DNM=4-216	DS 1C	DISP				
DNM=4-239	02	FAC-PROT-DARK-MDT	BL=1	109	DNM=4-239	DS 1C	DISP				
DNM=4-266	02	FAC-PROT-SKIP	BL=1	10A	DNM=4-266	DS 1C	DISP				
DNM=4-289	02	FAC-PROT-SKIP-MDT	BL=1	10B	DNM=4-289	DS 1C	DISP				
DNM=4-319	02	FAC-PROT-SKIP-BRT	BL=1	10C	DNM=4-319	DS 1C	DISP				

Figure 10-7   Compiler output for the mortgage-calculation program (part 7 of 9)

```
13        MORCAL1      14.45.40     OCT 18,1983

REGISTER ASSIGNMENT

REG 6   BL =1

WORKING-STORAGE STARTS AT LOCATION 000A0 FOR A LENGTH OF 00260.
```

Figure 10-7 Compiler output for the mortgage-calculation program (part 8 of 9)

```
14        MORCAL1      14.45.40     OCT 18,1983

                CONDENSED LISTING
```

Line	Verb	Address	Line	Verb	Address	Line	Verb	Address
160	ENTRY	00090E	161	SERVICE	000926	162	SERVICE	000926
166	IF	000926	167	PERFORM	000938	169	PERFORM	00095C
170	CALL	00097A	171	PERFORM	000984	175	MOVE	0009A2
176	CALL	0009B2	184	MOVE	0009E2	185	MOVE	0009F2
186	MOVE	0009F8	187	CALL	0009FE	192	PERFORM	000A40
193	IF	000A5E	194	PERFORM	000A68	195	IF	000A86
196	PERFORM	000A90	197	MOVE	000AAE	199	MOVE	000ABE
200	MOVE	000AC8	201	PERFORM	000ACE	203	MOVE	000AF2
205	PERFORM	000B02	213	MOVE	000B26	214	CALL	000B2C
215	GO	000B56	222	MOVE	000B86	223	MOVE	000B96
224	MOVE	000B9C	225	CALL	0009A2	227	GO	000BEC
231	MOVE	000BF2	232	GO	000BF6	236	MOVE	000BFC
237	MOVE	000C00	238	IF	000C06	242	EXIT	000C16
246	MOVE	000C1C	250	MOVE	000C2E	251	MOVE	000C3C
252	MOVE	000C42	253	IF	000C48	255	IF	000C5E
256	MOVE	000C6E	257	MOVE	000C74	258	MOVE	000C7A
260	IF	000C90	261	MOVE	000C9E	262	MOVE	000CA4
263	MOVE	000CAA	266	IF	000CBA	267	MOVE	000CC8
268	MOVE	000CCE	269	MOVE	000D00	271	IF	000CEA
272	MOVE	000CFA	273	MOVE	000D2E	274	MOVE	000D06
276	IF	000D1C	277	MOVE	000D4A	278	MOVE	000D34
279	MOVE	000D3A	282	IF	000D64	283	MOVE	000D58
284	MOVE	000D5E	285	MOVE	000D90	287	IF	000D7A
288	MOVE	000D8A	289	MOVE	000DBE	290	MOVE	000D96
292	IF	000DAC	293	MOVE	000DDA	294	MOVE	000DC4
295	MOVE	000DCA	298	IF	000EC2	299	MOVE	000DF0
303	COMPUTE	000DFA	318	MOVE	000EDE	319	MOVE	000ED2
320	MOVE	000ED8	321	MOVE	000F5E	322	CALL	000EE4
328	MOVE	000F54	329	MOVE	000F84	330	MOVE	000F6E
338	MOVE	000F74	339	MOVE	000F96	340	MOVE	000F8A
341	MOVE	000F90	342	CALL	00101C	354	MOVE	001006
355	MOVE	001016	356	CALL				
```

**Figure 10-7** Compiler output for the mortgage-calculation program (part 9 of 9)
```

```
TRANSACTION: MOR1    PROGRAM: MORCAL1    TASK NUMBER: 0000214    DISPLAY:  00
STATUS:   PROGRAM INITIATION

     EIBTIME      = +0153926
     EIBDATE      = +0083287
     EIBTRNID     = 'MOR1'
     EIBTASKN     = +0000214
     EIBTRMID     = 'H401'

     EIBCPOSN     = +00004
     EIBCALEN     = +00000
     EIBAID       = X'7D'                      AT X'001895EA'
     EIBFN        = X'0000'                     AT X'001895EB'
     EIBRCODE     = X'000000000000'             AT X'001895ED'
     EIBDS        = '........'
  +  EIBREQID     = '........'




ENTER:  CONTINUE
PF1 : UNDEFINED            PF2 : SWITCH HEX/CHAR      PF3 : END EDF SESSION
PF4 : SUPPRESS DISPLAYS    PF5 : WORKING STORAGE      PF6 : USER DISPLAY
PF7 : SCROLL BACK          PF8 : SCROLL FORWARD       PF9 : STOP CONDITIONS
PF10: PREVIOUS DISPLAY     PF11: UNDEFINED            PF12: UNDEFINED
```

Figure 10-8   EDF display at program initiation

A second way to use EDF is called *two-terminal checkout*. When you use two-terminal checkout, you run EDF at one terminal and the task you're debugging at another. For example, suppose I want to debug a task that's running at the terminal named H400. I place my terminal into EDF mode by entering this transaction:

```
CEDF H400,ON
```

Then, EDF responds with this message:

```
TERMINAL H400: EDF MODE ON
```

Now, I can debug the task running at terminal H400 from my own terminal.

Once you've started EDF and the task you're debugging, but before the first instruction of your program is executed, EDF displays a *program initiation screen*. Figure 10-8 shows a sample program initiation screen for the mortgage-calculation program. This screen shows the contents of the fields in the Execute Interface Block. For example, the shaded area of figure 10-8 shows that the value of EIBCALEN is zero, indicating that a communication area isn't passed to the program.

```
    TRANSACTION: MOR1    PROGRAM: MORCAL1    TASK NUMBER: 0000214    DISPLAY:  00
    STATUS:  ABOUT TO EXECUTE COMMAND
    EXEC CICS SEND MAP
    MAP ('MORMAP1')
    FROM ('..................................................PRESS CLEAR TO'...)
    MAPSET ('MORSET1')
    CURSOR
    TERMINAL
    ERASE




    OFFSET:X'000FEE'    LINE:00181          EIBFN=X'1804'


    ENTER:  CONTINUE
    PF1 : UNDEFINED
    PF4 : SUPPRESS DISPLAYS   PF2 : SWITCH HEX/CHAR    PF3 : UNDEFINED
    PF7 : SCROLL BACK         PF5 : WORKING STORAGE    PF6 : USER DISPLAY
    PF10: PREVIOUS DISPLAY    PF8 : SCROLL FORWARD     PF9 : STOP CONDITIONS
                             PF11: UNDEFINED          PF12: ABEND USER TASK
```

Figure 10-9   EDF display before execution of a SEND MAP command

The bottom of each EDF display shows the meaning of each enabled key. For example, the ENTER key means to continue execution of the program, PF2 allows you to switch the display from character mode to hex mode, PF3 ends the EDF session, and so on.

As your program executes, EDF intercepts all CICS commands and displays two screens—one before and the other after the execution of the command. For example, figure 10-9 shows the screen displayed before the execution of a SEND MAP command. As you can see, EDF shows you the command and all of its options along with their values. In addition, it shows you the command's statement number (LINE) from the translator listing (*not* the compiler listing).

Figure 10-10 shows the EDF screen displayed after the command is executed. This screen indicates whether the command executed successfully. Here, RESPONSE: NORMAL means the command was successful. If an exceptional condition is raised by the command, the condition name (NOTFND, for example) is displayed as the RESPONSE.

If you're using EDF for single-terminal checkout, the map sent by this SEND MAP command is displayed between the before and after EDF displays. For two-terminal checkout, the EDF displays are sent to the terminal running EDF, and the map generated by

```
TRANSACTION: MOR1    PROGRAM: MORCAL1     TASK NUMBER: 0000214   DISPLAY:  00
STATUS:   COMMAND EXECUTION COMPLETE
EXEC CICS SEND MAP
 MAP ('MORMAP1')
 FROM ('.................................................PRESS CLEAR TO'...)
 MAPSET ('MORSET1')
 CURSOR
 TERMINAL
 ERASE




 OFFSET:X'000FEE'     LINE:00181          EIBFN=X'1804'
 RESPONSE: NORMAL                         EIBRCODE=X'000000000000'

 ENTER:  CONTINUE
 PF1 : UNDEFINED         PF2 : SWITCH HEX/CHAR      PF3 : END EDF SESSION
 PF4 : SUPPRESS DISPLAYS PF5 : WORKING STORAGE      PF6 : USER DISPLAY
 PF7 : SCROLL BACK       PF8 : SCROLL FORWARD       PF9 : STOP CONDITIONS
 PF10: PREVIOUS DISPLAY  PF11: UNDEFINED            PF12: ABEND USER TASK
```

Figure 10-10   EDF display after execution of a SEND MAP command

the SEND MAP command is sent to the program running the task being tested. As a result, when you use two-terminal checkout, the map sent by your program doesn't appear at the terminal running EDF.

In pseudo-conversational programming, your program issues a RETURN command to terminate the task after each SEND command. When EDF detects that the task is being terminated, it displays a screen like the one in figure 10-11. Here, you must enter YES in the REPLY field; otherwise, EDF ends when the task ends.

Figure 10-12 shows the screen EDF displays when an abend occurs. The shaded portions of figure 10-12 indicate the important information the screen contains: the abend code is ASRA (meaning a program check has occurred), the offset is E7A, and the interrupt was caused by a decimal-divide exception. In other words, the instruction at offset E7A tried to divide by zero, an operation not allowed by the System/370.

To find the source statement that caused the abend, you look in the CLIST for the statement with an offset closest to the offset on the EDF screen, but not exceeding it. For example, the COMPUTE statement shaded in part 9 of figure 10-7 has an offset of DFA, less than the offset on the EDF screen. Since the offset of

```
    TRANSACTION: MOR1                      TASK NUMBER: 0000214   DISPLAY:  00
    STATUS:   TASK TERMINATION




















    TO CONTINUE EDF SESSION REPLY YES                          REPLY: YES
    ENTER:  CONTINUE
    PF1 : UNDEFINED           PF2 : SWITCH HEX/CHAR   PF3 : END EDF SESSION
    PF4 : SUPPRESS DISPLAYS   PF5 : WORKING STORAGE   PF6 : USER DISPLAY
    PF7 : SCROLL BACK         PF8 : SCROLL FORWARD    PF9 : STOP CONDITIONS
    PF10: PREVIOUS DISPLAY    PF11: UNDEFINED         PF12: UNDEFINED
```

Figure 10-11 EDF display at task termination

```
    TRANSACTION: MOR1   PROGRAM: MORCAL1   TASK NUMBER: 0000227   DISPLAY:  00
    STATUS:   AN ABEND HAS OCCURRED
        COMMAREA      = '.'
        EIBTIME       = +0154339
        EIBDATE       = +0083287
        EIBTRNID      = 'MOR1'
        EIBTASKN      = +0000227
        EIBTRMID      = 'H401'

        EIBCPOSN      = +00259
        EIBCALEN      = +00001
        EIBAID        = X'7D'                                  AT X'001895EA'
        EIBFN         = X'1802'   RECEIVE                      AT X'001895EB'
        EIBRCODE      = X'000000000000'  NORMAL                AT X'001895ED'
        EIBDS         = '........'
    +   EIBREQID      = '........'
    OFFSET:X'000E7A'                     INTERRUPT: DECIMAL DIVIDE
    ABEND :   ASRA                       PSW: X'478D0000 004A7ED0 0006000B'

    ENTER:  CONTINUE
    PF1 : UNDEFINED           PF2 : SWITCH HEX/CHAR   PF3 : END EDF SESSION
    PF4 : SUPPRESS DISPLAYS   PF5 : WORKING STORAGE   PF6 : USER DISPLAY
    PF7 : SCROLL BACK         PF8 : SCROLL FORWARD    PF9 : STOP CONDITIONS
    PF10: PREVIOUS DISPLAY    PF11: UNDEFINED         PF12: REGISTERS AT ABEND
```

Figure 10-12 EDF display at program abend

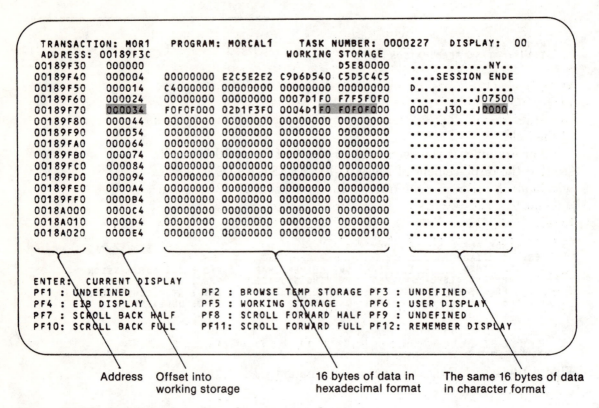

```
  TRANSACTION: MOR1    PROGRAM: MORCAL1    TASK NUMBER: 0000227    DISPLAY:   00
    ADDRESS: 00189F3C                      WORKING STORAGE
  00189F30   000000                                         D5E80000    ............NY..
  00189F40   000004    00000000 E2C5E2E2 C9D6D540 C5D5C4C5   ....SESSION ENDE
  00189F50   000014    C4000000 00000000 00000000 00000000   D...............
  00189F60   000024    00000000 00000000 0007D1F0 F7F5F0F0   ..........J07500
  00189F70   000034    F0F0F000 02D1F3F0 0004D1F0 F0F0F000   000..J30..J0000.
  00189F80   000044    00000000 00000000 00000000 00000000   ................
  00189F90   000054    00000000 00000000 00000000 00000000   ................
  00189FA0   000064    00000000 00000000 00000000 00000000   ................
  00189FB0   000074    00000000 00000000 00000000 00000000   ................
  00189FC0   000084    00000000 00000000 00000000 00000000   ................
  00189FD0   000094    00000000 00000000 00000000 00000000   ................
  00189FE0   0000A4    00000000 00000000 00000000 00000000   ................
  00189FF0   0000B4    00000000 00000000 00000000 00000000   ................
  0018A000   0000C4    00000000 00000000 00000000 00000000   ................
  0018A010   0000D4    00000000 00000000 00000000 00000000   ................
  0018A020   0000E4    00000000 00000000 00000000 00000100   ................


  ENTER:   CURRENT DISPLAY
  PF1 : UNDEFINED               PF2 : BROWSE TEMP STORAGE PF3 : UNDEFINED
  PF4 : EIB DISPLAY             PF5 : WORKING STORAGE     PF6 : USER DISPLAY
  PF7 : SCROLL BACK HALF        PF8 : SCROLL FORWARD HALF PF9 : UNDEFINED
  PF10: SCROLL BACK FULL        PF11: SCROLL FORWARD FULL PF12: REMEMBER DISPLAY
```

Address Offset into   16 bytes of data in   The same 16 bytes of data
         working storage   hexadecimal format   in character format

Figure 10-13   EDF display of working storage data

the next statement in the CLIST (EC2) is greater than E7A, you can tell that the abend occurred during the execution of the COMPUTE statement.

By examining the COMPUTE statement in the source listing, you can conclude that one of the values entered by the operator had to be zero for a decimal-divide exception to occur. Since the program was to edit all of the fields to see that none of them were zero, you can also assume that one of the edit routines didn't work. But which field—principal amount, number of years, or interest rate—is invalid?

To find out, press PF5 to display the contents of working storage. Figure 10-13 illustrates the screen EDF displays. Here, working storage data is displayed in four columns: (1) the address of the data in hexadecimal, (2) the displacement (or offset) of the field in working storage in hexadecimal, (3) 16 bytes of data in hexadecimal format, and (4) the same 16 bytes of data in character format.

To find a particular field in the display, you first determine the field's displacement in working storage from the DMAP. Then, you scan the offset column on the screen EDF displays, looking for a value that's closest to but not greater than the displacement of the field you're looking for. The field will be on that line, but you have to count over the correct number of bytes to find the exact position of the field.

For example, if you refer back to part 7 of figure 10-7, you'll see that the displacement of MCM-D-INTEREST-RATE is 3F (hexadecimal). By scanning the offset column in figure 10-13, you can see that the fifth row begins with offset 34. Then, counting over 12 bytes to byte 3F, you can see that MCM-D-INTEREST-RATE contains a value of zero (hex F0F0F0F0).

Now that I've located the field containing invalid data, it's a simple matter to look back to the source code to determine which statement caused the abend. If you look at a portion of the source listing in part 5 of figure 10-7, you'll see that line 260 is this:

```
ELSE IF MCM-L-INTEREST-RATE NOT > ZERO
```

This statement is in error—it should test the interest rate's data field (MCM-D-INTEREST-RATE), not its length field.

Note that when you use EDF, you don't have to worry about the contents of the base locator to find a field in working storage. That's because EDF takes care of that automatically. As you'll soon see, finding a field in a storage dump is more difficult.

As you can imagine, EDF is a powerful debugging tool. However, it has two limitations. First, EDF only traces execution of CICS commands. COBOL statements are not traced. Since there may be many COBOL statements between two CICS commands, it may be difficult to isolate a bug. Second, in my experience, EDF doesn't always work properly for same-terminal checkout in a TCAM environment (it works fine for two-terminal checkout, however). If you encounter a bug you can't solve because of these limitations, you have to use a storage dump.

The storage dump

A CICS *storage dump* (sometimes called a *transaction dump*) is like a regular OS or DOS storage dump, so I'm not going to go into the details of interpreting it here. There are three debugging techniques I want to cover, however. They are (1) determining the cause of an

ASRA abend, (2) determining the instruction that caused the program check, and (3) locating a field in working storage. After I
show you these techniques, I'll show you how to get a trace table
along with a storage dump and how to get the storage dump in the
first place.

How to determine the cause of an abend   The first step in determining the cause of a CICS abend is locating the abend code. It's
easy to find, since it appears in the heading line of each page of the
storage dump. Figure 10-14 is a portion of a CICS storage dump
for the mortgage-calculation program presented in figure 10-7. In
part 1, item 1 shows that the abend code is ASRA.

For an ASRA abend, you need to determine which program
check caused the abend. You can find this by looking at the program status word (PSW), item 2 in part 1 of figure 10-14. Here, a
one-character code indicates which program check occurred. Figure
10-15 lists the meaning of each program check code. In this example, B means that a decimal-divide exception occurred.

How to determine the instruction that caused the abend   To determine the instruction that caused the abend, you need the interrupt
address (item 3 in part 1 of figure 10-14) and the program load
point (item 4). Then, you subtract the load point from the interrupt address, like this:

$$
\begin{array}{r}
4A7ED0 \\
-\,4A7050 \\
\hline
E80
\end{array}
$$

Thus, the interrupt occurred at the instruction whose displacement
is E80. Now, you use the CLIST to find the COBOL statement
that caused the abend, just as when you use EDF.

How to locate a field in working storage   To locate a field in
working storage, you must first determine the value of the field's
base locator. To illustrate, suppose you want to locate the field
MCM-D-INTEREST-RATE. According to the DMAP in figure
10-7, that field's base locator is 1 (BL = 1). According to the
REGISTER ASSIGNMENT output, base locator 1 is assigned to
register 6. So, the base locator value for MCM-D-INTEREST-
RATE is 18904C (item 5 in part 1 of figure 10-14). To determine

CUSTOMER INFORMATION CONTROL SYSTEM STORAGE DUMP   CODE=ASRA   TASK=MOR1   DATE=10/14/83   TIME=17:14:10   PAGE   1

SYMPTOMS= AB/UASRA PIDS/5740XX100 FLDS/F000KC RIDS/MORCAL1

CICS/VS LEVEL = 0160

```
PSW            478D0000   004A7ED0   0006000B   00000000

REGS 14-4      5052A522   604A88F8   00000168   004A7E4A      004A7B42   00000168   0018451C

REGS 5-11      80188FC8   0018904C   001894B3   001894B4      004A812E   004A7050   004A7050

TASK CONTROL AREA (USER AREA)           ADDRESS 00184140 TO 00184EEF    LENGTH 000DB0

00000000   00184000 004D5E8C 01531278 0055BE70   00184680 00000000 14006500 043100A0   *.. ..(;.....................*   00184140
00000020   0554C8F8 00000000 00000000 00000000   00000000 00000000 00000000 00000000   *..H8........................*   00184160
00000040   00000000 00000000 00000000 00000000   00000000 00000000 5052A522 00189590   *.........................V...N.*  00184180
00000060   4052A3B4 C1E2D9C1 00000168 00006000   0052ABE8 00000006 004D5BF0 0052A154   * .T.ASRA......-....Y....($0...*  001841A0
00000080   FE000000 00000000 C5E3F140 C1E2D9C1   478D0000 004A7ED0 0006000B 00000000   *.......ET1 ASRA.......=......*   001841C0
000000A0   5052A522 604A88F8 0000C168 004A7E4A   004A7B42 00000168 0018451C 80188FC8   *..V.-H8........=.........H*    001841E0
000000C0   0018904C 001894B3 001894B4 004A812E   004A7050 004A7050 18020000 0000077E   *...M..M..A................=*   00184200
000000E0   00189590 8C0000A8 24F40000 00000000   00000000 00000000 00000000 00000000   *..N....Y.4..................*  00184220
00000100   00000000 00000000 00000000 00000000   00000000 00000000 00000000 00000000   *............................*  00184240
00000120   LINES TO 000002E0 SAME AS ABOVE                                                                              00184260
00000300   8B000028 00184440 00000000 00528BE4   00000000 00000000 00000000 00000000   *........ .......U..........*   00184440
00000320   00000000 00000000 00000028 00184440   00000190 00184470 001845D0 00000000   *...........  ..............*  00184460
00000340   00000000 00000000 00000000 40404040   00531278 00000000 00000000 00000000   *...............  ...........*  00184480
00000360   00000000 00000000 00000000 00000000   00000000 00184F80 00000000 00000000   *...........................*  001844A0
00000380   00000000 00000000 00000000 00000000   00000000 00008200 00140000 00000000   *..........................B*   001844C0
000003A0   00000000 00184EF0 00000000 00000004   00000000 00000000 00000000 001845D0   *.....+0...................*   001844E0
000003C0   80188FC8 001892AC 0018904C 00000000   004D5BF8 001892AC 5055952A 004A7050   *...H..K..........($8..K...N....*  00184500
000003E0   004D5BF8 C018451C 004A7090 00189010   004A7098 0052B760 00184000 004A7050   *.($8..........Q...-.. ...*    00184520
00000400   005592E4 004A795E 00528A98 80184470   00184140 00000000 00000000 00000000   *..KU..;..Q.................*   00184540
00000420   00000000 00000000 0018451C 80184520   00000000 00000000 00000000 00000000   *.........................*   00184560
00000440   00000000 00000000 00000000 00000000   001845D0 00189558 00000000 00000000   *......................N....*  00184580
00000460   00000000 00000000 40C4C6C8 C5C9C240   0171410C 0083287F D4D6D9F1 0000244C   *.... DFHEIB .....C...MOR1....*  001845A0
00000480   C8F4F0F0 00000103 00017D18 02000000   00000000 00000000 00000000 00000000   *H400....'..................*   001845C0
000004A0   00000040 40404040 40404040 00000000   00000000 00000000 00000000 00000000   *...  ......................*  001845E0
000004C0   000001B0 00184470 00000000 0017D790   00000001 0017C82C 00000001 0017C92C   *.............P......H.......I.*  00184600
000004E0   00000001 00000000 00000000 00000000   00000000 00000000 D3C9C6D6 E2E3D6D9   *..........................LIFOSTOR*  00184620
00000500   42000068 00000000 FF1846E8 5051FA9C   9051FBAE 00000005 00189558 0018928C   *...........Y...........N...K.*  00184640
00000520   00189274 0018906C 00189284 00182000   00000002 00559C2C 0051F9B0 00531278   *..K......KD...........9....*  00184660
00000540   00184470 00184140 0055B870 FE1846E8   F000D2C3 005578E0 00000000 00000000   *.........YO.KC...........*   00184680
00000560   00000000 00000000 48000060 00184680   FF184748 4051D538 5051D428 00000054   *...........-....N..M....*    001846A0
00000580   00184000 0051D674 00189274 00184680   00189284 00184000 48000060 00559C2C   *.. ...0..K.......KD.. ...-...*  001846C0
000005A0   00000000 00531278 01531278 00184140   0055B870 FE184748 FA00D4C3 0051D674   *.....................MC..O..*  001846E0
000005C0   01000000 00000000 480001D8 00184140   FF184920 4052B09C 00503F74 C0000200   *........G..Y...........*    00184700
000005E0   00184130 0052ABE8 8052AF94 004D5BF0   0052A154 00184000 480001D8 00000002   *.....Y..M.($0....... ...Q....*  00184720
00000600   000003A8 0052AC90 8052B058 00184140   0055B870 FE184920 FA00D4C3 005211A0   *...Y................MC.....*  00184740
00000620   01020000 00020505 00000020   C1D3F140 00531278 D4D6D9D4 C1D7F140   *...............AL1 ....MORMAP1*  00184760
00000640   D4D6D9E2 C5E3F140 005592E4 FFFFFFFE   00000000 00184810 00000000 00000000   *MORSET1 ..KU...............*  00184780
00000660   00000000 001809E0 00531284 00000000   00000000 07800000 00000000 00000000   *..............D............*   001847A0
00000680   00000000 00000000 001809E0 00184814   00000000 00000000 00000000 00000000   *..........................*   001847E0
000006A0   00110000 00000000 00000000 00000000   00000000 00000000 00000000 00000000   *..........................*   00184800
                                                                                                                        00184820
```

Figure 10-14   Part of a CICS storage dump (part 1 of 2)

CUSTOMER INFORMATION CONTROL SYSTEM STORAGE DUMP   CODE=ASRA   TASK=MOR1   DATE=10/14/83   TIME=17:14:10   PAGE 8

Figure 10-14 Part of a CICS storage dump (part 2 of 2)

Program check code	Meaning
1	Operation exception
2	Privileged operation
3	Execute exception
4	Protection exception
5	Addressing exception
6	Specification exception
7	Data exception
8	Fixed-point overflow
9	Fixed-point divide exception
A	Decimal overflow
B	Decimal-divide exception
C	Exponent overflow
D	Exponent underflow
E	Significance exception
F	Floating-point divide exception

Figure 10-15   Program checks indicated by ASRA abend

the address of the field, you add the base locator to the field's displacement (from the DMAP), like this:

```
    18904C
+       3F
    18908B
```

So, the address of MCM-D-INTEREST-RATE is 18908B.

   To locate the field in working storage, turn to the portion of the dump labelled:

    TRANSACTION STORAGE —USER

If more than one section has this label, refer to the one that contains the address you're looking for (the section's heading specifies the range of addresses included in it). The transaction storage section that contains the address 18908B is shown in part 2 of figure 10-14.

   Once you've located the correct section of the dump, scan the address column (the rightmost column of the dump) until you find the largest address that's smaller than the address you're looking for. The data is on that line, but you still have to count over the correct number of bytes to find its exact location. In part 2 of figure 10-14, item 1 shows the address (189080) for the line containing MCM-D-INTEREST-RATE. Counting over 12 bytes to get to 18908B, item 2 shows the hexadecimal contents of the field, and item 3 shows the character equivalent.

The trace table   CICS maintains a listing of all its operations in a special *trace table* that can be printed as part of a transaction dump when a task is terminated. The trace table can be helpful when you're debugging a complex problem. Figure 10-16 shows one page from a typical trace table.

I'm not going to give you the details of the trace table because its format is complex, and you won't need to use most of the information it contains anyway. That's because most of the trace entries are made by other CICS activities. Briefly, then, the column I've labelled "1" identifies the CICS module that created the trace entry. All trace entries generated by CICS commands in your application program have EIP in this column (EIP stands for Execute Interface Program).

The column I've labelled "2" identifies the CICS command that caused the trace entry. For each CICS command, two entries are made. The one labelled ENTRY is generated *before* the command is executed; the one labelled RESPONSE is generated *after* the command is executed.

For a trace table to be included in the transaction dump, you must activate the trace option. You do this by entering the transaction:

    CSMT TRACE ON

or:

    CEMT SET TRACE ON

To turn off the trace option, you run the same transaction, but with the word OFF instead of ON.

How to obtain a storage dump   CICS automatically adds all storage dumps to a special file called a *dump data set*. This file accumulates all of the storage dumps produced during an execution of CICS. When CICS is terminated, the dumps are automatically printed. As a result, you may have to wait until the end of the day to get your dump.

CUSTOMER INFORMATION CONTROL SYSTEM STORAGE DUMP CODE=ASPA TASK=MOR1 DATE=10/14/83 TIME=17:14:10 PAGE 6

TIME OF DAY	ID	REG 14	REQD	TASK	FIELD A	FIELD B	CHARS	RESOURCE	TRACE TYPE	INTERVAL
17:14:10.914496	EA	70557368	0003	TCP	01040100	0055C300	......C.	MOR1	TMP PCT LOCATE	00.000032
17:14:10.914560	EA	405428D0	0005	TCP	01040100	0052C8AC	......H.		TMP RETN NORMAL	00.000064
17:14:10.914592	F1	405574CC	EA04	TCP	00000EE8	00531278	...Y....		SCP GETMAIN CONDITIONAL INITIMG	00.000032
17:14:10.914784	C8	5052E762	0004	TCP	00184000	8A040EE8	.. ....Y		SCP ACQUIRED TCA STORAGE	00.000192
17:14:10.914848	D0	50558178	0604	00244	C8F4F0F0	D4D6D9F1	H400MOR1		KCP CREATE	00.000064
17:14:10.914880	EA	405578D4	0003	TCP	0C000100	0052C8AC	......H.	MOR1	TMP PCT TRANSFER	00.000032
17:14:10.914912	EA	405428D0	0005	TCP	0C000100	00000000	....		TMP RETN NORMAL	00.000032
17:14:10.915840	F0	40549662	4004	TCP	40000000	00533160	......-		KCP WAIT DCI=LIST	00.000928
17:14:10.915904	FC	0554C8F8	0503	00244	00010000	00531278	....		ZCP ZSUP START UP TASK	00.000064
17:14:10.915968	E5	4054C9AA	CC03	00244	00000000	00000000	....	MOR1.*..	XSP SECURITY	00.000064
17:14:10.916000	E7	0054D064	0004	00244	00000000	00000000	....		ERM ENTRY	00.000032
17:14:10.916000	E7	0054D064	0004	00244	00000000	000000FF	....		ERM RESPONSE	00.000000
17:14:10.916032	F2	5054D096	8804	00244	00000000	00000000	....	MORCAL1	PCP XCTL-CONDITIONAL	00.000032
17:14:10.916064	EA	4052B09C	0003	00244	01000300	001841C4	.......D	MORCAL1	TMP PPT LOCATE	00.000032
17:14:10.916128	EA	405428D0	0005	00244	01000300	00528A98	....		TMP RETN NORMAL	00.000064
17:14:10.916160	F1	60528B2E	8C04	00244	0000057C	01531278	....		SCP GETMAIN	00.000032
17:14:10.916480	C8	5052E762	0004	00244	00189000	8C000588	....		SCP ACQUIRED USER STORAGE	00.000320
17:14:10.916640	E1	504A7B96	0004	00244	0018904C	00000206	....		EIP HANDLE-AID ENTRY	00.000160
17:14:10.916672	F1	60559F0C	CC04	00244	0000007F	01531278	....		SCP GETMAIN INITIMG	00.000032
17:14:10.916704	C8	5052E762	0004	00244	00184EF0	8C000088	..+0....		SCP ACQUIRED USER STORAGE	00.000032
17:14:10.916704	F1	60559F0C	CC04	00244	00000040	01531278	... .		SCP GETMAIN INITIMG	00.000000
17:14:10.916736	C8	5052E762	0C04	00244	00184F80	8C000048	....		SCP ACQUIRED USER STORAGE	00.000032
17:14:10.916768	E1	504A7B96	00F4	00244	00000000	00000206	....		EIP HANDLE-AID RESPONSE	00.000032
17:14:10.916800	E1	504A7C2C	0004	00244	0018904C	00001802	....		EIP RECEIVE-MAP ENTRY	00.000032
17:14:10.916832	FA	5051FA9C	0003	00244	00020505	00000020	....		BMS MAP MAPSET MAP-FROM IN	00.000032
17:14:10.916832	FA	4051D538	0003	00244	00020505	00000020	....		BMS MAP MAPSET MAP-FROM IN	00.000000
17:14:10.916864	F2	50520438	0404	00244	00000000	00000000	....	MORSET1	PCP LOAD	00.000032
17:14:10.916896	EA	4052B09C	0003	00244	01000300	001841C4	.......D	MORSET1	TMP PPT LOCATE	00.000032
17:14:10.916928	EA	405428D0	0005	00244	01000300	00528BE4	.......U		TMP RETN NORMAL	00.000032
17:14:10.916992	F1	605205FC	C504	00244	000000D0	01531278	....		SCP GETMAIN INITIMG	00.000064
17:14:10.917024	C8	5052E762	0004	00244	001809E0	850000E8	.......Y		SCP ACQUIRED TERMINAL STORAGE	00.000032
17:14:10.917088	F1	50520A22	4004	00244	00182000	01531278	....		SCP FREEMAIN	00.000064
17:14:10.917120	C9	5052E798	0004	00244	00182000	850009D8	.......Q		SCP RELEASED TERMINAL STORAGE	00.000032
17:14:10.917280	FA	4052104E	0005	00244	00000000	00000000	....		BMS RETN	00.000160
17:14:10.917280	FA	4051D556	0005	00244	00000000	00000000	....		BMS RETN	00.000000
17:14:10.917312	F1	50559F0C	4004	00244	001809E0	01531278	....		SCP FREEMAIN	00.000032
17:14:10.917344	C9	5052E798	0004	00244	001809E0	850000E8	.......Y		SCP RELEASED TERMINAL STORAGE	00.000032
17:14:10.917376	E1	504A7C2C	00F4	00244	00000000	00001802	....		EIP RECEIVE-MAP RESPONSE	00.000032
17:14:11.108352	F2	80509F78	6004	00244	C1E2D9C1	00000000	ASRA....		PCP ABEND	*00.190976
17:14:11.108384	F1	4052A3B4	CC04	00244	000000A0	01531278	....		SCP GETMAIN INITIMG	00.000032
17:14:11.108448	C8	5052E762	0004	00244	00189590	8C0000A8	....		SCP ACQUIRED USER STORAGE	00.000064
17:14:11.108480	F4	5052A522	FE04	00244	00000000	C1E2D9C1	....ASRA		DCP TRANSACTION	00.000032
17:14:11.127616	F0	4050B6FC	4004	00244	80000000	004D5FD4	.....(.M		KCP WAIT DCI=SINGLE	*00.019136

Figure 10-16 Part of a CICS trace table

However, in some installations, it may be possible to print the dump data set while CICS is operating. CICS can be configured to maintain two dump data sets. At any given moment, one of them is active, and the other can be printed. When a task is terminated, the dump is written to the active dump data set. To print the dump, you switch dump data sets by issuing this transaction:

```
CSMT SWI
```

or:

```
CEMT SET DUMP SWITCH
```

Then, you can run a batch job to print the dump data set.

Discussion

Quite frankly, CICS debugging is complex, and I've only covered it briefly here. Fortunately, you can solve most CICS abends using the Execute Diagnostics Facility. And EDF is easy to learn.

Furthermore, many of the skills required to interpret a CICS dump are similar to those required for a standard OS or DOS storage dump. So, if you know how to add and subtract in hexadecimal, how to find the instruction that caused the interrupt, and how to locate a field in working storage, you can quickly learn how to interpret a CICS storage dump.

If you don't have these basic debugging skills, I recommend you read *OS Debugging for the COBOL Programmer* by Wayne Clary, available from Mike Murach & Associates. This book covers basic storage dump analysis procedures and outlines the most likely causes of various program checks.

Terminology

abnormal termination
abend
abnormal termination message
abend message
abend code
program check
data exception

base locator
Execution Diagnostics Facility
EDF
same-terminal checkout
two-terminal checkout
program initiation screen
storage dump
transaction dump
trace table
dump data set

Objective

Given a CICS program abend involving an exceptional condition or
a program check, locate the statement that caused the abend and
the values of any relevant fields in working storage.

Appendix

CICS Command Summary

This appendix summarizes the CICS commands presented in this book. For each command, you'll find a complete format as well as a chapter reference that will help you find more detailed information for the command. You can use this summary as a quick refresher on how to code a particular command or option.

The ADDRESS command   Chapter 8   Topic 1

```
EXEC CICS
    ADDRESS CWA(pointer)
END-EXEC
```

The DELETE command   Chapter 8   Topic 2

```
EXEC CICS
    DELETE DATASET(alphanumeric-data-value)
        [RIDFLD(data-name)]
        [RRN]
END-EXEC
```

The HANDLE AID command   Chapter 6   Topic 3

```
EXEC CICS
    HANDLE AID option(procedure-name)...
END-EXEC
```

The HANDLE CONDITION command   Chapter 8   Topic 1

```
EXEC CICS
    HANDLE CONDITION condition-name(procedure-name)...
END-EXEC
```

The LINK command   Chapter 8   Topic 1

```
EXEC CICS
    LINK PROGRAM(alphanumeric-data-value)
       [COMMAREA(data-name)          ]
       [LENGTH(numeric-data-value)]
END-EXEC
```

The READ command   Chapter 8   Topic 2

```
EXEC CICS
    READ DATASET(alphanumeric-data-value)
        INTO(data-name)
        RIDFLD(data-name)
       [RRN]
       [UPDATE]
END-EXEC
```

The RECEIVE MAP command   Chapter 6   Topic 3

```
EXEC CICS
    RECEIVE MAP(alphanumeric-data-value)
            MAPSET(alphanumeric-data-value)
            INTO(data-name)
END-EXEC
```

The RETURN command   Chapter 6   Topic 3

```
EXEC CICS
    RETURN [TRANSID(alphanumeric-data-value)]
        [COMMAREA(data-name)           ]
        [LENGTH(numeric-data-value)]
END-EXEC
```

The REWRITE command   Chapter 8   Topic 2

```
EXEC CICS
    REWRITE DATASET(alphanumeric-data-value)
            FROM(data-name)
END-EXEC
```

The SEND MAP command   Chapter 6   Topic 3

```
EXEC CICS
    SEND MAP(alphanumeric-data-value)
        MAPSET(alphanumeric-data-value)
        FROM(data-name)
        [MAPONLY/DATAONLY]
        [ERASE/ERASEAUP]
        [CURSOR[(numeric-data-value)]]
END-EXEC
```

The SEND TEXT command   Chapter 6   Topic 3

```
EXEC CICS
    SEND TEXT FROM(data-name)
        LENGTH(numeric-data-value)
        [ERASE]
        [FREEKB]
END-EXEC
```

The UNLOCK command   Chapter 8   Topic 2

```
EXEC CICS
    UNLOCK DATASET(alphanumeric-data-value)
END-EXEC
```

The WRITE command   Chapter 8   Topic 2

```
EXEC CICS
    WRITE DATASET(alphanumeric-data-value)
        FROM(data-name)
        RIDFLD(data-name)
       [RRN]
END-EXEC
```

The XCTL command   Chapter 8   Topic 1

```
EXEC CICS
    XCTL PROGRAM(alphanumeric-data-value)
       [COMMAREA(data-name)          ]
       [LENGTH(numeric-data-value)]
END-EXEC
```

Index

Comment Form

Your opinions count

If you have comments, criticisms, or suggestions, I'm eager to get them. Your opinions today will affect our products of tomorrow. If you have questions, you can expect an answer within one week of the time we receive them. And if you discover any errors in this book, typographical or otherwise, please point them out so we can make corrections when the book is reprinted.

Thanks for your help.

fold

Mike Murach
Fresno, California

Book title: CICS for the COBOL Programmer, Part 1

Dear Mike: _____

_____

_____

_____

_____

_____

_____

fold _____ fold

Name & Title _____

Company (if company address) _____

Address _____

City, State, Zip _____

Fold where indicated and tape closed.

No postage necessary if mailed in the U.S.